FRAUD

MIHIR BOSE
—AND—
CATHY GUNN

FRAUD

UNWIN

HYMAN

LONDON   SYDNEY   WELLINGTON

First published in Great Britain by the Trade Division of
Unwin Hyman Limited in 1989.

UNWIN HYMAN LIMITED
15–17 Broadwick Street
London W1V 1FP

Allen & Unwin Australia Pty Ltd
8 Napier Street, North Sydney, NSW 2060, Australia

Allen & Unwin New Zealand Pty Ltd with the Port Nicholson Press
Compusales Building, 75 Ghuznee Street, Wellington, New Zealand

British Library Cataloguing in Publication Data

Bose, Mihir, *1947–*
Fraud
I. Title   II. Gunn, Cathy.
364.1'63

ISBN 0-04-440299-6

Typeset in Garamond 11 on 13 point by
Computape (Pickering) Ltd, North Yorkshire
and printed at the University Press, Cambridge

To David Dein for all his help,
and Edward Russell for his encouragement

Contents

Acknowledgements

This has not always been an easy book to write, perhaps because we never really planned to write it. It came about as a result of our growing shared interest in fraud and some of the cases we found ourselves reporting as they unfolded.

A lot of people were very generous with their time, assistance and patience when we were researching this book. Some of them do not want to be thanked publicly. They each know who they are: thank you for everything. On the record, we would particularly like to thank Malcolm Campbell, Brian Cooper, Michael John, Eric Ellen, Barry Rides, and the staff of *Financial Weekly* during our time there, who tolerated our obsession and fielded some delicate phone calls.

Mihir Bose and Cathy Gunn

Introduction

That fraud is a growing reality of modern life cannot be doubted. It is not, however, quite as recent as some writers would like to make out. You can find fraud cases in Roman and Byzantine times, and forgery and counterfeiting was made a treasonable offence by the Statute of Purveyors of 1350. To obtain goods and money by false pretences was a crime even in the middle ages.

What is different is the nature, growth and the increasing international dimension of fraud. The figures as are available indicate that such frauds are increasing dramatically. In the UK, recorded fraud has increased by an average of 5 per cent since 1980 with what is called other fraud, other than false accounting and that committed by company directors, having increased from 93,187 in 1980 to 120,758 in 1985. There are blips and oddities in these figures. For instance, in 1980 there were 30 frauds committed by company directors, in 1985 this had gone up to 37, having peaked, it seems, at 71 in 1984. But this as the Home Office, which collects these figures, says may be due to the way fraud is recorded and the 'variations in recording practice'.

The international figures indicate a steady growth pattern. The figures collated by Michael Levi, with the help of Interpol, show that the industrial countries of North America and Europe are now showing a huge boom in 'recorded fraud'. The words need to be put in inverted commas because what may be recorded as fraud in one country may not be fraud, but some other offence, in another country. Or sometimes what is recorded as one offence may, in fact, be several. This can lead to some strange conclusions. Sweden, for instance, saw fraud, other than embezzlement, increase from 14,653 cases in 1950 to 91,080 in 1984. So a Swedish citizen was four times a likely as the English or the Welsh to fall to a fraudster, and 44 times more susceptible than an Italian. But if international comparisons are not very valid, nevertheless Levi's research shows that in almost all the industrialised countries the period 1977–1982 showed a huge increase in fraud. Only in countries like Taiwan, Chile, Israel and Zambia did the rate of recorded fraud per 100,000 of the population fall.

In that sense this is not so much the century of the fraud as the era of the international fraudster. Living as we do in Marshall McLuan's global village where a famine, or a riot, or an election in a distant part of the world is an instant, digestible two minutes of television news, it is hardly surprising that a national of one country can operate from another and commit a fraud that affects a third country far removed from the other two.

Indeed, if there is a distinctive feature of the frauds we discuss and describe it is this international dimension. This brought the two of us to the reporting of fraud and first inspired us to think of writing such a book. It also cuts across what may be called the political divide of fraud. This has led to a very interesting way in which fraud is reported in the press.

For sections of the press, particularly the down-market tabloid press, the fraud that has most impact are the 'fiddles', the social security fiddles by the unemployed or the worker fiddling his employer. This sort of fraud is ideally suited for the emotional treatment that is much favoured. Yet, for all the emotional force that can be generated by stories of fiddlers and scroungers, such frauds represent a small element of the broader picture.

This is filled by what may be called the rich man's fraud, those committed in the City, in the boardroom, by the businessman as he makes a deal. Stories of the rich and powerful being tripped up by their crooked actions always make compulsive reading or viewing, a 'Dallas' or 'Dynasty' of fraudsters would be an instant hit, since it makes us feel that greed has had its come uppance. Some also see it as the natural excess of capitalism, particularly if it is not restrained by law. John Kenneth Galbraith, the distinguished American economist, has argued that it is the theological disinclination of the Reagan-Thatcher era not to have any regulation that is one reason for fraud.

We are not interested in discussing theological points. What seems to us obvious is that that high-value fraud committed in the international business world is not reported adequately, or its consequences properly analysed. A good illustration is provided by our very first example. This concerns a fraud perpetrated in London by a national of another country, trading with a third country. The case started early in 1984 and as we write this in the winter of 1988, there have been four years of police investigation amounting to thousands of hours and extensive travel in this country and overseas, two trials with another pending and innumerable hearings in magistrates courts, two fugitives in a foreign country awaiting extradition, and creditors still trying to recover their money.

The plight of one of the creditors illustrates how complicated and involved such frauds can be. David Dein, a sugar trader, is owed $16 million on this multi-million fraud which led to the principal suspect, Rajendra Sethia of Esal, becoming the world's biggest bankrupt. For four years Dein, with tremendous energy and at great expense, has been orchestrating a legal campaign to recover his and other creditors' money. The paperwork generated by this fight fills one whole wall of his London office, and with top lawyers in this country, the US and elsewhere involved, the legal fees for Dein and his fellow-creditors have already reached several millions. Yet the wheels of justice have turned very slowly. Only one man has been convicted, and he was conditionally discharged with the judge giving almost a character reference.

This, of course, points to the major problem with fraud: getting a conviction. A study by the Home Office of those convicted in 1982 showed that courts are much more likely to jail those who commit burglary or robbery than those who commit fraud and forgery. Partly this may be because those who are convicted of fraud and forgery are often first-time offenders, while often burglars and robbers are in front of the judges for what seem regular appearances. But even that is not the entire explanation. Michael Levi in *Regulating Fraud* says, 'Over the period 1977–82 the proportion of first offenders imprisoned for fraud remained constant at 10 per cent (though fines dropped, to be replaced by suspended sentences). For burglary and robbery, however, the rate of imprisonment for first offenders shot up from 13 per cent in 1977 to 24 per cent in 1982, while suspended sentences also increased from 11 per cent to 22 per cent.'

Levi's argument is that to the extent that each white-collar crime is less likely to be defined as such, reported and prosecuted than any street or household crime 'this gives the fraudster something of an advantage, almost a bias'. Some feel that judges can more easily identify with the social world of the fraudster – particularly the fraudulent professional person – than that of the burglar.

Yet the effects of the fraudster's crime can be felt no less keenly than that of the common thief. In the case we have mentioned and which we discuss more fully later, one of the consequences of the fraud was that several people not connected with it lost their jobs because the firms they worked for had to shut down. Robbery or burglary may have a more dramatic, immediate effect; fraud is more insidious but just as damaging.

Our book is an exploration of this world through an examination of some of the most dramatic examples of recent times. It is by no means an exhaustive list but we followed all these examples from the moment they emerged, and one or two emerged as full-blown cases because we persistently reported them. They also illustrate the nature and force of international fraud.

1

The Tip of the Iceberg

Fraudsters, like the poor, will always be with us. If, as Tristan Bernard said, God created the world but it is the Devil who keeps it going, then fraud is the necessary lubrication. This may seem unnecessarily pessimistic and moralistic but, in fact, fraud, in some form or other, seems to be very much part of everyday life. Some researchers have suggested that fraud could well turn out to be the great crime of the twentieth century. Certainly its expansion this century has been remarkable. Recorded fraud has increased by an average of five per cent annually since 1980. A 1987 study by accountants Ernst & Whinney, updating their earlier study of 1985, notes that in the intervening two years there has been 'substantial evidence of an increase in the level of suspected fraud within companies in Britain', with more businessmen both aware of fraud and fearful of its consequences. Two out of three companies consider themselves vulnerable to fraud. Companies with a turnover in excess of £35 million feel most at risk and a fifth of companies suspect that they may currently be the victim of fraud. The traditional areas of worry have always been stock/stores, accounts and petty cash, but there is growing awareness that the modern fraudster is sophisticated and has a lot of tricks up his sleeve. A single fraud on an average can cost a company as much as £15,000, much more than the average for other crimes, and in case of big frauds the total could run into millions.

There are few reliable figures on fraud. In 1985 the Fraud Squad estimated that total fraud in England and Wales came to £2 billion. But this did not include social security fraud which is probably around £100 million or cheque and credit fraud (around £50 million), or any of the frauds investigated by the Department of Trade and Industry, like insider trading. Since 1985 fraud in the Metropolitan Police Area has risen to £1½ billion, which suggests that the figure for country-

1

wide fraud, taking everything into account, could run into several billions.

The 1986 joint Home Office Police Foundation survey conducted by Dr Michael Levi and James R. Morgan found that two-thirds of the businessmen questioned thought that fraud was much more common now than ten years ago. But despite this, neither the Department of Trade and Industry nor many police forces regularly compile statistics on the cost of fraud. Yet such figures are available for property crime. The attitude is all the more odd given that figures recorded by the London Fraud Squad show that commercial fraud costs three times the total cost of all other property crimes in London. There is good reason why the police have traditionally seen fraud as a second division crime. As Levi and Morgan say, it is 'partly outside the action-oriented culture of police work, and partly because there has been at least until very recently (and then only in London) little political pressure for fraud work from the media and police authorities. This is reflected in the number of personnel allocated to fraud squads: about 5% of CID manpower in London and nationally.' As we shall see later this perspective is changing, but generally fraud investigations do not lend themselves very readily to the Z-car or Sweeney treatment.

But this police attitude may reflect the fact that deep down we still treat the fraudster on a different level to other criminals. It was affection for the fraudster which made Michael Gilbert, a crime writer – and a founder of the Crime Writers' Association – to turn from describing gruesome murders to what is almost a fond resumé of the century's leading fraudsters. Early on in his book *Fraudsters*, Gilbert declares his change of allegiance:

> Should it be asked why, after a writing life-time largely devoted to real and fictional murderers, I should turn now to swindlers, the answer is simple. I find them more agreeable as characters and a great deal more interesting as performer . . . so far as likeableness goes, it is a walk-over for the swindlers. Tennyson Jesse may insist that 'everyone loves a good murder' but how can we love the murderer?

Gilbert then contrasts some horrible murderers with swindlers like Ernest Terah Hooley, who was so lovable that Norman Birkett wrote to his wife, 'Hooley is a charming man and I like him very much. He smiled now and then with a quite radiant smile. I can well understand how he got his money from susceptible people.' Gilbert is so taken by the idea of the lovable rogue – an idea that, obviously, dies hard – that he comes close to excusing some remarkable swindles.

This romantic attachment to fraudsters explains why Gilbert launched an extraordinary attack on the 1958 Prevention of Fraud (Investments) Act, blaming it for causing John Stonehouse problems and seeing it as final proof of the reprehensible British love for a nanny regime. Gilbert's argument is that the idea of protecting a man with money from losing any part of it is a sign of paternalism and 'symptomatic of the British weakness for taking a good thing too far'. True, as crimes go, fraud is fairly recent. Murder has not only been most foul but recognised as such from time immemorial. Until about the seventeenth century, fraud was not a crime and the feeling was that it was up to the individual to look after himself; after all, 'A fool and his money are soon parted.' But as London became an international financial centre and the City maxim 'My word is my bond,' came under strain through the invention of financial devices, so fraud became the natural home of the dishonest. As the financial instruments became more sophisticated, so did the fraudster, quick to find a loophole in the most intricate law. Gilbert could argue that it was the creation of such laws that provides fertile ground for the fraudsters, but while this has some romantic charm it is clearly useless in an effort to understand this major crime of our times.

Another barrier to understanding fraud is its nature. We all think we know what fraud means but there is no universally acceptable definition of fraud. *The Shorter Oxford English Dictionary* has five definitions of fraud, one of which is considered obsolete. They range from, 'the quality of being deceitful', to the colloquial expression used in relation to a person as in, 'you are a fraud', meaning a humbug. Interestingly, the expression seems to have come into vogue in 1850 just when the financial world was acquiring some of the accoutrements that make up the modern shape, and in the process creating the first ripples of fraudulent behaviour.

Since this is not a historical study we shall not consider the hoary old tales of past frauds. In any case, modern frauds lack nothing in originality, variety and scope. Frauds can range from the petty to the serious, the complicated to the ridiculous. For thirteen years a Port Talbot housewife used the same 10p coin in her gas meter. When she was finally caught, she admitted she had enjoyed 'free' gas and was conditionally discharged. In a similar vein, if on a much larger scale, are fraud cases like that of the toll bridge collectors on the Mersey Tunnel who pocketed over a million pounds paid by those who used the tunnel. Or the story of the Gingerbread Man who kept on running. In April 1987, Keith Norkett set up The Gingerbread House. One night in October of the same year he, his wife and baby son vanished leaving behind twenty-three workers who had not been paid and debts all round of nearly £100,000. As the papers put it, the dough was really missing.

At this level we are dealing with the very basic kind of fraud, they make interesting little stories in the newspapers but do not require a great deal of thought or planning. More often frauds require a bit more ingenuity, but even then not a great deal more. Just before Christmas 1987 three major banks fell victim to a gang using the sort of technique that would hardly rate as a plot for a B movie. A man posing as a representative of the chartered accountant firm McNair, Mason phoned the firm's bankers, the Royal Bank of Scotland. They gave the correct account details and arranged for the release of £250,000 in French francs, which was collected by another member of the gang who had a bogus letter on company paper. The same gang had also got away with £236,000-worth of deutschmarks belonging to a construction company from a branch of the Midland Bank, and £300,000 belonging to a Japanese company. In these cases all they needed, it seemed, was a nice telephone manner and a few bits of bogus paper. As often happens with such frauds, their success left the police furious and the banks keen to cover up any bad publicity.

In many ways the oldest fraud is the one where the insurance company is the victim. The story of priest David Asvat could have come straight out of Hollywood. He insured his life for more than a million pounds, paying out over £1,160 a month in premiums to eight insurance companies covering some of the biggest names in the business. In March 1985 he and his wife took a holiday in India. The British High Commission in Bombay told him that it was easy to get death certificates in India and the Asvat plan swung into action. Within two days of arrival Asvat 'fell ill'. At hand was his brother-in-law who worked as a doctor. He helped Asvat fake his death, writing out a certificate saying he had died from pneumonia and heart failure. Asvat's wife returned to England to claim but the insurance companies, by now suspicious, decided to investigate. He was found living in an

Indian village and his explanation was the time-honoured one: he had done it to provide for his wife.

But despite the amounts involved and the judge's description of it as a deeply laid plot, it is difficult to see it as more than a typical attempt to defraud insurance companies. Some frauds, however, do seem cruel and touch a nerve, like that of the father swindling a retarded son of his fortune or a conman exploiting the generosity of a gullible public. This was very much the story of David Raines, owner of an East London medical agency, British Euro Medi-Vac, who saw his opportunity when an earthquake hit Mexico in September 1985. He got various drug companies, like Wellcome and Boots, to give him nearly £210,000-worth of drugs to airlift to the disaster zone where 4,000 people had died. Raines never intended to pay for the drugs, which were believed to have been sold in Mexico. At his trial he was shown to be a consumate conman, with fourteen previous convictions.

Frauds of this nature provoke judicial moralising tirades about the 'scandalous state of affairs'. But on this occasion Judge Marcus Anwyl-Davies' comment that the public ought to be protected from the likes of David Raines seemed justified. All the more so as there is growing evidence that there are quite a few Raines around able to take advantage of the British public's generous instincts.

The country's charities have a combined turnover of £10 billion, with another £2 billion in tax concessions and other support. But in early 1988 the House of Commons Public Accounts Committee found that at least £100 million had been creamed off charities by expert swindlers. The Charity Commission was helpless to stop it. It is not hard to see why. The Commission has to cope with 200,000 charities without a qualified accountant among its 330 staff, the register is hopelessly out of date and fewer than twenty-three per cent of charities have submitted accounts in the last five years.

A somewhat different type of fraud that also excites a great deal of interest and lurid headlines is the social security fraud. As in the 1980s, the Thatcher era has not only brought back mass unemployment but along with it the social stigma that goes with not being able to find a job. Inevitably there are those who find the temptation of claiming unemployment benefits, even when they have a job, far too great. A Government White Paper released early in 1988 estimated that one in five of the long-term unemployed fraudulently claimed benefits, amounting to half a million of the 2.7 million unemployed. There have been periodic government 'crackdowns on dole scroungers', as the tabloid press likes to describe it, with varying results. In 1986 the Department of Employment ran nine pilot schemes in which the long-term unemployed were asked to come for interviews. This resulted, as the department put it, in the claimants 'melting away like the snow'. Not long after that a fourteen-strong government fraud squad investigating the activities of agricultural gangmasters in the fens surrounding the Wash in East Anglia found 300 claims for unemployment benefits totalling nearly £10,000 a week. The gangmasters employed teams of freelance workers, often from areas of high unemployment in the North, to pick flowers and vegetables in the fenlands of Lincolnshire, Cambridgeshire and Norfolk. They were paid low wages and encouraged to supplement their incomes by claiming unemployment and social security benefits. The investigations had almost a nineteenth-century feel about them: the government's fraud squad investigators would drive out each day and stop at selected sites to check records; as the workers realised what was going on they would run across fields or hide in barns to escape questioning.

Such frauds make good journalistic copy and provide wonderful anecdotes – for example, the taxi-driver who parks his car a couple of minutes from the Social Security office and walks there to claim his benefit; or the roofing contractors who, in between doing jobs, also pay a visit to the dole office. They are all part of the growing black economy in which defrauding the Social Security goes hand in hand with not paying income tax or VAT. In the picture that is often drawn, the typical inhabitant of this nether world of the 'no cheques please, we prefer cash', is probably a redundant tradesman who is playing the Thatcherite game to the full. He has got on his bike and is working fulltime freelance while still claiming unemployment benefit. How big a part he plays in the black economy is hard to say, but it forms a growing section of the £4,000 million lost to the Revenue through unrecorded economic activity.

There is a perception that Social Security fraud is a victimless crime. The experience of the DHSS has been that magistrates are more likely to be harsh on shoplifters, even if they are first-time offenders, rather than on those who seek to defraud the taxpayer. The DHSS prosecutes only a fraction of those caught and even then finds it difficult to get convictions. In the summer of 1987 an investigation along south coast towns found that nearly a quarter of 4,400 people on unemployment

6

benefit had jobs. Some seventy were prosecuted, a third of them ended up in court and even then some were acquitted. Of course the very structure of the system makes this a messy fraud. The DHSS relies on information from neighbours or acquaintances with grievances, and the very nature of the investigation gives it the unpleasant feel of snoopers prying into people's lives. Also while such frauds raise the emotional temperature, compared to commercial frauds they are very minor.

If Social Security fraud concerns the lower paid, then the mortgage fraud involves the somewhat better-off. This, in some ways, is a crime of affluence. The sustained rise in house prices in the south of England means that it is very difficult for those who live in the north to buy houses in the south. Norman Tebbitt may say, 'Get on your bike and look for a job', but high southern house prices have made this almost impossible. One way out is for employers to certify that the overtime employees earn is part of their basic salary. This may boost their chances of getting a mortgage, but it comes close to being a fraudulent act.

In most cases mortgage frauds are more deliberate, exploiting both the rise in house prices and the relentless competition between financial institutions to lend money, which has seen building societies measure success by the sheer number of mortgages they grant. The amount of money available through tax relief also makes it attractive. MIRAS tax relief costs the taxpayer some £4.5 billion each year and a percentage of this is probably siphoned off in frauds. In 1987 MIRAS frauds involving home improvements alone were said to amount to more than £100 million a year. All this has meant that this type of fraud, almost unknown a few years ago, has become the fastest rising 'white-collar' crime, partly because it is so easy to operate. For example, a mortgage may be obtained on one property, then it may be sublet as a bedsit. In quite a few cases the person who obtains a mortgage then stops paying and flees the country. Or the person lies in order to get a mortgage, as one Peter Treadwell did. He told the Anglia Building Society that he was a £220-a-week builder when he was really unemployed. He got a £29,500 loan, paid two repayments and then stopped. The Anglia repossessed and sold the house, but by the time this happened the south-east factor had worked in Treadwell's favour. The house in Cheltenham had risen in value and Treadwell made a profit of £6,000. He was given a suspended jail sentence and fined £1,000, but his economy with the truth had meant an overall gain of £5,000.

Most mortgage frauds involve a certain amount of collusion, for instance a dishonest surveyor might overvalue a property or a corrupt solicitor help the same property to be mortgaged to several building societies. This can result in cases that range from what the police call 'mundane mortgage frauds' (where a man with an income of between £12,000 to £13,000 a year has mortgages on thirty houses) to complex frauds run by rings of professionals. One ring obtained 1,500 mortgages on as many houses. It is the involvement of professionals helping to perpetrate such frauds that worries the authorities. The professional may be a solicitor, a branch manager of a building society, or very often a professional mortgage broker or insurance broker. The problems worsen because societies very often do not check the credentials of these people, and the changed world of post-Big Bang de-regulation does not help. As Detective Chief-Superintendent David Stephenson, head of the Fraud Squad's non-investment division, says, 'Mortgage frauds have always been around, but without any doubt whatsoever, there has been a tremendous increase post de-regulation.' In 1987 such activities led to the Metropolitan and City Fraud Squad setting up a team of ten detectives to break rings of mortgage fraudsters. Some £120 million of frauds were investigated. But, given the size of the mortgage market and the scope for fraud, this represented the tip of the iceberg.

Another very modern 'white-collar' fraud is the credit-card trick. The cashless society has spawned its own enemy. Every year British banks are estimated to lose £100 million through credit-card swindles, a figure that has been rising steadily in the last few years. The frauds take various forms. Each day banks send hundreds of credit cards through the post to customers and thieves have found ways to spot the envelopes and remove the cards. The Post Office has always consistently denied that their workers are involved, claiming that most of these losses are in bedsits or blocks of flats where the mail is left lying on a communal table. Access and Barclays have taken steps to combat this, disguising envelopes, sometimes handwriting the address or, in some cases, getting the cardholder to collect the card from his or her local branch.

In the USA even such precautions have not worked. There fraudsters exploit the carbons found in credit card authorisation slips. We may consider them an irritant and throw them away, but in the USA they are collected by gangs who then use the impression of the card on the carbon to fabricate duplicate cards. This has resulted in the system where in America it is common for card-users to be asked for some identification – passport, driving licence, etc. – and for the cardholders themselves to destroy the carbons. In the UK, Access and Barclaycard use holograms on their cards to prevent forgery, together with a special strip on the back which shows if someone tries to erase the signature. Card companies lay great store by the hologram, which involves placing a three-dimensional image on the card with sophisticated laser technology. But how much protection this offers is debatable; in one case a cardholder experimenting with a different holographic foil image on top of the original card found it went undetected in London for months.

In many cases, of course, the credit-card fraud may be committed when the card is issued. Credit scoring, where points are awarded on the basis of a questionnaire, has clearly failed to keep out the undesirables. It may be an efficient and economical system to cope with the demand for credit cards but, unlike humans, computers cannot identify a fraudulent application. Fraud investigators believe that in some cases it would be better to have a manual vetting system which would be a version of red linning where certain areas are considered high risk. However, with the credit-card fraudster moving round the country, this would mean different areas would come under scrutiny.

But in this as with other frauds, progress is limited because companies will not spend money trying to combat fraud. They would rather write off their losses as bad debts. With no central bureau to pool information about suspects, similar to police records, and with companies reluctant to combat such crime, credit cards remain a potent fraud area.

Sometimes the complexities of government rules can open the door to fraud as with, for example, the rules governing exports from the EEC. If you want to export beef from the UK there are forty-three separate EEC regulations you have to fulfil. These are further subject to eighty-two permanent and 145 temporary amendments. The EEC has a complex system of granting rebates, refunds and duties, and this provides great scope to any fraudster. Here is one example: pigs are smuggled into Northern Ireland; they are then legally re-exported to the Irish Republic, qualifying for an EEC grant. Again, exports of cheese to the Caribbean gets subsidy, but this cheese then finds itself diverted to the USA and Canada. The subsidy for bacon varies by 50% depending on whether it is smoked or not. Between 1980 and 1985 there were some £60 million of irregularities in the EEC. Of these,

West Germany owned up to some £31 million, Britain just £1.8 million. In one of his last reports before retiring, Sir Gordon Downey, Comptroller and Auditor General, was convinced that Britain's share was grossly undervalued and represented just the tip of a vast fraud iceberg. Neither the Ministry of Agriculture nor Customs & Excise can cope with the immense amount of paperwork involved in following EEC regulations, and the delays and confusion involved means that not only are frauds committed but the fraudster often gets away with it. It costs the EEC dear and in 1986 refunds on food exported to non-EEC countries cost the European taxpayer £4,800 million.

So far we have been dealing with what may be called simple frauds that grab the headlines, cause a lot of distress but in many ways do not involve huge sums of money, the EEC frauds notwithstanding. The real paydirt is in commercial and City frauds. If all frauds are important, then some are more important than others. Or at least the crooks get away with a lot more money.

The City of London is one of the greatest money machines the world has ever seen. The city state of Venice under the Doge may have been more powerful politically, but the City of London undoubtedly makes more money as one of the three great financial centres of the world, the other two being New York and Tokyo. There is a certain symmetry in that trio. Fifty years ago London, as the centre of the British Empire, was the financial capital of the world. It was to London that the modern forms of tribute in dividends and remitted profits came, and London in turn arranged the transfer of capital to far-flung parts of the world. Britain's decline affected London and as America replaced Great Britain as a world power, so New York supplanted London as the financial capital of the world. In recent years as the American Empire has declined and Japan has threatened to become the great superpower, so Tokyo is rivalling New York as the world's financial centre.

At one time in the mid-1980s it seemed that London would have to accept a second-class status as a financial centre, but the Big Bang changes ushered in 1986 were designed to prevent that. Initially meant to do no more than abolish the minimum commissions rule of Stock Exchange transactions, they have brought in a whole raft of changes including outside ownership of Stock Exchange firms, the virtual elimination of the old club tradition of the City and a massive injection of capital, all of which is helping London to compete with New York and Tokyo.

If the changes were inevitable they have also provided scope for the fraudsters, sometimes in the most unexpected fashion. Thus the government's policy of privatisation, which made the sale of shares comparable with filling in football pools coupons, has inevitably produced its own crop of fraudsters. As private investors rushed to subscribe to these issues, so high-street share shops opened giving a service similar to a bookmaker but offering shares instead of betting slips. The story of City Investment Centres, which opened two such share shops in Finchley Road and New Bond Street, illustrated the problems for the private investor. The share shops proved very popular and the company's turnover jumped from £67,000 to £57 million as 1,100 people bought and sold shares through their high street shop-window operations. The success was too good to be true and in the summer of 1986 the Department of Trade and Industry started an enquiry. In November 1986 CIC was closed down, the company put into liquidation with a deficit of £1.13 million and its founder, Chander Singh, a Nigerian businessman, left the country for India. Some 1100 people who had bought shares through CIC never received share certificates or, if they had used the share shops to sell, they never saw any money. The only paper they owned turned out to be worthless contract notes.

If this was an extreme result of the craze for privatised shares, the very concept of privatisation opened a fraud window which in some ways was the most curious. New issues are much sought after in the City. Properly handled they can make a lot of money and City investors have always looked to 'stag' new issues, to sell them at a profit almost as soon as dealings start. It had always been the practice to make multiple applications for such share offerings. Sometimes the multiple applications were made in the same name, sometimes in different names, very thinly disguised. The reason for the multiplicity of applications is that if the issue is heavily oversubscribed then often there is a ballot to decide who gets the shares: the more applications in the ballot the more the chances of getting the shares.

Until the autumn of 1984 few in the City saw anything wrong in this. Merchant banks handling the new issues were grateful for multiple applications because this helped to get the issue underway, often leading to an oversubscription which did wonders for the banks' macho image as efficient handlers of new issues. But then the government decided to privatise British Telecom with an unprecedented media campaign aimed at the small private investor. For twenty years the private investor had been squeezed out by the relentless advance of the institutional investor; now the small investor was about to strike back. The government saw de-nationalisation as a powerful instrument with which to provide capitalism with a human, profitable face. This process received a further impetus when little more than a year after the sale of British Telecom, British Gas was brought to the market and television commercials indulged in a nationwide search for Sid, the elusive private investor. He was eventually lured from his mountain fastness to invest in this bonanza.

Not surprisingly, perhaps, this evangelical mission to popularise share ownership came heavily laden with moral sermons: multiple applications were ruled illegal. Under the old City system the private investor would have been overwhelmed by the well-trained army of City stags who knew all about making the most of new issues. The government was determined to prevent this, and as British Telecom shares were promoted there were dire warnings that those who indulged in the favourite City game of making more than one application would be prosecuted. Since then the Fraud Squad has been busy and, like the Orwellian thought police, has been going into areas where no investigator has ever reached before.

In the process we have had a fascinating glimpse of those whose greed has led them to break the law. The most famous of them was, undoubtedly, Keith Best. A barrister and Tory MP for Anglesey, Best used a variety of names and a variety of addresses including his law chambers in Brighton, his constituency base in Anglesey and his mother's home in West Sussex together with four bank accounts to make six applications for British Telecom shares. He was entitled to 800; he fiddled his way to 4,800. Eventually, when he was caught, he had to resign his seat and was fined. Yet his downfall showed the thin line between profit and penalty. When Jaguar had been floated, a few months before British Telecom, Best had made four applications and there had been no comeback. But that privatisation was before the government took a moral stance on multiple applications and unleashed what may be called the 'share police' upon the investing world.

The publicity surrounding the Best prosecution made the government re-emphasise its warnings about multiple applications, and since then there have been stringent searches to find culprits. Some of the police activity on this has been very similar to their approach to apprehending drug-dealers. In one raid at a home near Bolton in Lancashire, police found 360 allotment letters for shares in the British Airports Authority. The fraud involved a ring of people in a pyramid selling operation throughout the North-West of England. Fictitious names coupled with genuine addresses were gathered by paying the ring's agents £5 for each sealed envelope with a share application inside made out in the fictitious name. The shares were sold and the proceeds handed over to the organisers. Money left over from the unsuccessful applications was returned to the ring. The same system was also used for share offers in the private sector, including Richard Branson's Virgin Group. The ring made 450 applications for a total of 72,000 BAA shares and was allocated 27,000 shares. For Rolls-Royce the ring applied for 67,500 shares and got 45,000. In each case the money invested in a share issue plus the profits were rolled over into a fresh wave of multiple applications in the next share issue.

Since then there have been several prosecutions and all kinds of people have been exposed as share-swindlers. They range from estate agents to a teacher at a comprehensive school who hoped to make a profit of £3,360 in order to pay for his daughter's private education, to a former Stock Exchange tea-boy who found it very difficult to shake off an old habit. The story of a former tea-boy now turned estate agent, illustrates the curious nature of this fraud. He made 446 applications to obtain Britoil shares giving various addresses. 410 of them were successful. Yet even when he was found guilty he could find nothing wrong in what he had done. Multiple applications were an accepted practice in the Stock Exchange that he had grown up with, and he said, 'I didn't give it any thought to be truthful. When you have been brought up for fifteen years to accept the way that things are done by people far more intelligent, it is an accepted thing and I saw and see nothing wrong at all.' This is an argument that would not appeal to the nation's moralists, but it expressed the confusion caused by changing values, and indicates how yesterday's clever trick could become today's fraudulent act.

There was, of course, City fraud long before Big Bang and privatisation. However, the revolutionary changes wrought by Big Bang and privatisation produced conditions that made fraud more attractive and provided the fraudster with greater opportunities. In one simple but devastatingly effective case it involved the reappearance of George Bernard Shaw and the clever exploitation of Stock Exchange rules. In this case the share crook GBS first approached a broker, saying that he wanted to sell some privatised shares. This got him onto the books of a stockbroker. He then bought shares, always buying in parcels of less than £10,000, and sold them within the account period. The Stock Exchange share trading system works within an account period of two weeks – three weeks if a bank holiday Monday intervenes. If you buy at the beginning of the period and the price goes up during the two weeks and you sell before the end of the account, then all you do is receive the difference, less just one set of trading costs. In this case GBS took the profit if the share prices rose during the period, but if they fell and he had to pay for the shares then GBS vanished leaving the broker to follow a trail of addresses and aliases.

Frauds such as these could have taken place at any time in the Stock Exchange's history, but Big Bang has raised the stakes. Turnover, even after the crash of Black Monday, stayed much higher than it was before Big Bang for a while and now the City slogan is: trade, trade, trade. The emphasis is on getting more business, trying to entice more of those attracted by privatisation to deal in stocks and shares. The more people deal, the more commission income is generated and this keeps the engine of the new City going. Yet the systems, despite the changes made, remain more geared to a City before Big Bang and before the massive increase in private investors – up to nine million from just over two million before 1984 and the British Telecom privatisation. This has already led to the system breaking down and producing absurd results: for example, a shareholder who did not own privatised shares receiving dividends; another able to sell shares he did not own. With the rush to get as much business as possible, and the checks and balances necessary to cope with the growth in paperwork still to be put in place – there is, for instance, no mechanism which will help a broker quickly check whether a new client has a past record – scope for fraud is considerable.

Big Bang has also added an international dimension. The investor, much more easily than in the past, can trade in shares in various parts of the world. The craze for little-known Australian mining shares is not confined to a small group of people in the Home Counties: with the twenty-four-hour stockmarket almost any share in any market is accessible and this, of course, increases the possibilities for fraud.

Consider the case of a Fort Lauderdale stock promoter Carl Porto and his associates who recruited people willing to provide sample signatures and biographical details in return for cash. The names were then supplied to the authorities as being those of company directors and forged copies of the signatures were used to open bank accounts. The Securities & Exchange Commission which brought the case told the Chicago court that the fraud began in December 1985 when Mr Porto offered a New Yorker Dominic DeFilippo $3,000 for the use of his name. Mr DeFilippo agreed and recruited his son Paul, one of his employees, Undine Dressler and Charles Clark, a maintenance man who looked after the building in which DeFilippo had his office.

A few weeks later a company called Chatsworth Enterprises was formed with Dominic DeFilippo, Undine Dressler and Jack Hauser as officer and directors. Chatsworth never traded or earned any revenue but still earned glowing reports in tip sheets such as The Swiss Analyst, published by Equity Management Services of Geneva. By the time the SEC stepped in and stopped Chatsworth shares from being traded they were worth $2.50 each – 100 times their book value. Dominic DeFilippo, listed as President, had never heard of the company or of Jack Hauser. Son Paul had also, without his knowledge, become a director of Vanguard Financial whose President was the maintenance man Mr Clark. A Chicago public relations firm hired by Porto claimed that Vanguard was about to take over a British textile firm Tex-Tech, which has premises in various parts of the north of England. Vanguard shares were worth $3.37 each, 100 times the book value when the shares were suspended. Both companies and some others had their shares sold in Britain and around the world and the SEC believes that investors could have lost millions.

Since the case was filed in January 1988, Porto and his associates have consented to the entry of an order permanently enjoining them for further violations of Federal security laws as alleged in the complaint. The companies have also been enjoined. A receiver has been appointed and Porto has agreed to pay back $150,000. But with investors likely to have lost nearly $100 million, few will get any money back.

The sort of fraud possible here and the ones we have been discussing confirms the popular prejudice that fraud means having one's hands in the till. We all know what theft is: taking what does not belong to us. That is the classic definition of theft in Continental legal codes. Yet, under English law, theft has a much wider meaning. Thus Section 1 of the 1968 Theft Act says, 'A person is guilty of theft if he dishonestly appropriates property belonging to another with the intention of permanently depriving the other of it.' Section 12 goes further and makes it clear that it does not matter whether the appropriation is made for the thief's gain or benefit. Appropriation is defined as the assumption of the rights of another.

This point is of particular interest because the idea that fraud must mean the accused has personally benefited from his crime is very common. Indeed when Ernest Saunders, the former Chairman of Guinness, was charged with various acts of theft he loudly protested that he had not put his hand in the company's till to enrich himself. That may well be so, but his alleged role in paying people to buy Guinness shares and thus boost the share price during Guinness' takeover battle for Distillers was seen as a manipulation of the market and a possible violation of the law of theft. Similarly, also in relation to Guinness, when Lord Spens was charged under the Theft Act he was alleged to have committed illegal acts which helped boost the drinks company's share price by arranging for the purchase of a crucial block of 2.15 million Guinness shares for £7.6 million, also during the takeover of Distillers. He was alleged to have committed various acts that benefited his then firm, merchant bankers Henry Ansbacher, but there was no suggestion that he had derived personal profit.

To the public, everyone accused of fraud may be a criminal but there are clearly different kinds of fraud. This is well understood by the executives of British companies. The survey by Levi and Morgan found that there was a strong feeling that action should be taken against fraudsters whatever the consequences. But, as the authors say:

> Executives treat fraud seriously and in a discriminating manner. Frauds involving professional people were viewed as being particularly serious. Perhaps, more surprisingly, in the light of arguments that 'new' and 'technical' crimes lack moral support, insider trading is also rated high up the scale and in absolute terms. Both income tax fraud and frauds [by businesspeople] against insurance companies were regarded relatively lightly, though more seriously than joy-riding or smoking cannabis.

Unlike the wider public who tend to paint all fraudsters with the same brush, the executives realise the need to differentiate between crimes. They are aware not only that different crimes carry different penalties, but that, whatever the lurid headlines may suggest, social security frauds cost a lot less than commercial frauds. So it is commercial frauds upon which we intend to concentrate, for they go to the very nature of the financial system, how it operates and how it is manipulated.

2

A King's Ransom

On the bright, cold winter afternoon of Thursday 26 January 1984 a young trainee solicitor from the City firm of Linklater & Paines set off for Dunkirk. For most of us such a journey would combine history and nostalgia, but the young man, Tim Bardwell, was in a hurry and the quickest way to Dunkirk was a flight to Brussels and then a drive to the French port. The drive was through flat, uninteresting countryside, but as Bardwell sped through Belgium and France in his hired Hertz Ford he could review the events that had sent him scurrying to France.

It had begun a few days earlier when Allied Arab Bank, an Arab bank in the City, had rung Linklaters about a problem they were having with one of their clients. The client, Esal Commodities, was a well-known multi-million dollar London-based commodities group involved in shipping various goods to Nigeria and other Third World countries. It had only recently become a client of Allied Arab – in March 1983 – but the various amounts it had borrowed since then had all been promptly repaid. The bank had been so pleased with its new client that it had steadily increased its limits and, in December 1983, it had lent Esal $9.6 million for the shipment of sugar to Nigeria. But on 20 January 1984 Esal had confessed that it was having difficulty repaying the amount. There had just been a coup in Nigeria and this had placed the company in a very difficult situation. Could they please have another thirty days?

Allied Arab's new chief executive, Graham Butler, was worried about the Nigerian coup. Even at the best of times it could be difficult to get money out of that country; now the coup leaders were making all sorts of statements. Allied Arab could not easily afford to lose $9.6 million, or have it blocked in Nigeria indefinitely. Though backed by Barclays, who owned 20%, Esal was a big exposure for a bank whose capital was just £16 million. Butler decided that if Esal could not repay

18

then the bank should seize the sugar which was the security for the money. According to the bank's records several ships were carrying the sugar to Nigeria and Butler was concerned that the bank should get hold of the sugar before the ships left Europe. This was the task given to Linklaters.

The ship selected was the MV *Sea King* in Dunkirk and Bardwell was on his way to Dunkirk to effect a '*Saisie Conservatoire*', an exotic French term which for lawyers is a variation on an old theme. Debt collectors seize cars, houses or other possessions; Bardwell had to seize a cargo of sugar. If Bardwell, a smart, bright young man – well known in the firm for his stylish clothes – felt a sense of excitement it was because this was a foreign jaunt and the sort of operation that Linklaters had begun to specialise in. Little did he realise that his actions in Dunkirk over the next few hours would lead to one man entering the *Guinness Book of Records* as the world's biggest bankrupt, the disclosure of 'telephone number' debts that would shock a high court judge, and the start of what has proved to be one of the longest and most sustained fraud investigations seen in London.

Bardwell arrived in Dunkirk late on Thursday evening to find that steps had already been taken to arrest the cargo. The next morning Bardwell made sure of the arrangements and decided to see the ship's agents. Their offices were set back some 200 metres from the quayside and as Bardwell walked along the harbour front that morning all he could see and feel was the cold, windswept bleakness of this particular part of the French coastline. Not a ship was to be seen – the *Sea King*, itself, was a few miles offshore. Barren docklands and mountains of coal gave an atmosphere that made Bardwell feel that this was indeed an Orwellian 1984-ish vision of desolation and emptiness. But it was here that Bardwell was to encounter the first of many Esal surprises.

At the agents, Dewulf's, bright, modern, open-plan offices Bardwell was met by Charles Henri Tourillion, a fluent English-speaker with a delightful French accent. The Englishman had just drawn up his chair to sit alongside Tourillion when he noticed a set of bills of lading on the desk. They seemed to refer to the same cargo that Bardwell had just arrested.

The bill of lading that Bardwell had stated that the *Sea King* was loaded with 11,800 metric tonnes of sugar. The bills of lading on Tourillion's desk showed 10,290 metric tonnes of sugar on the ship. The *Sea King* could at best carry 16,000 tonnes and there was no way both Bardwell's and Tourillion's bills could be right. As Tourillion would later tell the police, 'He showed me documents which he believed were original documents related to the goods loaded on the *Sea King*, whereas in fact they were completely different from the documents signed on board (typing, stamp, signature, etc.). It was clear to me that these were not the correct documents.'

Tourillion insisted he had the proper bills of lading that gave the title to the goods though he refused to give them to Bardwell. But he did give Bardwell a copy of the stowage manifest which shows how the cargo is distributed on a ship. Again the stowage manifest Tourillion had was very different to the one Bardwell had been given in London by Allied Arab. So for the same cargo on the *Sea King* there seemed to be two totally different bills of lading and two different stowage manifests. But who had the right documents? Was it possible that Allied Arab had lent money to Esal on the basis of wrong documents? Something was dreadfully wrong. This was now no longer a case of arresting a cargo of sugar, this had the whiff of fraud about it and Bardwell quickly informed London before setting off on his return journey.

Saturday brought even worse news from Dunkirk. Another Englishman, quite unconnected with Linklaters, had descended on Dunkirk in search of the same sugar. He was Alaistair Tainsh, accounting manager of sugar traders Cargill. Just as Bardwell had set off for Dunkirk, rumours reached Cargill that Esal had been trying to raise money by presenting a full set of original bills of lading relating to sugar on the *Sea King*. It was as a reaction to this that Tainsh had travelled to Dunkirk to deliver notarised copies of bills of lading, proving Cargill's ownership, to their French lawyer. Cargill's information was that another sugar-trader called Rionda Da Pass was claiming the sugar. Though Tainsh had only schoolboy French, he understood enough of the court proceedings to realise that it was not another sugar-trader claiming the cargo but a bank. Worse, the bank had already arrested the cargo.

Saturday's news set Linklaters humming. Their great expert in litigation, Christopher Stiles, was back from Vancouver and an awesome operation was started. On Friday night they had issued a writ against Esal. Over the weekend they went for the kill. It was classic litigation work of the type of which Perry Mason would have been proud. True there was no Paul Drake or Della Street, but there was no

20

dearth of investigative activity. While a whole army of paralegal staff kept Stiles and his colleagues well fed on sandwiches and Big Macs, the legal machine set to work. On Sunday another Linklater contingent – this time a team of three – set off for Dunkirk to determine who owned what. Just as they were leaving, Stiles was finalising affidavits to obtain two special injunctions: *Mareva* and *Anton Piller*. Both are named after court actions that created them and are extremely powerful remedies. The Mareva freezes the assets of a company from the moment it is served; an Anton Piller order is like a civil search warrant. Marevas are not uncommon in civil actions.

Linklaters had been building up quite a picture of Esal Commodities. It seemed to shelter a whole rabbit-warren of companies: Global-bridge, which owned the *Sea King*, Levenco, Quoteberry and White Cross Development Corporation all seemed to be connected with it. Then there were the banks to which Allied Arab had paid the monies it had lent Esal. They were mostly London branches of Indian banks, and Stiles advised Allied Arab to name them in the injunction. This, thought Stiles, would help in tracing the money – a matter of some importance if there had indeed been a fraud.

Mr Justice Mars-Jones, the duty judge at the Royal Courts of Justice in the Strand, was playing golf, but he agreed to see Stiles and his team at 6 p.m. that Sunday evening. After an hour's hearing he granted Allied Arab an Anton Piller to search Esal Group's premises and a Mareva freezing the assets of five of its companies and its accounts in four London banks: Grindlays, Punjab National, Central Bank and Union Bank.

Stiles and his colleagues returned to their office to plan Operation Esal. This was just the sort of thing Linklaters did so well, and throughout Sunday night the phone lines at their Gresham Street offices in Barrington House fairly buzzed as Stiles gathered together his team for what promised to be a momentous start to the week.

At 7.30 the next morning, Monday 30 January 1984, over twenty lawyers gathered in the offices of Linklaters to be divided into eleven teams. Each of the teams was armed with a copy of the Mareva injunction and the Anton Piller order and their task was simple and dramatic. At precisely 9.14 a.m. eleven teams rang eleven doorbells – either of an Esal company or an Esal banker. Some of the doorbells turned out to be worthless, no more than accommodation addresses in the East End, but Esal's main offices at 19/20 Noel Street in the West

End provided drama that would dwarf everything that had gone before.

Noel Street in Soho was like most Soho streets: a ragbag of scruffy shops, offices and neon lights. From the outside the Esal offices looked just as unprepossessing, but this concealed the crucial fact that the offices backed on to flats in D'Arblay Street at the back, and which meant you could walk in through the Noel Street entrance and exit through D'Arblay Street. Before the morning was over this simple fact was to acquire tremendous significance.

The Linklater team that had arrived at Esal that morning consisted of two recently qualified solicitors. Clarke Miller was a thoughtful, rather chunky man; his great friend and colleague, Dominic Helps, was very much more extrovert. They had been shown into quite a palatial executive office: several Reuters' screens displayed the maze of numbers that indicated sugar prices, and there was a large desk behind which sat a shirt-sleeved executive. He identified himself as Fahim Nasim, an Esal director, and he simulated a convincing show of anger about the Mareva and Anton Piller orders. But a quick call to Tringham, Esal's solicitors, established that these orders had to be obeyed and soon Miller and Helps were busy going through the various offices, looking through files and photocopying important documents.

Miller had been doing this for about an hour when the photocopying took him to the fifth-floor offices of Allan Dean, Esal's shipping manager. He had just left Dean's office and stepped into the corridor when he found he was being followed by a man who looked like he was a rugby prop forward. Actually he was a 15½-stone former back-row player with a directness of style and conversation that matched his physique. 'Who are you?' he asked Miller. When Miller explained, the man introduced himself: 'Detective Inspector Brian Cooper, Metropolitan Police Fraud Squad.' Miller was too well-trained as a lawyer to betray an instant reaction, but he knew he had to ring Stiles so he and Cooper went down to the first floor to make the call. Stiles' reaction, 'Oh, shit!', overheard by Cooper, seemed to sum up the situation. What had started as an interesting debt collection exercise had now turned into a police fraud investigation.

In many ways Cooper's presence there was something of an accident. In those days the Met's Fraud Squad offices in Holborn maintained a skeleton Saturday service and the previous Saturday afternoon it had been Cooper's turn. He had just had a sandwich lunch when Scotland Yard referred a call from Cargill to him. The call was the result of

Tainsh's discoveries at Dunkirk and Cargill's fears that they might be the victims of an Esal insurance fraud. The natural instinct would have been to begin investigations at once, but CID overtime was an escalating cost and it was decided to wait until Monday. So Cooper agreed to meet a Cargill representative outside Esal's offices at 10.30 on Monday morning in what was meant to be a hand-holding exercise. He was shown into Dean's offices where it was soon clear that hands were not so much being held as wrung in desperation. Dean was in quite a state and there was a rather grim-looking man sitting in the office looking for all the world like a fierce minder. Cooper was intrigued by the man's refusal to reveal anything about himself and wondered if he was from the Department of Trade or even, perhaps, the City Fraud Squad. Was a raid on? Cooper saw Miller enter, photocopy some documents and leave. It was after Stiles had exclaimed, 'Oh shit,' that Cooper discovered that the grim-looking minder, with an apparent vow of silence, was a Linklater assistant.

So far in our story the lawyers have made all the running, now Cooper quickly took charge. As he was speaking to Stiles on the telephone, an official of Esal interrupted him. Cooper forcibly reminded him of his manners, then, when Dean rushed up threatening to throw everybody out, Cooper adopted the classical attitude of British policemen: 'I am a police officer. All of you are nicked.' Kalim Nasim, now playing the innocent, said, 'I'm sorry, I don't know much about the law. What does "nicked" mean.' 'It means,' said Cooper, 'that nobody moves out of this building till I have had some explanations.'

The next few hours, indeed days, were spent in seeking explanations. Dean was taken to the Fraud Squad's offices in Richbell Place, where he made a statement – the first of many such statements from many people that Cooper would collect over the next three years. There were visits to the offices of Cargill and Allied Arab. If there had been a fraud then they, not Cargill, were the ones who had been duped. On Wednesday 1 February Allied Arab formally lodged a complaint. Finally, on the morning of Wednesday 8 February 1984, Cooper led a team of forty officers in raids on several Esal addresses ranging from drab, dingy holes in the East End to sumptuous houses in London suburbs. A great number of books, documents and papers were taken away but only two directors were arrested: Ashish Banerji and Rajendra Bhutoria, the latter almost accidentally as he just happened to be passing through London when Cooper's men raided. Bhutoria, a plump Indian who normally lived in Nigeria, betrayed no emotion, but two distinct drops of tears formed under Banerji's eyes and trickled slowly, gently, down his bearded face. It was, is, the face of a very proper even professorial man suggesting dignity and calm. The sight of those teardrops was so incongruous that it made a dramatic impression on Cooper.

But the biggest prize of all eluded Cooper: Rajendra Sethia, the boss of Esal. Indeed even as Cooper had been playing the classic police role on that historic Monday, Sethia had been making just as classic an escape. Later, stories would sweep through London's commodity markets elaborately describing Sethia's escape. And, like all such stories, every teller improved on the previous version, adding an extra dash of colour. One story had it that, even as Cooper made his dramatic intervention, Sethia nipped out of the D'Arblay Street exit into a waiting Rolls and headed straight for Heathrow. He arrived just as the lunch-time flights were leaving for the United States and by nightfall he was in New York. Another version painted him as a more frightened fugitive seeking sanctuary in a friend's house – and hiding under the stairs there – before taking a night flight to Spain. Whatever the truth, by the time Cooper and the Fraud Squad came calling on 8 February, Rajendra Sethia had long gone. Over the next three years, as Cooper investigated what was to turn out to be the biggest fraud investigation seen in London, he must have often bitterly regretted the fact that he had not been allowed to begin his investigations the moment Cargill rang on that Saturday afternoon.

Our story would have been simpler if Sethia had stayed to face British justice, but his escape, colourful and dramatic as it was, was more in keeping with the flamboyance and style of the man. Like Lazarus he had risen from the dead, repaying in full all the creditors of his first bankruptcy. Now, even as stories circulated about Sethia's escape, many creditors believed that lightning would strike twice. He would not only return, they argued, but answer all the questions and settle all the debts. Indeed within days of the Fraud Squad raid, Sethia was holding a meeting with his bankers in a Copenhagen hotel. As news of this reached London those who knew Sethia shook their heads in awe. This was certainly the Raj they knew and feared. A few months before the collapse, Sethia had taken friends to the Royal Exchange Building he had just acquired and, pointing to the Bank of England across the road, said, 'When I open my offices here, opposite the Old Lady, everybody will know I am the King.' One companion, recalling the scene later, would be convinced that Sethia saw the building as did Fitzgerald's Gatsby when he picked out the green light at the end of Daisy's dock. Sethia, like Gatsby, felt he had arrived only to discover that what was waiting round the corner was not the gilded royal carriage but the bankrupt's dust-cart. The man who wanted to be King was to end up as King of the bankrupts.

Some months after the events we have just described, when Rajendra Sethia had at last entered the *Guinness Book of Records* as the world's biggest bankrupt, and police on three continents were seeking him, it became fashionable to talk about the end of the Raj. This was, of course, a clever pun on his name for since his childhood Rajendra was known as Raj by both friends and foes. Raj is a regal name in India and, it was perhaps appropriate that Rajendra Sethia was born, just four months after the British Raj ended, into a Marwari business family. Few men could have been so well equipped for business as Raj Sethia was. In India the Marwaris, a tightly knit community, are credited with fantastic business skills and no little business ruthlessness. The joke is that if you are in a jungle and see a Marwari and a tiger approaching you, be sure to shoot the Marwari first. The pot-bellied Marwari, forever counting money with his greasy palms and prepared to suck the last penny from the tearful widow, is part of the demonology of modern India. He is as often the baddie in Indian film melodramas as he is in the Indian parliament, a convenient scapegoat for all the country's economic problems. Many of the Marwaris had shrewdly financed Gandhi and the right-wing of the Indian freedom movement and, despite all the talk of socialism that swept newly independent India, the Marwaris were able to cash in their chips. Just as the Indian nationalists took over from the departing English administrators, so the Marwari business Raj mopped up the jute mills and engineering factories being sold by the departing Scottish financial Raj. The basic difference between the Scots and Marwaris was that while the Scots were industrialists, the Marwaris were essentially traders who made their money buying and selling other people's products – the classic middle-men.

Sethia's father was already well established as a jute trader in London by the time Raj, the youngest of four sons, was born, but the dictates of the extended Indian family system made it more convenient for Raj's early education to be at an essentially Marwari school in Calcutta. He arrived in London at the age of eleven and began to experience something like the conventional education that the well-off classes in this country enjoy: a couple of years in a London school, then a boarding school in Norfolk for his 'O' and 'A' levels and, finally, a degree in economics from London University's Queen Mary College.

The death of his father in December 1967 had lured him to the family business, jointly managed by uncles and older brothers. He was still a student at Queen Mary's and he was also something of a stock market punter. This was the era of Poseidon, the Australian nickel share that started at a few coppers and ended at £126, and Raj both made and lost money on it, eventually buying it at £124 and then seeing it sink to £10. Later he would boast the deal had cost him £50,000.

In 1973 the family decided to go their separate business ways and Raj took over Rusel Fibre Dealers Ltd, a jute trading firm set up by his father. He aggressively diversified it into sugar, just in time to taste the sugar boom years of 1974 and 1975. Raj's forte was the 'forward trading market'. Here, the trader promises to buy sugar, or some other commodity, at today's prices with a delivery date several weeks hence. By this time the sugar price might be much higher, but the buyer pays the price he had promised and sells at this higher price. This is a very proper and normal business transaction and, of course, sweet, sweet profit requiring nothing more than a steady nerve. By the middle of 1974 Raj had a new company, Metacom, also making forward deals in commodities, and by the end of 1974 he was a millionaire several times over. Then suddenly the price collapsed, and Raj was left with 200,000 tonnes he had to buy at a higher price and debts of around £8 million. Metacom and Rusel Fibre went under, and Rajendra Sethia was made bankrupt.

Raj, clinging to the essence of the Hindu faith, blamed it on his karma and spent dreary hours in the central London library of a Hindu Institute where his sister worked, or at dingy bookies' offices trying to pick winners. Then he decided to visit Nigeria and though he returned to London a sick man – it was months before he was fully fit – he had made contacts there, of all places in a Lagos casino, that pointed the way forward. His brothers, Ranjit and Nirmal, were willing to help and by 1976 Raj was once again making money, first for his brothers, then for himself.

He did not, could not, forget his creditors and, as his business expanded, his list of creditors diminished. Companies were created in Nigeria in collaboration with Nigerians, and in 1977 Esal Commodities was formed in London. It had a capital of £5,000 and three directors: Raj, his wife and another Indian. In 1979 yet another Nigerian company, Nimpex, was formed, again with Nigerian collaborators. By then, Rajendra Sethia was no longer a bankrupt, having repaid all his creditors with interest – as he boasted later – and Esal was making a name for bold, successful deals.

Raj had called the company Esal because the way he pronounced the name it sounded like S.L., which were also his father's initials. As in the great Hindu legends it seemed the son would make the father's name famous. Nigeria, blessed with oil, was booming, and Sethia's hour had struck. Or so it seemed.

As Esal expanded – by 1982–83 the capital had increased to £5 million, the turnover was several times that figure – Raj Sethia's gestures seemed to display a touch of royal caprice. On one occasion returning late from a Mayfair casino he crashed one of his cars against a bollard. He cursed the bollard, the car and the world in choice Hindi abuse, then just abandoned the car and the next day bought another. It was around this time that he bought a Rolls almost as an alternative to some strawberries and cream. His friend Jayant and he had gone to the annual Berkeley Square ball – quite a haunt for the rich Asians of this country. Jayant had suggested that they buy some strawberries and cream and sample the local talent when he suddenly found Raj interested in a Rolls that was being auctioned. Even before Jayant realised what was happening Raj had bid £35,000 to add yet another Rolls to his collection. Explaining it later to Jayant, he said he saw it as a dare. The Arabs dominated such auctions and Raj was determined to show them that when it came to extravagance he could match any sheikh. By the time Cooper and the Fraud Squad arrived Raj certainly had enough cars to match the sheikhs: nine in all, three of them Rolls, one a two-tone pink and yellow Rolls that boasted the number plate ESA 1, complete with all mod cons: stereo video, cocktail cabinet and telephone.

Sethia had originally made friends with the London manager of the Central Bank of India, one Bhaskar Ramchandran Patankar. He had then used his friendship to gain entry into several London Indian banks, one of them being the Punjab National Bank. Though PNB was one of the great banks of India it had limited international experience at that time. The increasing business activities of Indian expatriates through overseas British banks had convinced the bank that it should open a branch in London. On 10 July 1976 it opened its first international branch in London on a suitably modest scale. It had a paid-up capital of £200,000, a first month business loss of £50,000 and the manager, A.K. Talwar, was housed in rented accommodation in Leytonstone where he had to keep a ready store of coins to obtain heat and light from slot machines. In April 1980 Talwar was replaced by Amarjit Singh with Talwar staying on in London as an employee of Rajendra's brother Ranjit. This was the great turning point for Esal and Rajendra Sethia.

It is easy to see in retrospect that Singh, Sethia and, to an extent, the Punjab National Bank were made for each other. Thin, austere and perpetually chain-smoking, Singh may not have had the outward flamboyance and dash of Sethia, but like him he had burning ambition and London in the early 1980s provided the ideal opportunity. Amarjit Singh arrived in London to find PNB firmly established and Rajendra Sethia a client, having been provided a loan of $500,000 against the security of his office property at Bedford Row. But within a few months Singh had doubled and trebled the loans to Sethia. By the time the bubble burst, in January 1984, PNB had lent Esal nearly $130 million and established a relationship that was to end, as we have seen, in tears.

When precisely the Sethia–Singh relationship developed from a conventional banking relationship to an extraordinarily unconventional one is not that clear, but sometime towards the end of 1981 Amarjit summoned his then loans manager, Swami Satsanghi, and asked him to send a telex to the Central Bank of India and the United Bank confirming that PNB would pay $2.5 million into Esal's account within eight to ten days. Satsanghi was warned that guarantees were not to be entered in the guarantee register or any other books of the bank. This was the first of many 'future dated bank pay orders' games which enabled Raj Sethia to indulge in even more paper chasing operations through the banks.

As Sethia's business empire expanded through the early 1980s there seemed no danger to the Singh–Sethia relationship. Outwardly, Esal Commodities could not have appeared stronger or healthier. Its first accounts, covering the period 1 October 1977 to 31 March 1979, had shown a turnover of £6.767 million and net profits of £123,326. By the end of March 1982 turnover had risen to £143,284 million and net profits to £3.372 million. The turnover was double that of 1981, profits nearly 5 ½ times that of the previous year. Of course, none of the Esal accounts had been agreed with the Revenue, but this seemed a small matter. The amount set aside for taxation in the 1981 accounts was a modest £70,000 and for 1982, £100,000.

But loans from the banks were mounting and 1982 provided the first signs that not everything was wonderful in the Nigerian garden. In April of that year, President Shagari, worried by the enormous capital outflows, imposed emergency economic measures and Sethia's paper chase ran into some problems.

Throughout the early part of 1983 tiny cracks were beginning to appear in the Sethia empire, but outwardly it appeared so secure that no doubts surfaced. In December 1983 Raj Sethia seemed to have achieved his great ambition. His brothers had imposing London buildings as headquarters of their offices: Ranjit Sethia, opposite *The Times* and the *Sunday Times* in Gray's Inn Road, and Nirmal was located in Sethia House near Clerkenwell Road. Raj was going to best them all and in December he acquired the freehold of 1 and 2 Royal Exchange Buildings and the leasehold of 3 and 4 Royal Exchange. These buildings are, of course, opposite the Bank of England and as soon as he had secured the deal he brought one of his contacts to the building. Then, looking across at the Bank of England building, he said, 'Now they will believe me. I have arrived. I am the King.'

One only had to look at some of the prestigious City names that had helped him with the financing to confirm that. The first mortgage had been done through merchant bankers Hill Samuel with bridging finance provided by Amas S.A., a Geneva-based company controlled by Hindujas, one of the most successful Indian businessmen in this country. The Hindujas are so well connected that every autumn, around Guy Fawkes night, they hold a party to celebrate Diwali, the Indian festival of light. These parties have been attended by Denis and Mrs Thatcher and Norman Tebbitt. Lately the Hindujas have become embroiled in a controversy about the supply of Swedish Bofors guns to the Indian army, a controversy that nearly brought down Rajiv Gandhi's government.

But even as Sethia gazed at the Bank of England and planned the most extravagant office the City had ever seen, the first public exposure of his unsavoury activities appeared, appropriately perhaps, in the most unlikely of places. On 30 November 1983 the *Free Press Journal* of Bombay published an article about Esal and its relationship with the

Central Bank of India. Obviously fed by an inside source, it had sensational revelations about Esal's Central Bank problems: vast amounts owing on overdue bills, Reserve Bank of Indian concern, apparent lack of action by Central chairman Sonalkar and suggestions that fraud may have been committed and connived at by bank officials.

In India the Reserve Bank was stirred into belated action and in London, where the article was telexed by Central's head office, it created what one insider would later describe as 'a panic situation'. Though the allegations concerned Central, other banks felt the draught, particularly Punjab. Its exposure to Esal was three times that of Central, getting on to $130 million as opposed to Central's $50 million. Some $40 million of the monies lent by Punjab was very simply Amarjit Singh doling out money to his friend Rajendra without any head office approval and far in excess of sanctioned limits. Unless something was done the 31 December year-end figures – due in a few weeks – would reveal this and, almost certainly, raise very awkward questions with auditors.

Singh's solution was window-dressing – one of the most notorious of dubious practices that students of auditing are warned about. It means monkeying with the figures so that the auditors will think the account is in a far better shape than it really is. Companies in trouble do try window-dressing, but any reasonable auditor would be able to detect that. In this case Singh, with the resources of a bank and its many customers at his disposal, was in a much better position. All he had to do was persuade some of his other customers to 'accommodate' Esal by lending a few millions to cover the crucial year-end period. They would have the money back once the year-end fuss was over. It was Singh's own version of robbing the rich to help out 'poor' Esal. The first Punjab customer Singh decided to put the bite on was Tulsi Brothers, another Indian trading company in London.

On the morning of either the 20 or 21 December Amarjit Singh rang his former assistant Swami Satsanghi, who was by now finance director of Tulsi Brothers. Could he and his boss, Mr Vaswani drop in at the bank? There was something he wanted to discuss. Vaswani was away but that afternoon Satsanghi, popularly known as Sami, went to see his old boss. Amarjit wanted Tulsi Brothers to lend Esal $5 million. The loan was to be for only three weeks and Tulsi would have the money returned to them by 21 January. Singh freely confessed to his former assistant that this was all part of 'window-dressing'. Satsanghi was not very receptive but promised to discuss it with Vaswani. The next day Vaswani returned to London and they both went to see Singh.

Esal already owed Tulsi Brothers $3 million and Vaswani and Satsanghi decided this might be a good opportunity to try and reclaim the money. Yes, they said, they would 'accommodate' Esal provided they got a bill of exchange worth $6.5 million. This was a lot more than Amarjit was prepared for and they haggled over the terms. By the time Vaswani and Sami got into their car to travel the short distance from Punjab's offices in London Wall to their own at High Holborn, they had agreed that in exchange for a bill of exchange of $5 million Tulsi would lend Esal $5 million. But nothing came of it and no money was ever lent by Tulsi to Esal. The arrangements with Tulsi involved too many commitments being put on paper, and Singh had found another customer he could more easily put the bite on. It was Raj Sethia's brother Nirmal.

On Tuesday 20 December Nirmal Sethia received a phone call from his brother Raj. The two had not always got on very well and it was only in August of that year that Nirmal and Raj had started speaking to each other again. For almost eight long years previous to that the brothers had been virtual strangers, and in the late 1970s Nirmal had fought legal battles with Ranjit. But then their mother fell ill and the quarrels were patched up. Now Raj wanted to borrow $3 million for ninety days. He had to pay the money to Punjab before 31 December.

For Nirmal Sethia this was a large sum of money. His company, also in commodity trading, was nowhere near as big as his brother's and he told Raj he would have to consult another director. The next day Nirmal rang back to say that he was prepared to lend the money provided Punjab agreed to guarantee the loan. Raj was sure the bank would agree and rang on 22 December to confirm that this was fine by the bank.

But Amarjit was not that happy and he rang Nirmal to wonder why he wanted Punjab to provide a guarantee. After Nirmal had explained, Singh suggested it would be better all round to accept a bank payment order dated either for the 30 or 31 of March. This would be a piece of paper saying pay to Sethia (London) Ltd by order of Esal the sum of $3 million and would be signed by Amarjit Singh on behalf of Punjab. So if Esal failed to repay the loan Punjab would be liable. This may appear identical to a guarantee but in this form Punjab was countersigning an

Esal document and to Singh, who was terrified of recording things and putting commitments on paper, this was preferable.

The next day, Friday 23 December, Nirmal's nephew delivered to Punjab a letter authorising the bank to transfer $3 million to Esal. He returned with the bank payment order which Nirmal, having checked it was signed by Amarjit Singh, put in his safe. Everybody seemed happy and Amarjit's window-dressing to fool the auditors and head office appeared to have worked beautifully.

Six days later, however, something very odd surfaced. On 29 December an accounts officer in Nirmal's firm suddenly came to see him. He had just received a very disturbing bank advice from the Punjab. This informed Sethia (London) Ltd that its company's account at Punjab had been debited by $5 million. Nirmal asked his account officer to make sure that such a debit had actually been made, then tried to ring Amarjit Singh without any success. The next day Nirmal Sethia wrote a letter, formally addressing it to the general manager of the Punjab National Bank, protesting about this wholly unauthorised debit and asking it to be reversed. Though the whole thing came as a shock and $5 million was a huge amount to be wrongly debited to the account, Nirmal saw it as no more than a mistake by the bank. As planned he left for India on 3 January.

His finance director Virendra Ahuja was also on holiday then. They were both back at work on 9 January and it was decided that Ahuja would pursue Punjab about the wrong debit. Ahuja was one of that tribe of Indian managers who had come to London as an official of an Indian government-owned bank, then left it to join Nirmal's firm. He was, obviously, very familiar with banking practices and had also discovered that the bank payment order guaranteeing the $3 million loan was wrongly dated.

For the next few weeks letters, telexes and telephone calls poured out from Sethia (London) Ltd trying to get Punjab to correct the un-authorised debit and reverse any interest that might be charged on it. Ahuja consulted solicitors, but by Monday 30 January the entry had still not been corrected. That was the day, as we have seen, that Allied Arab Bank imposed a Mareva injunction on Esal and froze everything. Nothing would ever be the same again.

Ever since he had arrived at Esal's offices on that Monday morning, Detective Inspector Cooper had felt that here was something big. There were a lot of questions, but very few answers and the more he investigated the more disturbing the shape of the final answer seemed. It was rather like a Hercule Poirot situation: something nasty has happened, perhaps murder, but who has been murdered? An answer to that would go a long way in explaining how, even why. As in the classic detective novel, particularly the ones popular in the 1930s, Cooper's biggest problem was to find the body.

Of course, the biggest suspect, Rajendra Sethia, was out of reach. As we have seen, on Wednesday 8 February Cooper and some forty officers had raided Esal and the next day warrants were issued for the arrest of Sethia and other Esal directors.

That weekend the main Esal bankers started gathering in Copenhagen where Raj Sethia had holed up in a hotel. It was an impressive list: Ian Fraser of Johnson Matthey Bankers; Richard Williams of Oriental Credit; a Mr Tara from the Union Bank of India; Shetty from the Central Bank of India and Ian Mitchell of Middle East Bank. Also present was Raj's brother Ranjit, who had flown in from India along with his wife and Jim Coote, an accountant who owned a company with whom Esal had had dealings.

Rajendra had hired a conference room at the hotel and on Monday morning, 13 February, the two-day meeting began. Allied Arab's actions and the police raid had done nothing to dent Sethia's confidence. He may have fled London like a common criminal but here at Copenhagen he was oozing confidence and charm in equal measure. There was nothing to worry about, he told the bankers. All this Allied Arab action and police action was nothing; he could explain everything. Surely the bankers knew him, he had made massive profits for them. They knew his track-record and he would repay the whole lot of them, every creditor down to the last penny. In fact, though he had no books and records to help him, he had produced figures which proved his point.

The figures that Sethia showed his bankers were later to be described as 'an unauthenticated Statement of Assets and Liabilities', and this had Esal's liabilities at $212.215 million, assets at $206.704 million, the difference being 'profits which have not yet been accounted for'. Sethia was confident that in 1984 he would make profits of $60–$65 million. This may strike us as a bit of Sethia in wonderland, but Amarjit and the other bankers still seemed to treat Esal as if it was any other trading group. They accepted that Esal Group's profits were 'principally generated from their trading activities', and that it 'was particularly difficult to project estimated profits for future periods with any real certainty'. But, just to be on the safe side, Amarjit and his friends discounted Sethia's profit figures from $60–$65 million to $50 million. In making this remarkable concession the bankers felt they were acting 'in the interests of prudence and having regard to the current circumstances'. But Amarjit and his friends like Ian Fraser had sufficient faith in Sethia to assume that a similar profit would be made in 1985. Of course Nigeria was unstable and estimates uncertain, but they hoped that 'the creditors and unsecured Banks would be paid in full, or at least substantially, by the end of December 1985'.

So this remarkable bankers' wonderland of a meeting went on discussing Raj's figures and Esal's glorious future to come. The minutes that recorded the figures and the future course of action are certainly quite the most extraordinary ever produced. Though they filled nineteen pages, there was no reference to the events of 30 January, no indication that police had raided Esal and issued warrants for the arrest of Raj Sethia and some of his fellow-directors. In fact, the minutes do not even mention where the meeting was held, or name the individuals present, only the banks. And the only possible reference to the police action is this coy statement explaining the need for 'unauthenticated Statement of Assets and Liabilities prepared by Raj Sethia'. According to the minutes, 'as the records and the papers of the Esal Group were unavailable it was understood that the unauthenticated Statement had been prepared on the basis of the information available to Mr Sethia and his knowledge of the affairs of the Esal Group, and, as such, he warranted its accuracy, completeness and reliability, subject to discrepancies of not more than, nor less than, 5%'. Given the 'current circumstances', the banks were quite happy with that.

Most mysteriously, the minutes spoke of an earlier meeting held just two days after the Fraud Squad raids 'in London on Friday 10 February 1984'. According to the minutes, that London meeting decided that 'no legal action would be commenced or continued against Esal (Commodities) Ltd and other members of the Esal group for a period of one month pending discussion and resolution of the proposed Creditors' scheme'. It was, probably, this meeting, initiated by Amarjit Singh, that had led to the Copenhagen meeting. Certainly, the thrust of both the meetings was simple: stop the actions being taken by Allied Arab and the police. Give Raj Sethia time and everything would work out all right.

But Brian Cooper was already loose, looking for the body he knew existed, and the people who had committed the murder. Amarjit Singh, outwardly a respectable banker of an Indian government-owned bank, could not publicly oppose Cooper and his investigations, but privately he fought against it tooth and nail, feverishly promoting the Esal rescue. So, through the spring, summer and early autumn of 1984, London witnessed an extraordinary spectacle: Cooper busy burrowing away to discover what had happened, Singh just as busily going to creditors' meetings and seeking to stitch together a new Esal. While Cooper went round meeting creditors, bank officials and whoever would tell him who murdered Esal, Singh almost in parallel pretended there had been no murder, just a fainting spell and the patient could be revived with some more money. As ever the legal men were the ones who made money as some of the most expensive, prestigious lawyers from the best law firms in the City argued about the rescue package that Singh was convinced would save Esal and thwart Cooper.

Amarjit's ploy was very simple. On 2 March 1984 Punjab presented a winding-up petition. To the innocent this may have suggested that Punjab wanted to liquidate Esal. But there was no intention of that. This was just a legal device to prevent a creditor who might really want to wind up Esal being in the 'saddle', the phrase Mr Justice Harman later used to describe Punjab's tactics. As Harman said, 'This was a game we played as juniors. If you can't complete, issue a writ for specific performance.' For Amarjit the game was essential if his Esal rescue plan was to succeed.

The rescue, known legally as the contractual scheme, was the one agreed at Copenhagen. Esal would trade its way out of its problems, the banks would provide a further stand-by facility of $40 million and impose 'suitable controls' on the 'management of the group'. On 19 April most, but not all, creditors were circulated about the rescue and Amarjit came within a hair's breadth of success. He required 90% approval, he got 87%. But 78% of these were banks. Only 9% of the 22% unsecured creditors wanted the rescue. There had to be an alternative. On 8 May the first meeting involving all the creditors was held at the Barbican Conference Centre.

This was like Hamlet without the Prince. Raj Sethia hovered over the meeting in spirit, though he had friends who spoke up for him. One of the most influential was Ian Fraser of Johnson Matthey Bankers. Sometime before the meeting Fraser had met Sethia in New York and he now told the creditors' meeting that Sethia was fine and that he would be able to get everyone's money back.

Soon after this David Dein, the most important of the unsecured creditors, was invited to a meeting at the Punjab National Bank. Amarjit Singh and Ian Fraser pressed him very hard to agree the rescue package. But he could see it made no sense and resisted their blandishments. The rescue package could not generate immediate cash and it was not backed by tangible securities. Dein's refusal to agree proved a thorn in Amarjit's side, more so as Dein led the fight by the creditors against the PNB plan.

Amarjit and his friends tried hard to counteract this by fostering the image that if only Sethia was given more time, all would be well.

This was also the message nearly all those who visited Sethia brought back. Shuttling between Spain, Sweden and New York, where he calmly attended his offices, he told most of them, 'I am not going to pay any guy who is going to bust me or who is going to take action against me personally.' But despite these threats, not all the unsecured creditors could believe that lightning would indeed strike twice, that Sethia, having recovered from one bankruptcy, would come back again. They began to press for a proper winding-up. Amarjit's response was to change tack and propose a Scheme of Arrangement under Section 206 of the Companies Act. This needed to be approved by only 75% of the creditors and if the voting on the Copenhagen plan was repeated then there would be no problems. This new plan meant that a new company, Anglesharp, which had been incorporated on 12 March of that year, would take over from the Esal Group. Punjab and the other banks were to provide various credit facilities, but central to the financing of Anglesharp was $18 million of credit to be provided by unknown financiers. This was the bait that Raj Sethia and Amarjit offered to hook the other creditors.

At this stage Amarjit must have felt his cover-up plans were working. He had pushed, cajoled and occasionally browbeaten his fellow-bankers to accept the Section 206 rescue. So effective was Amarjit's hectoring and bullying tactics that even Allied Arab decided that perhaps it ought to withdraw the complaint it had made regarding Esal and Sethia. In early April Allied Arab wrote to Cooper saying that they no longer had a continuing interest in the criminal proceedings.

The Director of Public Prosecutions was most alarmed. If Allied withdrew then the case was as good as over. But there was some ambiguity about what Allied wanted to do and Cooper went to see Butler at Allied's offices in Cannon Street. Butler was accompanied by his legal advisers and after some discussion he said, 'Mr Cooper, we will support the prosecution.' It had been a close shave.

As Cooper left the Allied's offices in Cannon Street in the City he could not help contrasting this foreign bank's response to the one made by a very British bank. The bank was Johnson Matthey Bankers. Most of the banks who were involved with Esal were London branches of overseas banks. In the initial days of the investigation it was reassuring to find that there was one British bank prominent in that list. Sometime in February, an approach was made to JMB that, perhaps, they would be prepared to make a complaint. This would greatly assist in the fraud investigation. But they did not wish to make a complaint and, in effect, the Fraud Squad was sent away with the proverbial flea in the ear.

Cooper was aware he was dealing with clever men but it was soon painfully clear to him that these clever men were also heartless. What shook him and slowly drained much of his faith in the City and indeed the whole system was the way the major banks failed to provide any assistance. For them he was the flat-footed policeman who did not understand high finance and whose efforts to find Esal crooks was only messing up the whole thing.

But flat-footed policeman or no, Cooper was beginning to realise that some of the banks and their officers must have known all along what was happening. The more he examined the documents, the more he began to feel that some of Punjab's officials must have been up to something very crooked. This conviction was strengthened in March when Cooper visited Punjab's offices in the City for the first time. Armed with a Bankers Book Evidence order he went through the various Esal group accounts at the bank and began to experience that strange Esal feeling: this was not just a big one; this could turn out to be the biggest fraud investigation ever mounted in London. Time would prove him right.

Suddenly, Cooper found two crucial allies. Cooper had so far met polite bankers who just as politely pretended that there was nothing really wrong with Esal. The two new friends he made put flesh on his suspicious collection of bones. One was Talwar, Amarjit's precedessor, who had been alarmed at the way PNB was operating and who had tried to get somebody interested. He found Cooper a sympathetic listener, and Cooper found him a very informed man who could guide him through the maze. The other was probably the most remarkable man in the Esal story.

Cooper had been diligently meeting Esal's clients and customers. Some were more informative than the others. Among the most helpful was David Dein of commodity dealers London & Overseas Sugar and vice-chairman of Arsenal football club. Despite being threatened with ruin by Punjab for refusing to join the rescue package, he was leading a brave fight on behalf of the unsecured creditors. One day, on the way back from visiting Dein's offices in Pall Mall, Cooper decided to look up an Indian businessman whose name had cropped up in the Esal records.

The trader, operating from the West End not far from Esal's offices, was a short man with a merry laugh and a taste for perfume. So extravagant was his use of perfume that you could smell him half a block away. Compared to some of the others he met, Cooper was immediately taken by this man. He was refreshingly frank, never used two words when one would do, and very direct. Indians can be very direct in each other's company but in the company of strangers they often give cryptic answers. This man was not like that. He behaved with Indians as he did with Englishmen. Yes, he told Cooper, I have had dealings with Sethia. Esal owes me money; not as much as the banks are owed but for me it is a lot. I could make a statement but if you make me do that, then that will be it. I will not help you any more. But if you do not drag me into court then I can help you in many ways, help you explain the intricacies, tell you what is going on.

The man, of course, had done nothing wrong, but in the tightly knit Indian business world he could not afford to be seen babbling to the police. And Cooper could do with a man who knew the Esal crowd, who understood them but was willing to tell the truth. Cooper dubbed the man 'Umpire'. In cricket, when things are going right the umpire is not noticed; when things fall apart he is often at the centre of the storm. Over the months and years of his investigations Cooper's Indian umpire often performed this role – a natural middle-man who knew all the gossip and could adjudicate between Cooper and the complicated world of Esal.

So, through the summer of 1984 Amarjit and Cooper pursued their very different strategies. A small group of unsecured creditors led by David Dein opposed Amarjit's rescue package and there were several court hearings, but despite this it looked like succeeding.

One big thing going for Amarjit was that the press had taken little interest in Esal. Early reporting by some Indian journalists in London might have been ghosted by Amarjit so dutifully did they follow his line. One report by the *Times of India*'s London correspondent blamed other banks, in particular an unnamed Pakistani bank, a clear reference to BCCI, for Esal's fall.

Then, suddenly, we at *Financial Weekly* got involved. It was, like the best stories, quite accidental. In February Mihir Bose had to return to India to attend his father's funeral. There he read about Esal's problems and how the Indian banks were trying to mount a rescue. He was familiar with the names of both Esal and its boss Rajendra Sethia. He has a passionate interest in cricket and had come across Esal as book-makers and Rajendra Sethia as lavish host to Indian cricket teams touring England. But there was something about these Indian stories on Esal that worried him. They did not quite explain why Esal was in trouble; why the Nigerian coup should have so affected its fortunes that a massive rescue should be needed.

Mihir returned to find the British press showing little or no interest. In the summer, business friends arrived from India to wonder why. They also mentioned that Rajendra Sethia had fled the country to avoid arrest. They seemed surprised that this was not news in England. Why? they asked. There seemed no logical answer.

Financial Weekly had a reputation for researching business failures. Some spoke of it as the *Private Eye* of the City. Cathy Gunn had established excellent contacts in the Fraud Squad, and had also just become Features Editor of the weekly. In one of those 'Do you know what might be a good story' conversations that journalists always indulge in, Mihir had spoken to Cathy about Esal. Many such ideas are bounced around a newspaper office, but somehow this one was followed up. On the morning of Thursday 14 June we arranged to meet Detective Inspector Cooper and Detective Chief Inspector Smith.

We were shown to a sixth-floor office in a building that had once housed the Yard's forensic experts but now bristled with officers of C6, the Metropolitan Police Fraud Squad. Neither of us knew Cooper or Smith. We were told that they had agreed to see us only after checking out our credentials and finding them to be satisfactory. In a long exploratory conversation the ground rules were explained. The Fraud Squad has a reputation of always being helpful to responsible journalists, but they could not say anything that would jeopardize their investigations or break confidentialities. Also, they did not want to be quoted, and would prefer to confirm or deny the accuracy of any information we may gather rather than provide us with information.

We confirmed some of the impressions we had and found other leads. Mihir knew a young lady with good commodity-market contacts and she brought in interesting information from the sugar market. The juiciest titbit was how Sethia was supposed to have jumped out of a window to escape the Fraud Squad. Like all newspapers *Financial Weekly* is insured for libel and the policy requires that articles are 'lawyered' before publication. In other words a proof of what is being printed is read by a barrister before it is printed. Despite our nervousness, not too many changes were made.

Our story appeared on 29 June. Good stories create a certain frisson both for those who write them and for those, like the editor of the paper, who have ultimate responsibility for printing them. Right from the beginning Esal seemed to have such a quality. *Financial Weekly* was then a small, struggling paper where senior journalists were always under pressure and whole teams could not be assigned for weeks to put together major stories. Both Cathy and Mihir had enough on their plates covering their regular slots. But almost as soon as the first story appeared Mihir started getting calls offering information and suggesting that there was even more to the story than had been reported.

The calls that Mihir was getting were mainly from the Umpire. In the previous three months he had scoured Fleet Street to find a reporter who would be interested in Esal but nobody seemed to find it 'sexy'. He had never heard of *Financial Weekly* until somebody had brought the issue of 29 June to his notice. The Umpire had a wealth of information, but he was afraid. Raj Sethia was supposed to have underworld contacts, links with the old Kray brothers gangs still ruling the East End. If he heard someone was talking about him to the press there could be trouble. Then there was the other kind of pressure Amarjit could exercise. The Umpire was well aware of the Amarjit blackmail that was forcing many of the unsecured creditors to accept the rescue package. Some of them were customers of his bank and they were being told if they did not toe the line, then they had better find another banker. Tulsi Brothers had been reluctant to sign the rescue package; they saw little merit in it. Amarjit warned both Satsinghi and Tulsi boss Vaswani that if they did not sign then not only would they get nothing more but that he would tell other Indian banks to freeze them out. Tulsi knew Amarjit had enough clout with other managers to enforce the threat.

So the first calls Mihir received from the Umpire had what seemed an excessive degree of secrecy. He would not give his name. If Mihir was not there he would not leave a message. 'Your Indian deep throat called,' became something of a joke at *Financial Weekly*, recalling in jest that other more famous deep throat of Watergate. When he did give Mihir a name he pretended he was someone else. The early meetings with the Umpire followed a pattern. Generally they were held in lobbies of hotels: the Great Eastern near Liverpool Street or the Churchill in the West End. The Umpire would always arrive in a taxi. He would walk quickly through the length of the lobby and refuse to acknowledge Mihir until he had made sure there was no one in the hotel he knew. Then he would beckon Mihir furtively into a corner. At Esal creditors' meetings or at court hearings the Umpire always ignored Mihir. It was after the two had been meeting for some weeks that the Umpire provided a phone number, but since he had given a false name this only created comical confusion.

Some of the pressures became evident when, quite suddenly, on Wednesday 25 July, Mihir had a message to ring a Dr Ray. He had never heard of him before and Dr Ray would not say who he was, or what it was about, just that he wanted to come and have a chat. The meeting was arranged for 3.30 on Thursday 26 July at the offices of *Financial Weekly*. Dr Ray turned out to be a comfortable, middle-aged Bengali with an equally comfortable girth. But very quickly he warned Mihir to lay off Esal — if he knew what was good for him. The problems of Esal were no more than a domestic tiff with its bankers and Cooper should keep his nose out of the affair.

Cooper was now concentrating on what was becoming the central thrust of his investigation. Did the Punjab National Bank help defraud creditors by monkeying with Esal's accounts even after the Mareva had been imposed? There was nothing to be got from Amarjit on this. So, on the morning of 18 July, Cooper, accompanied by some officers, went to the Punjab's offices. He had come armed with a search warrant and this was a raid to get to the heart of the Punjab–Esal relationship. How fraudulent was it?

Punjab was embarrassed and angry about the raid — the first time such an indignity had been suffered by an Indian bank in London — and tried to hush up the whole thing. It pretended that Cooper had not really raided and continued with the rescue as if nothing had happened. In the High Court the arguments continued.

Financial Weekly had not had an Esal story for a couple of weeks, which was considered so strange that Dominic Helps of Linklaters had rung with the comment, 'What's the matter? Where is our weekly Esal fix?' Then, on Tuesday 21 August, the Umpire rang with what he excitedly described as 'hot news'. Punjab had been raided. This was indeed big and either that day or the next day Mihir checked with the Fraud Squad and spoke to Chief Inspector Smith. Smith said that the Fraud Squad had executed a search warrant. Does that mean they have raided Punjab? He replied, 'I believe you journalists use the word "raid" when we execute a search warrant.' The definition of what constitutes a raid was to acquire great significance soon. We ran the story in our issue of 24 August and were caught up in the Esal saga.

The crucial creditors' meeting to vote on Amarjit's Section 206 rescue was to be held on 6 September. Two days before the meeting, Linklater & Paines wrote to Slaughter and May. They referred to our 24 August article, then said, 'We find it extraordinary that the fact of the Fraud Squad's investigation of PNB and the search of PNB's premises have not been disclosed by your clients or to the general body of Esal's creditors . . . The failure of your clients to disclose the fact of the Fraud Squad's investigation further emphasises the need for full investigative powers of the Administrator under the Scheme. We request, therefore, that PNB provide to creditors a full explanation as to the nature of the Fraud Squad's investigations. We need hardly point out to you that under the terms of the Scheme, PNB has been designated the agent bank and that Mr Singh, its General Manager, will be one of the first members of the steering committee. What steps have Fraud Squad taken with relation to your client? Has anyone been charged?' Linklaters sent a copy of the letter to the Department of Trade and Industry. *Financial Weekly*'s Esal stories were now being used by those who opposed Amarjit's plans for an Esal rescue.

Slaughters replied on 5 September:

The truth is that, entirely contrary to your own suggestions, the Fraud Squad has not been investigating PNB. All that happened was that, consistent with the Fraud Squad's continuing investigation of the affairs of Esal (an investigation which has been continuing for many months as you well know following your own clients' involvement with Esal), the Fraud Squad visited the premises of PNB at Moor House asking for certain documents relating to Esal. Being very properly aware of the fact that our clients would be unable to supply the information without Esal's consent, the police had obtained a search warrant relating to these documents. The police were given full facilities to examine the papers in which they were interested . . . Needless to say, no one on PNB's staff has been charged or even questioned and our clients take exception to the suggestion in your letter that this is even a possibility.

The next day, 6 September, Amarjit scored a single public triumph. The long heralded creditors' meeting was held. In an irony that did not go unnoticed, it was held in the Spanish Rooms located in the basement of Barrington House, whose upper floors housed Linklaters. The meeting was presided over by Raymond Mackie, a prominent chartered accountant, with Richard Youard, senior partner of Slaughters sitting next to Mr Mackie and acting the legal expert. The meeting revealed for the first time the public anger of the unsecured creditors led by the articulate Keith Berman, the New York-based English solicitor representing Creedex.

The focus of the stormy meeting was a Scheme of Arrangement under the Section 206 rescue. Jim Coote, who was running Esal in the absence of the directors, had produced a scheme document. Much of the arguments raged round this document. An apparently impressive-looking document, fifty-one pages with several schedules, it asked more questions than it answered. Who were the financiers willing to pay $18 million to Anglesharp which was supposed to replace Esal and help get all the creditors' money back? And what role was Rajendra Sethia going to play? Berman said he should return to England, Youard agreed. Singh, looking lean and hungry, stubbed out one cigarette after another as he listened to the debate. Very reluctantly he rose to speak, but insisted that 'without Raj Sethia there can be no business in the company'. But to other angry queries about the Coote document Singh maintained a stony silence.

Coote, himself, was the subject of an extraordinary interlude. Berman had described the Coote document as having been produced by banks, being 'the machinations of their tiny minds'. The directors had fled, he asserted, why even Mr J.A. Coote, under whose signature the plan appears, is not present. 'Could anybody tell me where he is?' For a

few minutes the creditors' meeting debated Coote's whereabouts.
Mackie explained, to some astonishment, that he thought Coote was in
China. Berman was appalled. 'China? Is that for business or, as I
suspect, because that is the furthest point he can go from this meeting?'
Later a call to Mrs Coote revealed that her husband was at Esal's
registered office at Bedford Row, a ten-minute drive from Gresham
Street.

Some months later Mr Justice Harman would find it 'startling' that
Coote could not 'vouch for the accuracy' of his document and that 'he
chose not to attend and chose to do nothing'. But even some of those
present were shy of publicity. We were the only newspaper present, the
only one to report the meeting, but one pro-Esal man threatened to hit
Financial Weekly's photographer as he attempted to photograph the
participants. Ranjit, prominent in his handle-bar moustache, was
particularly camera-shy, dodging behind pillars as we tried to record
his presence.

But even if the publicity and arguments were now going against
Amarjit, he had got the votes. Effectively marshalling the banks and
blackmailing creditors, like Tulsi Brothers, he secured sufficient votes
to have the Section 206 rescue scheme approved. Later that week
Amarjit, along with chairman S.L. Baluja, who had been seeing
Rajendra in New York, celebrated the victory with a lavish party at a
West End club. It had been a struggle but now the worst was over, or so
Amarjit must have felt.

But, as ever, Cooper had been planning a counter-punch. Twelve
days later at precisely 9.00 on the morning of 18 September Cooper and
a couple of officers went to the Regent Street offices of Atri. Cooper's
target was Vijay Kumar, who had left the bank to come and work for
Atri, suspected of being owned by Abdul Shamji. In a straightforward
and undramatic arrest Cooper told Kumar that they wanted to question
him in connection with Punjab–Esal dealings. He then cautioned him
saying, 'You are not obliged to say anything unless you wish to do so,
but what you say may be put into writing and given in evidence.' He
then brought him back to Richbell Place. Kumar was questioned and
later released.

Now there was no alternative to the hard graft of interviewing as
many PNB people as possible. However, as a result of the material
Cooper's raid on PNB had unearthed he could glimpse the outlines of
his case. There had been something very fishy going on at the bank on

30 January? Were entries backdated? If so what happened to the computer? How was that fiddled?

This was probably the most difficult part of the investigation, also the most sensitive. Cooper had to talk to the ordinary clerks and operators at the bank. Amarjit and the bosses were telling him nothing. Would these low ranking bank employees prove more useful? Would they dare? How effective would their testimony be against the silence of the bosses? If the bank had fiddled the books once, then with Amarjit in charge could they not do it again?

Cooper could not go to the bank to talk to them. That would alert Amarjit. So for the next few weeks he toured the various suburbs of London visiting the homes of computer operators, clerks and junior Punjab officials to try and piece the whole thing together. For these employees a visit from Cooper was a shock. Hardeesch Ghanty would later tell an Old Bailey jury her reaction on seeing Cooper, whom she had never met, outside her front door one evening: 'I was shocked to have the police turn up about something that had happened at the Punjab National Bank.' But after the initial shock they realised Cooper was after the truth. Most of those questioned were helpful; some were relieved to tell the story of that amazing Monday when the bank was turned upside down.

Cooper was not the only one plotting Amarjit's fall. At the creditors' meeting, Mr Roberts of Linklaters had observed, 'The scheme document as it stands is woefully silent on the question of tax.' Roberts' interjection led to a debate on tax but there was no satisfactory answer. However, it would come back to haunt Amarjit. Like Al Capone, he would discover that there was no escape from the tax man.

This was the tax time-bomb that had been ticking away under Esal ever since the company started. Despite reporting colossal profits, the company had never paid any taxes. None of its accounts had ever been agreed with the Revenue. During the debate about taxation at the creditors' meeting in the Spanish Rooms, the chairman, Raymond Mackie, had confessed he did not know the tax history of the company or the taxation position of the scheme. This was an answer that Mr Justice Harman, while giving judgment on costs with regard to the winding-up, would describe as 'an extraordinary statement'.

Worse was to follow. Mr Silver of Tringham's, Esal's solicitors, had told the meeting that, 'I believe the Revenue has been represented in Court on every hearing of the petition to date.' This, said Mr Justice

Harman, 'was untrue. The Revenue was never represented at all. How Mr Silver made this statement I do not know but it was clear that it was wholly false. It may have been a misunderstanding or it may not.'

The Revenue were not amused when they heard what had happened in the Spanish Rooms. They had already had some discussions with Esal about back tax. They had queried certain deductions in the accounts described as commission, but which the Revenue suspected were bribes and wanted to disallow. After the creditors' meeting the Revenue raised assessments of nearly £20 million. Amarjit was most upset. He had expected that Esal would have tax losses which Anglesharp, the new company, could inherit. Instead these assessments could jeopardize any chance of getting Anglesharp off the ground.

After the creditors' meeting, discussions with the Revenue and Amarjit continued, with Revenue officials visiting the offices of the Punjab in the process. On Friday 12 October an even more crucial meeting took place. Treasury Counsel Mr John Mummery called a meeting of all counsels acting in the Esal case and told them that there were several things about the scheme worrying the Department of Trade. Before the summer adjournment of the Esal winding up saga, Mr Justice Vinelott had suggested that perhaps the Department of Trade should examine the public interest aspects of the rescue. It was an unprecedented reference but then Esal was an unusual case as solicitors of the DoT discovered when they spoke to the Fraud Squad. The Mummery meeting was a result of that reference. What was worrying the DoT was never made public, but they probably centred round the uncertainty of the $18 million Anglesharp was to receive, the Fraud investigations and Inland Revenue's claims.

Four days later on Tuesday 16 October, DoT counsel Rayner James told Mr Justice Harman that the Secretary of State felt the scheme should not be approved, and that the Inland Revenue were also in favour of winding-up. Mr Justice Harman ruled that it would make more sense to have David Dein's firm, which really wanted to liquidate Esal, take over the winding-up petition from Punjab, which had no intention of doing so. The hearings on the scheme were adjourned for another thirteen days.

Cooper intervened before they resumed. Early in the morning of 5 November two teams from the Fraud Squad travelled in different directions from their headquarters in Richbell Place, Holborn. One headed east to the offices of the Punjab National Bank in the City to carry out another raid; another, consisting of two cars travelled to a house in North London. There it waited discreetly outside until the man they were looking for got in his car and drove to town. For a mile the police followed, being always careful to maintain their distance and give no cause for the man to suspect anything. Then the man stopped at traffic lights. As he did one of the cars rolled up alongside, a detective got out, tapped the window of this man's car, showed his badge, and got into his car. Then the detective warned the man in the familiar language used by policemen when arresting a suspect.

The man was Jinendra Jain and his arrest had come after painstaking work by Cooper and colleagues on several Punjab employees and ex-employees over several weeks. Cooper must have planned Jain's arrest carefully. To arrest him at home might alert other people, so he had to be arrested while he was travelling, and also he wanted to co-ordinate this with yet another raid on the Punjab which the other team was carrying out as Cooper tailed Jain.

Jain was taken to Richbell Place and at 5 that evening Cooper and Detective Constable Archer began their interrogation in the interview room on the 10th floor. But Jain had his solicitor, Mr Simon, present and Cooper had little joy out of this shrewd banker. The next day, 6 November, the questioning was resumed. Jain presented such a dead bat that he even refused to acknowledge that Esal was in any particular financial difficulties as the 1983 year-end approached.

6 November was proving quite a crucial day for Punjab. As Jain was being questioned the banks that had stuck with Amarjit and his rescue plan were meeting at Slaughter & May's offices. In the past ten months they had often met there to discuss the latest twist and turn but now they had come to the end of the road. The Inland Revenue wanted £20 million and would not go away, the DoT did not like the rescue and the $18 million that mysterious friends were supposed to invest in Anglesharp to get it going was proving, like all Raj Sethia promises, very illusory. The banks had been told this would be in clean securities. They turned out to be two hotels in New York, Aberdeen and Kenmore, one a leasehold, the other with a mortgage on it. By evening, the banks like Middle East and others had made it clear that the rescue was dead. As the telexes went out from Punjab that evening informing the creditors, particularly those whose arms had been twisted by Amarjit to get them to sign the package, he and his assistant Uppal sought solace in a few drinks.

About closing time that Tuesday evening Cooper and a colleague emerged from the Queen's Head, a pub next door to his office. It had been a long day and they had managed only to get a dinner break at about 10 that night. As Cooper stepped onto the pavement he noticed a Mercedes car parked by the side of the kerb. It contained Amarjit and Uppal. Cooper went up to the car and knocked on the window. Amarjit stepped out of the car, and he seemed rather eager to talk. Cooper suggested they talk inside the station where Singh argued with Cooper about Jain's arrrest. 'You've made a terrible mistake. It was all operational errors.' Amarjit promised to return in the morning and provide all the explanations. For a fleeting moment Cooper thought about arresting Amarjit there and then and holding him overnight. But he did not and must have bitterly regretted this ever since. It was late, it had been a long day, it could wait until tomorrow.

Amarjit did return the next day, 7 November. But he came with his solicitor and had nothing to say. Jain also still saying nothing, was produced before the Magistrates Court and charged with false accounting with regard to the payment of an insurance premium to Fieldings. While this was going on, Esal was finally coming to an end. Mr Justice Harman heard that, with the banks withdrawing their support, there was no rescue possible. Soon he ruled there should be no Esal. The company that had traded in millions was going down with what Mr Justice Harman had, himself, called telephone number debts: nearly $400 million.

Esal's winding-up was a great victory for David Dein who had, against all odds, pursued it. He was also pursuing Rajendra Sethia. The two had once been great friends, socialising frequently and enjoying games of tennis as doubles partners. But Raj's collapse had threatened to pull David down. The very day that Esal fell he secured bankruptcy judgment against Rajendra Sethia.

On Friday 18 February 1985 at a private hearing of the London Bankruptcy Court Sethia was finally declared bankrupt with debts estimated at £140 million. Ten days later his trustee in bankruptcy, George Auger, produced a statement which showed that Sethia had at last achieved his moment in history. Since 1976 the *Guinness Book of Records* had featured a former Harvard Law school graduate and property developer William Stern as the world's biggest bankrupt with debts of £118,690,524. Sethia had easily topped him coming in at £168,551,823.30. He wanted to be famous; now he was notorious.

Newspapers which had hardly bothered about the Esal story now sent teams of reporters to cover the sensational discovery of the world's biggest bankrupt. The *Sun* and the *National Enquirer* rang us to discover details; others merely cribbed. Sethia, his wife and his two children all featured, and Lakshmi as a dutiful wife explained it was all due to her husband not being very good at paperwork. There were others who thought he was a bit too good with paperwork, if of the wrong kind.

By the time the world caught up with Sethia he was back in India. It meant re-union with Amarjit, who seemed as powerful as ever though he had just managed to get away from Cooper.

Cooper had kept a beady eye on Amarjit, who had not been arrested due to lack of evidence that could convince the DPP. The airport police had been told to watch out for any attempt by Amarjit to leave the country. They were meant to watch flights to Delhi. On 2 January 1985 Amarjit easily fooled the airport police by boarding a flight to Paris, then changing there for Bombay and eventually Delhi. Heathrow's police did not realise until long after he had gone and Cooper must have felt even more frustrated about missing Amarjit on that Tuesday night in November.

On 18 February 1985 the Indian Finance Ministry announced that Baluja, chairman of Punjab and Sonalkar, chairman of Central, were to be sacked. Baluja had another sixteen months of his three-year term to serve, Sonalkar another twenty months. The government gave no official reasons but the same day the Reserve Bank of India issued a directive that executive directors and chairmen of banks are 'morally and constitutionally' responsible for the effective supervision and monitoring of large advances made by the banks. Inspired leaks in the Indian press made it clear that Baluja and Sonalkar had lost their jobs because of Raj Sethia.

The sackings of the chairmen made the Esal saga front page news in India for the first time. For the Indian government Sethia, free, was an embarrassment. But what could they arrest him on? Amazingly none of the Indian banks had charged him with any offence. Then somebody thought, could not the Fraud Squad make an extradition request? If they did the Indians could then arrest Sethia. The question was who would start the process. The Indian government could hardly request the Fraud Squad. So a high Indian official asked the new chairman of the Central Bank to use the bank's London solicitors, Stocken & Lambert, as the go-between. The senior partner of the firm, Mr

Hiranandani, a large, plump Indian who had been acting for Central over the Esal saga, got in touch with Cooper.

On 1 March, Ashok Malhotra of the Indian Central Bureau of Investigation, the country's FBI, accompanied by a few policemen hurried to the Maurya Sheraton. Malhotra waited until Sethia had gone up then followed him. At first Sethia refused to open the door. A journalist had been trying to interview him and he probably felt it was the same person, but when Malhotra insisted saying he was from the Indian CBI Sethia relented. Sethia was taken to CBI's central Delhi offices and the long, slow process of interrogation began.

Meanwhile, Malhotra's men searched the room. They were just about to give up when one of them, more in frustration than anything else, yanked up the blankets from the bed. Underneath were several goodies: a passport and a Swissair ticket which would enable Sethia to fly from Calcutta via Delhi, Bombay, Cairo, and Geneva to New York and back. The passport was in the name of Raj Kumar Dugar and issued in Calcutta on 13 February. The photograph of Sethia showed him without the beard and wearing spectacles.

Initially, Sethia told Malhotra little or nothing, but when he was confronted by the false passport he caved in and began a long confession. The passport had been arranged by a friend in Calcutta, another had signed a document saying he worked for his firm and helped him get visas for several countries. He wanted to visit Cairo to meet Kalim Nasim and get some papers signed, and New York to dispose of his hotel. And as he gave the passport details he gave other details and made a long confession implicating, among others, Amarjit Singh. Sethia was produced before magistrates and remanded in police custody. This in Delhi means the notorious Tihar jail, the home of conmen, murderers and all types of suspects. Sethia found himself in a 9 ft by 2 ft cell with communal toilets and with suspected spies and Mrs Gandhi's assassins as his companions.

Elsewhere, banks were trying to pick up the pieces after the Esal fall-out. Allied Arab had to be rescued through a £41 million rescue package arranged by Barclays and other, Arab, investors. Oriental Credit and Commerce had to shut their doors and went into liquidation. The three Indian banks who were so heavily involved with Sethia, were closed down on 31 December 1986. Creditors led by Dein have issued a writ against Punjab for negligence, claiming nearly $150 million. The banks lost $200 million between them to Sethia, but their behaviour had so worried the Bank of England that it had been discussed at the highest levels involving senior ministers in both the British and Indian governments. The Governor of the Bank of England had told the Indian Reserve Bank in no uncertain terms that they either shut the branches of these banks in London or else.

Sethia, it could be said, has already paid for his misdeeds. He spent two years in the notorious Tihar jail while waiting to be tried. Sethia has often said that once he is free he would return to London. That is where he belongs, 'where my family and interests are'. His bail conditions do not allow him to do that. It is interesting to speculate what might have happened had he not fled through the Esal back door to the waiting Rolls in D'Arblay Street and then New York on that January day. The way British justice has coped with Esal it is quite likely that he might have been a free man by now ready to start all over again.

Since the events we have described there have been two Esal trials and several other court hearings. In one, as we have seen, Vijay Kumar obtained a conditional discharge and Jain walked away free. In another, the judge threw out the charges against Bhutoria, Banerjit and Gopal saying there was no case to answer. In April 1987, Nirmal Banthia was arrested and charged, but the DPP decided not to proceed with the case. In the summer of 1987, Kalim Nasim was arrested, but was discharged after a three-day hearing at Wells Street Magistrates Court. Babulal Bengani is on bail in India awaiting extradition to Britain.

In both the trials Sethia was presented as the boss man, Amarjit as his Svengali and the others as minions. In the first, Kumar and Jain made much of the fact that Amarjit was powerful, ruthless and brooked no opposition. In the second, the defendants saw themselves more as cheque-signing machines. A Sethia trial at the Old Bailey would have been a very different affair and would undoubtedly have attracted much attention. None of the papers reported the first two Esal trials. Despite that, who is to say whether, had Sethia stayed put that Monday morning in 1984, he would by now be starting Esal Mark II? In his early jail days Sethia carried round with him a copy of *Shōgun*, whose last line reads, 'I did not choose to be what I am. It is my karma.' He clearly identified with that sentiment, but then Hindu philosophy has it that a man's karma is shaped by his past sins. So if Sethia bemoans his fate, probably he brought a lot of it on to himself by his past behaviour.

But if Sethia has his karma to wrestle with, the implications of this amazing story are many and varied. It shows the complexity and sheer bewilderment of modern financial transactions and the scope for fraud. It demonstrates how difficult it is to trace these financial actions, let alone prove fraud has been committed. This becomes worse when international banks and several different governments with widely contrasting political motives are in play. And most dispiriting of all, it shows the near impossibility of getting justice in a fraud case. Vijay Kumar, the Punjab manager, was found guilty of trying to defraud creditors of several million pounds. Yet the judge, in giving him a conditional discharge, said, 'This was a serious fraud; you got no benefit from it. No employer need fear that you will do this again. I am satisfied you will never commit a criminal offence.' The words were spoken the same week that a woman was sacked for stealing a peanut after twenty years' devoted service.

In the second trial the judge, while throwing out the case, said that none of the three defendants, Banerjit, Bhutoria and Gopal 'stand in a white sheet. All the three defendants appear foolish and negligent; even, it could be said, they were criminal. But whatever the crimes they committed these are not the crimes they are accused of.' The trial turned on the definition of a forged bill of lading. The DPP's office was horrified by the judgment but decided not to go for a re-trial. It is not without significance that the trial was held at Newington Causeway, because the Old Bailey was taken up with other more important trials and clearly there were problems of explaining to the judge and jury what constituted fraud.

The Sethia saga shows how international and complex fraud can be, and how parochial and timid was the power of the law. That, at least, is changing as we write.

3

The Nigerian Connection

The fifth of July 1984 started as just another day at Stansted airport, east of London. Aircraft took off and landed and on the tarmac there waited a Boeing 707 belonging to Nigerian Airways. It had flown in from Lagos that very day and was due to take off again at 7 p.m. It had arrived empty but was due to collect four and a half tonnes of catering equipment – little more than a tenth of its normal cargo capacity. But shortly before 1 p.m. a telephone call came from the Essex police which was to make the airport world famous. The caller asked the airport authorities to keep a watch on flights to and from Nigeria. Would they particularly watch out for any unusual cargo, and prevent it from taking off? The caller made it clear that the request was over something quite serious and had, in fact, come from Scotland Yard.

At 4 p.m., a curious little convoy swung into the airport and drew up at the Servisair cargo terminal. A white container was escorted by two black Mercedes saloons bearing the numberplates of the Nigerian High Commission in London. A forklift truck trundled up to unload the van, which contained two pretty unexceptional-looking cargo crates. The only striking thing about them was they were labelled 'Diplomatic Baggage' and were addressed to the Ministry of External Affairs in Lagos.

Soon a Customs officer came to inspect the crates and he thought he spotted something odd. The phone call from the Essex police had already alerted him and the labels on the crate made him look twice. As diplomatic baggage they were inviolate, but there was something strange about the paperwork. One was labelled 'diplomatic property', the other 'diplomatic baggage', but the necessary papers were absent. The officer rang the police and told the Servisair people not to load the crates onto the aircraft. The men in the two limousines, by this time growing anxious that the flight was to be delayed, were asked to wait.

After hasty consultations it had been decided that the crates could not be given the status or immunity of diplomatic baggage.

Shortly after 7 p.m. the crates were opened. Inside the larger case was an astonishing sight: a heavily drugged Nigerian gentleman with a rubber endotracheal tube in his throat to aid his breathing, and other tubes inserted at various points in his body to top him up with drugs and fluid for the long flight home. With him, but conscious, was an Israeli equipped with more drugs and syringes. He turned out to be quite a well-known anaesthesiologist, there to keep the Nigerian alive, but asleep, on the unorthodox journey to Lagos. In the smaller case, just two feet six inches wide, unconscious and sandwiched together, were two more Israelis, one of Tunisian origin.

The Nigerian gentleman was one Umaru Dikko, an exiled politician. Over the next few days as Dikko recovered in hospital, lucky to be alive (said William Hucklesby, head of Scotland Yard's anti-terrorist squad), the story of how he got to be in the crate emerged, fuelling a diplomatic row between Britain and Nigeria. This brought into the open the fascinating world of Nigerian politics, corruption, international business links and fraud. Thus also was revealed the role played by London-based businessmen and banks in some of the deals that lay at the heart of the Dikko scandal and the corruption prevalent in Nigeria under President Shagari.

Dr Umaru Dikko was, reputedly, his country's wealthiest man. A former Transport Minister, he was pictured by political enemies as the very epitome of the modern Nigerian politician: unscrupulous, corrupt and always seeking to exploit the main chance in collusion with business. He vigorously denied the charges, but the 1979 Nigerian elections that had made Dikko's brother-in-law Shehu Shagari President had opened the floodgates for local and foreign businessmen. Nigeria, experiencing the heady delights of oil riches – 1.3 million barrels a day of production – began to import vast quantities of all kinds of goods. Dikko's opponents alleged that he had used this opportunity to exploit what looked like a Nigerian equivalent of the gold rush to line his pockets.

Dikko had been found guilty of corruption in 1975, but under the Shagari government he was put in charge of the rice distribution, always a potent source of making money in countries like Nigeria. Dikko's stewardship had coincided with dramatic price rises and he was widely suspected of taking bribes from rice importers and inflating rice prices thereby robbing the country of foreign exchange amounting to around 4 billion Naira, about £3.5 billion at the then exchange-rate. But in Shagari's regime it seemed that anything went, and in 1983 Dikko not only successfully masterminded the Shagari election campaign but, it seems, played a dubious role in rigging the ballot.

However, with Nigeria squandering its oil riches economic logic could be denied. Short-term debt was $5 billion and total debts were close on $21.4 billion. On New Year's Eve 1983 Shagari and his government were ousted in a bloodless coup led by Major-General Mohammed Buhari. Dikko, nicknamed 'Mr Corruption', was top of the military wanted list but after hiding in Lagos for a couple of days he managed to escape to London.

There he set himself up in splendid luxury in a home in Porchester Terrace, rebutting allegations of corruption by the new regime, yet plotting to overthrow it. In the summer of 1984 he was openly discussing ways of overthrowing the government and called for a Jihad, a holy war against the regime. The Buhari government accused him of inciting a junior officers' plot – Dikko denied this – and on the morning of 5 July Buhari's men struck.

As Dikko walked outside his Porchester Terrace home, several men leapt out from a yellow Ford Transit van, seized him and bundled him, violently struggling, inside the van. The van raced away on the first leg of the journey that was to take Dikko to Stansted. Fortunately for Dikko, who had feared something like this, the whole thing had been witnessed by his assistant Elizabeth Hayes. She immediately telephoned the police and this, as we have seen, led to the denouement at Stansted.

Dikko had survived but the Nigerian government were determined to get him. While Dikko's kidnappers were tried at the Old Bailey and received heavy jail sentences ranging from ten years to fourteen years, the Nigerians launched extradition proceedings against Dikko. Dikko, himself, sought political asylum in Britain. When this failed he appealed to the independent British tribunal set up to hear immigration appeals. This, after lengthy hearings, granted his right to stay. By this time the Buhari government had been replaced by another led by Major-General Ibrahmin Babangida.

However, the basic charge against Dikko of fraud on a giant scale would not go away. The sort of rice scams he was suspected of promoting and profiting from involved foreign exchange frauds that damaged both Nigeria, milking it of sorely needed cash, and other countries' agencies, including, as we shall see, Britain's Export Credit Guarantee Department. However, before we look at them let us examine the free-for-all that operated under the Shagari government which allowed various frauds to be perpetrated. Inevitably, Rajendra Sethia figured in some of them. With his base in London and growing and intimate connections with the City, he was in a marvellous position to make the most of the Nigerian El Dorado.

Sethia had set up a Nigerian company, Nimpex, backed by powerful local partners. It was Nimpex which was at the heart of the Sethia Nigerian deals. The methods were deliciously simple. Nimpex obtains the valuable 'M' form to import, say, $1 million worth of sugar. To obtain this it probably has to pay bribes, but that, with 'Shagari-Dikko' operating, is no problem. Nimpex is to buy this sugar from Esal Commodities in London, which in turn is to buy it from other dealers. Esal draws up what is known as a bill of exchange, a sort of post-dated cheque on Nimpex for $1 million. In a completely above-the-board transaction, Esal Commodities in London would use this bill of exchange to borrow money from a London bank to finance the purchase of $1 million worth of sugar. When this is shipped to Nigeria, Nimpex would deposit $1 million in favour of Esal in a Nigerian bank and this, in turn, would be sent to Esal's bankers in London to repay the $1 million loan Esal had taken. Their skill in the buying and selling of sugar at the right price together with the commissions on the deal would provide the profit for Esal and Nimpex.

But this was clearly not enough for a man who wanted to match the oil sheikhs. As mushrooming exports lead to a balance of payments problem and the institution of foreign exchange restrictions by Nigeria, Sethia found the ideal opportunity. Very simply it was the sort of black-market currency deals many tourists indulge in, but on a much bigger scale. At that stage, officially, one Naira was almost equal to $1. But on the black market you could get three Nairas for every dollar. Sethia used the existence of this black market to fashion a quite remarkable double-your-money business.

The first part of the transaction was as in the legitimate one. Sethia's Nigerian company Nimpex ordered sugar worth one million naira. Since this was meant to be a legitimate transaction going through recognised banks, one naira was equivalent to $1. So in London in the hands of Esal this became an order for $1 million of sugar. Esal used this to borrow $1 million from one of its London banks. But Esal did not go into the market and buy that amount of sugar. It would buy sugar of $300,000 worth but draw up documents, bills of exchange, invoices, etc., suggesting that sugar worth $1 million was being shipped to Nigeria.

Sethia now exploited the tremendous black market in nairas cleverly to make up the difference between the $300,000 dollars' worth of sugar bought and the $1 million shown in the documents as having been shipped to the country. What happened was this. Nimpex received $300,000 worth of sugar which it could use – and did use – to deposit 300,000 nairas into the bank in Lagos. The remaining 700,000 nairas came from the unofficial exchange Esal had bought from some Nigerian who wanted to get money out of the country. Generally, the deal was that Esal would pay this Nigerian some $230,000 into a Swiss bank account. This, at the black market rate of one dollar equals 3 nairas, would translate into 700,000 nairas. The Nigerian would pay Nimpex 700,000 nairas in Nigeria. Nimpex would deposit this sum in its Nigerian bank in the name of Esal as payment for the supposed one million nairas of sugar it had imported. So the Nigerian bank had 300,000 nairas from the sugar proceeds, and 700,000 nairas paid in by Nimpex.

The bank did not enquire where Nimpex had acquired this 700,000 nairas from and, of course, it was no concern of the bank. What mattered was that it had a million nairas which, according to the official rate of exchange, was $1 million. The Nigerian bank would notify Esal's bank in London accordingly and transmit the amount in dollars. Everybody had reason to be happy. The bank had made its commission on the deal, some rich Nigerian had got some valuable money out of Nigeria and Sethia had made an absolute killing.

Raj Sethia, of course, had benefited the most. He had borrowed $1 million, used $300,000 to buy sugar, $230,000 to buy nairas on the foreign exchange market and then used legitimate banking systems so well that he had repaid the $1 million but still earned a profit of $470,000. Unethical and sharp as this fiddling of the foreign exchange rules was, it was probably not fraudulent. Sethia certainly did not see it that way. After his arrest by Indian police he said, 'When you speculate in currency in Switzerland you are called a banker, in Nigeria you are called a criminal.' But soon he was to move into a world far removed from Swiss bankers and enter the murky waters of fraud.

The essence of the fraud lay in a simple question. Was it necessary to ship the sugar at all? The answer: no. Nigerian officials could be bribed just as easily to certify that a container full of junk contained valuable sugar as they had been bribed to certify over-invoicing of sugar in the double-your-money gambit. Indeed, as Sethia and other Indian businessmen were soon to discover, Nigerian officials could even be bribed to certify that non-existent containers had arrived at Nigerian ports and disgorged tons of sugar that never existed. The officials were not particularly greedy and did not demand exorbitant bribes to satisfy the growing greed of the Indians. Double your money had had some basis in reality and Sethia was not the only one to play it, but this new game was a rather deadly paper-chase where the only genuine papers were the monies Sethia persuaded the banks to part with.

Once again, the opening moves appeared above board and absolutely proper. Nimpex has permission to import sugar into Nigeria and approaches Esal Commodities. Esal approaches a bank, say A, and says the sugar for Nimpex is to be bought through Dollarscrown, not a formal subsidiary but as the Official Esal Receiver would put it 'entwined in a very complex manner'. The bank is requested to open a letter of credit in favour of Dollarscrown for, say, $1 million. Dollarscrown have to provide a whole sheaf of documents to the bank. These include invoices relating to purchases of sugar, bills of lading, insurance certificates, packing lists and weight lists, in other words all the necessary documents to prove that sugar worth $1 million has been bought and is being shipped to Nigeria. This evidence is the bank's security for the finance it is providing.

Dollarscrown would also have to present a bill of exchange drawn in favour of Esal for $1 million. The bank would sign and seal the reverse of the bill. Now, in very broad terms, a bill of exchange is something like a high-class post-dated cheque. One company giving another a bill of exchange might mean nothing or a lot depending on the status of the two companies. In this case both companies connected. However, bank A by signing on the back of the bill that it had 'accepted' it, made it a very special paper. It converted it into a negotiable instrument, which means it became something you could take to another bank and use to get money. A bill of exchange accepted by a bank has something like the status of a banknote.

If this were a normal, above-board transaction then Esal, Nimpex and Dollarscrown would not be related in quite the fashion they were.

More significantly, Esal would have used the money borrowed from the bank to buy sugar from Dollarscrown. This would have been shipped to its Nigerian customer which would gain possession and ownership of the goods by paying a bank in Nigeria $1 million in favour of A, Esal's London bankers. A would send the whole sheaf of documents received from Dollarscrown to Nigeria to establish the Nigerian customer's right to the goods.

But this was a Raj Sethia transaction. The goods never left for Nigeria and neither did the papers. They just became part of the great Sethia trick, a fascinating paper-chase that saw bills of exchange chase each other through various London and New York banks providing more finance for Raj Sethia. What Sethia did was this. He took the bill of exchange that bank A had 'accepted' to some other London bank, B say, and had it discounted. This, by itself, is not an unusual thing and Sethia would often use some very reputable banks with whom he had no particular trading links to discount the bill of exchange accepted by A. Bank B could often be Manufacturers Hanover, or Manny Hanny as it is known in the trade. Bank B would be happy to discount the bill, paying Sethia slightly less than the full value of the bill of exchange. Since this was a bill of exchange payable within ninety days Sethia would receive $1 million less ninety days' interest. In the previous ninety days Sethia had already worked this paper-chase scam at another bank, C. There a bill of exchange had fallen due and C wanted its $1 million back. Sethia would use the money he had obtained from bank B to repay C.

He would then immediately open a letter of credit facility at C to start the whole process again so that in ninety days he could repay A. And so it would continue. As long as the music continued, in other words banks were prepared to open letters of credit and sign bills of exchange, there was no reason why the paper-chase should ever stop. But a good bank manager, or even a clerk, would have noticed one oddity: that contrary to normal practice documents never left London for Nigeria as they were meant to. On day one Sethia would borrow money, on day ninety he would return the money and retrieve the documents when, of course, the documents, as we have seen, should have gone to Nigeria and the money come from there to London. Sethia was indulging in what is known as accommodation bills, with banks financing a transaction that was not supported by any physical trade. But every ninety days some bank or other in the City of London was repaid the money it was owed and as long as that happened nobody seemed to care.

What part Dikko played in the Sethia scams is not clear. Sethia knew him and had done deals with him. But under the regime that Shagari ran, the connections that businessmen had with Dikko provided the scope for major scams, aided to an extent by slack and at times fraudulent practices in London. Sethia was the most colourful but not the only one to make the most of the Nigerian gold rush. There were others, and one fraud actually came to light during the Shagari regime that illustrated how valuable foreign exchange could be spirited out of the country by unscrupulous, locally registered importers through a complicated set of international transactions.

In early July 1978, two ships, called the *Jal Sea Condor* and the *Delta Sigma Pi*, sank somewhat mysteriously in fine weather off the Angolan coast. Their cargo included a considerable quantity of parboiled rice, *en route* from Thailand to Lagos. The consignee and importer of the rice was a Nigerian-based company called Ceekay Traders, controlled by a Cayman Islands registered holding company owned by the Hiranwand Melwani trading family. There was also a London arm – and the head of the firm, though of Indian extraction, was a British citizen. Ceekay was insured through the Nigerian end of the huge American International Insurance business, and claimed HK$16 million for the lost cargoes. But AII, suspicious, disputed the size of the claim and refused to pay it. Ceekay took legal action to recover the money. By the time the case came to court, it was 1983. Shagari was by then in power. Produced in court were documents and bills of lading that just happened to reveal a substantial foreign exchange rip-off. This is how it worked. Ceekay bought the rice from a sister company, Commonwealth Traders of Hong Kong. Ceekay failed to declare the connection between importer and supplier, an omission that was itself a breach of Nigerian law. What the bills of lading produced in court for the hearings revealed was that while Commonwealth Traders had paid $315 a tonne including freight for the rice bought in Thailand (where the government-controlled rice price excluding freight was $265 a tonne), it had invoiced its sister company for the rice at $500 a tonne. Ceekay declared the $500-a-tonne price to the Nigerian authorities with the cargo's bill of lading as 'proof' – and the dollars (foreign exchange) the Nigerian company needed to buy in Naira, the local currency, to pay for the consignment of rice, were released: at $185 per tonne more than the rice had actually cost. It might look costly for Ceekay, but it was a handy little windfall for the parent company controlling both Commonwealth Traders, who received the cash, and Ceekay Traders, who conned the extra dollars out of the Nigerians – always assuming that all the dollars went to Commonwealth Traders. Given that the two companies were in cahoots, some of the extra hard currency may have stayed with Ceekay to grease a few palms in order to obtain permits to distribute the rice and generally make business run smoothly.

Ceekay admitted in court that it was associated with Commonwealth Traders – and furthermore that the bills of lading, as well as over-invoicing for the rice, were backdated to show that the rice was loaded not in April 1978, as it actually had been, but on 31 March. The reason? Nigerian customs' duty on imported rice was raised in 1978 from $10 a tonne to $40 a tonne: with the exception of rice loaded before 1 April. Failure to declare associations between exporters and importers, though illegal, was common at the time. It was Ceekay's presentation of the incriminating documents and its confession in court to over-invoicing and backdating the documents that came as a surprise. However, the Shagari government showed no outward signs of taking action against the perpetrators of this costly scam. It was only after Major-General Buhari and the military took power that things went sour for the Hiranwand Melwani family over Ceekay's rice consignment when the head of the family, Arjandas Melwani, was arrested on 18 April 1985 by the Criminal Investigations Department and held in detention for a month before being released on bail, charged with violations of Nigerian foreign exchange, customs and tax laws.

The *Jal Sea Condor* had belonged to a man called Paul Chang Pak Hoi. In 1980 he faced charges in Hong Kong of an attempted insurance fraud on the hull by scuttling the ship and claiming compensation from the insurers. He was eventually acquitted.

The Ceekay rice story was a curious episode that lifted just a corner of the veil on some of the things that can go on in world trade. One of the casualties of some of the scams that went on was Britain's Export Credit Guarantee Department. It had agreed to support UK-based exporters selling goods to Nigeria, and was unable to get the money back from individual Nigerian importers because of Nigeria's moves to limit the outflow of foreign exchange from the country while she tried to repair the gaping holes in her economy left by the fraudsters. But it was worse than that, for it later emerged that some of those ECGD loans had themselves been fraudulently obtained. Nigeria was not the only country to have been ripped off, and the proceeds of fraud against the ECGD had in some instances gone towards furthering fresh fraud in West Africa.

The ECGD was set up in 1919 to act as an export credit insurance operation. It offers a range of services from blanket, comprehensive cover to one exporter for a wide range of goods and contracts, to individual policies tailored to single trade contracts. It also helps foreign importers to borrow the cash for their purchases from UK banks and repay it in a series of stages, by providing the bank with guarantees. The British exporter, then, is able to negotiate a cash contract with the buyer, and even receive progress payments before the finished goods are delivered. The bank pays over the cash, supported by the ECGD guarantee, and the buyer pays off the bank loan in agreed stages.

The ECGD used to provide bank guarantees for exporters too – latterly on deals involving goods sold on credit terms of two years or more. But, as its promotional literature rather coyly says, 'these guarantees were being run at a loss', and in October 1985 the decision was taken to phase them out over the following two years.

One of the reasons these schemes were being 'run at a loss' was that sharp-eyed conmen were taking advantage of them to raise finance for some distinctly shady deals. The ECGD was being defrauded to the tune of many millions of pounds a year. A lot of the money it lost – on legitimate as well as dubious trade deals – was linked to trade with Nigeria.

Things that can genuinely go wrong on an export deal might include a buyer going into receivership and defaulting on his payments; his country suddenly imposing exchange controls; the sudden imposition of import restrictions on certain items – and so on. All these things happened in Nigeria in the early 1980s.

The ECGD will check a buyer's record for major contracts, but in the hurly-burly of world trade in consumer goods, for instance, it cannot keep a watch on everyone. So each policy allows exporters £5,000 (at the time of writing) leeway to trade with any buyer without referring each time to the ECGD. To go above this cover, the exporter must first agree a higher credit limit for that deal with the ECGD.

Some countries are also riskier trading partners than others, so the ECGD grades them into four categories and charges higher premiums on insurance in the higher risk areas. Insurance cover is for up to 90% of the value of the contract against the risk that the buyer of the goods or services will default in some way, and 90–95% of the value against the risk that the country of the buyer will encounter some problem or introduce some measure that will scupper the deal. Once there is a claim – and in 1984–85 the ECGD paid out £784 million in claims out of the £17 billion worth of exports for which it had provided cover – the ECGD pays out 90% (or whatever the proportion of the value was agreed in the first place) under the terms of the policy, and the exporter is able to keep on trading. The rest of his business is not threatened by this one incident. But the exporter is then supposed to take action to get the money back for the ECGD (which, in turn, will usually help to cover the costs of debt recovery).

In the early 1980s, however, some of the clever international trading groups, who had learnt their business skills in less-regulated places, came to the conclusion that the ECGD was a bit of a soft touch, especially when it came to the bank guarantees for exporters. At its simplest, an overseas importer might order goods and deliberately default on the payments – even going into receivership to avoid paying – and leave the hapless British exporter without his goods or his money.

If he was covered by an ECGD policy, the exporter would be able to claim and the ECGD would be left out of pocket, since the chances of recovering the debt would be minimal. Precisely to avoid attracting unscrupulous importing clients of this ilk to a company, the ECGD likes its provision of insurance cover on a deal to be kept confidential; and the idea that the exporter once he has claimed, is responsible for pursuing the debt helps to deter importer and exporter from acting in cahoots to defraud the ECGD – in theory, at any rate.

But where you have large import-export businesses trading all over the world, with sister companies in practically every port, and goods coming and going constantly, then the scope for collusion and fraud multiplies. A favourite trick that was played upon the ill-starred Johnson Matthey Bankers in the early 1980s was for an importer to purport to be buying goods through a sister outfit (though this relationship would be kept secret) in the UK. The sister company would pretend to act as the confirming house – that is, as the intermediary between the overseas 'buyer' of the goods and the (mythical) British supplier. It would provide documents (usually faked) and arrange the finance, preferably through the old ECGD-guaranteed exporter's bank loans. But instead of being paid to the non-existent UK supplier, the money would be passed by the confirming house to the 'importer'. Then, if an ECGD insurance policy was involved, the confirming house would claim that the import company had defaulted on the deal in some way and make a claim to the ECGD for the value of the contract. Or it would just default on the bank loan and leave the bank to battle it out with the ECGD when it finally realised that no stage repayments were forthcoming. Nothing but fresh air would have actually moved from one country to another – hence the nickname 'fresh air exports' given to these scams when they came to light.

If, as Johnson Matthey Bankers' rescuer, the Bank of England (no less), later found, the bank loans were linked to an ECGD insurance policy rather than a simple ECGD guarantee, and the confirming house had not kept paying the premiums due on that policy, then the cover was technically void and the bank was stuck with the loss, willy-nilly. In the JMB case (the full story is covered in more detail in the next chapter) the sums were so large – £130 million worth of its bad debts were linked to ECGD guarantees on policies, of which a cool £90 million related to trade deals with Nigeria alone – then negotiations over who bore which losses followed. JMB's total bad debt was £248 million, as it turned out, so the ECGD-related debts were a substantial part of the ill-fated trade bank's problems.

JMB had made the mistake of growing too fast in a notoriously difficult area of business, and not policing its clients, nor keeping its own records properly. But its experiences helped to expose the world of 'fresh air exports'.

Another nasty scam that exploited the ECGD was where the overseas arm of an international trading house 'ordered' goods through a sister operation in the UK. With no intention of taking delivery, the order would be placed with a UK manufacturer. The contract with him would provide the documents needed for the UK sister company to go to the ECGD for cover or guarantees, raise the finance from a bank with this backing, and vanish with it. In due course the manufacturer would fulfil the order and find it got no further than the British docks he sent it to. He did not get paid, since not being the direct exporter he had no ECGD cover, and he would have goods on his hands that might cost him extra money to store, and might have to be sold at a substantial loss to any takers later – or might never find another purchaser. That sort of trick can destroy a small business. Small companies in a difficult domestic trading climate, who are desperately seeking new overseas orders, may be particularly vulnerable and should check out a new client's past trading record carefully. Even in a large firm, jobs might be at stake in the plant that bears the cost of scam.

By the time some of these frauds and deceptions were coming to light, the ECGD was already under the microscope. ECGD guarantees covered far greater sums of money than did its annual policies, partly because they were often a cumulative exposure built up over fixed periods of time, and partly because by no means all the guarantees were linked with ECGD policies anyway.

The ECGD's income came from the premiums it charged on policies, and interest earned from the basic fund of money built up over the years – the Consolidated Fund – plus some interest from debts that were yet to be repaid but were not yet lost causes. Business had built up very fast in the 1950s and 1960s but slowed down in the 1970s when ECGD premium rates rose, on the back of a rising proportion of claims under ECGD cover.

By this time, interest from the Consolidated Fund provided almost a third of the ECGD's total income. But as the number of claims began to rise, it was to be whittled away completely. By the end of the 1970s, came the collapse of oil prices coupled with a deadly combination of rising inflation and recession in the industrialised nations. Interest rates rose and poorer Third World countries ran into trouble servicing the large foreign debts built up earlier in the decade when credit was cheap and plentiful. Their purchasing-power dwindled; so did the buying power of the oil-exporting countries.

The result, as far as the ECGD was concerned, was a decline in the volume of UK trade with other nations, and therefore less demand for its policies and fewer premiums coming in. At the same time there was a leap in the number of deals that fell through under the political risk cover section of ECGD insurance policies. It had to meet a much higher number of claims, reaching £734 million worth by 1984–85, against just £94 million in 1977–78 before the oil crisis struck.

By spring 1985, the amounts of money in trade deals that the ECGD had 'at risk' had risen from $15.3 billion in 1977–78 to $33 billion; and 60% of that was on deals with developing countries. Africa – mostly Nigeria – made up the largest amount at risk by geographical area. In the first nine months of the financial year 1984–85 (that is, by the close of December 1984) the ECGD had already paid out £535 million in political risk claims – 65% of that on deals with Nigeria, Poland and Brazil alone. By 31 March 1985 (the year-end) the Consolidated Fund was a consolidated loss of £392 million. It was a scandal.

But the ECGD was able to act fast to put its house in order. The reason was a major review of its operations that had been set up nearly two years beforehand, in August 1983, the then Trade Minister Paul Channon had appointed a committee led by Sir Peter Matthews to look into 'the structure, functions and status' of the department.

The result – known generally as the Matthews Report – was published in March 1984, just as the ECGD's financial year 1983–84 was ending: a year in which the beleagured Consolidated Fund had already slipped £42.3 million into the red because of transfers to pay out on rising claims. The Matthews Report was tactful but concerned. It found that while the ECGD did a reasonable job on the whole, it was not entirely efficient and could be more flexible and co-operative with the private sector. It needed a thorough overhaul.

The changes the report recommended included re-forming the ECGD not as a government department connected to the Department of Trade as before, but as a fully fledged, government-owned corporation in its own right to provide insurance and financial services 'in support of exports and to do so at a profit'. It also recommended that the new corporation's guarantees should be fully backed by Her Majesty's Government. In the event, Paul Channon set up another team to review the ECGD in the light of the Matthews Report, led by F.J. Chapman, an Under Secretary at the ECGD, with a team of management consultants, ECGD and Treasury officials.

They published their recommendations in June 1985, and work began on implementing them. The Chapman Report did not mince its words. It found 'a vacuum at the top' of the ECGD, recommended a new board structure, better methods of financial measurement and of assessing political risk, improved communications between staff and management, better delegation of work, more use of computers – and more. But it did not take up the suggestion that the ECGD become a separate corporation. It remains a government department. 'Our recommendations,' the report concluded, 'add up to a radical change in both the working methods and the organisation of the Department.'

Most were to be implemented within a year; the rest, within two. The ECGD had discovered the *sine qua non* of fraud: your own sloppy systems make you a sitting target.

By the time the swingeing Chapman Report came out, JMB had collapsed (at the beginning of the previous October). The City of London Company Fraud Squad was investigating alleged 'fresh air export' frauds against the ECGD, and found that one man at least had accepted a £50,000 bribe to smooth the passage of certain transactions. Some of the confirming houses under investigation were JMB customers, the Bank of England admitted to the magazine *Financial Weekly* in July 1985. Because some of the confirming houses involved in the ECGD scams were Asian trading families like the Sethias, the UK popular press nicknamed them The Magic Carpet Mob. The rug was being pulled from under these firms' mischievous activities. But the whole adventure had cost the ECGD and the British economy dear.

4

Trading Places

On Friday 28 September 1984 a stockbroker who handles a lot of private investors' business received a call from one of his clients. He was an employee of Johnson Matthey Bankers and for the past few days he had been noticing a lot of activity in the boardroom: directors bustling in and out, important-looking men arriving with set expressions and bulging brief-cases. For the employee the conclusion was obvious: there was a bid on. That was why he was on the phone to his broker to tell him to buy JMB shares. The broker, a shrewd man who knew about City rumours and how people got only half the story, advised caution. Why don't you sleep on it over the weekend? It turned out to be the best investment advice of recent times.

On Monday morning, 1 October 1984, at 8.30 the employee was proved right – but only in the most perverse sense. JMB was taken over by the Bank of England for the amazing consideration of £1. The bid signs that the employee had spotted were, in fact, a rescue. Johnson Matthey Bankers was bust and in normal circumstances might have been allowed to go to the wall. But its parent was bullion dealer Johnson Matthey and that last weekend in September, as the JMB employee pondered over the advice given by his broker, the Bank of England in a feverish burst of activity wrestled with the effect that JMB's collapse would have on the fragile, delicate institution known as the gold market. Midland Bank was still in the throes of its problems with its American subsidiary Crocker, and it was easy to imagine that if JMB was not rescued and the gold market was adversely affected, it could have an impact on the Midland and other high street banks.

From Saturday morning, 29 September, to almost breakfast time on Monday, the bankers and bullion men summoned to the Bank of England discussed various options. The Bank was inclined to let JMB go but the bullion men pressed for a rescue, fearing this could mean the

68

loss of the gold market to Switzerland, not least because JMB was one of the five banks that set the London gold price daily. The Bank of England had originally contacted Morgan Guaranty, the lead manager of an earlier syndicated credit to Johnson Matthey Group, and asked it and thirteen other banks to consider a rescue loan. Johnson Matthey, the parent company, estimated that even without its banking arm it would require a credit line of around £250 million. By Sunday evening it seemed a buyer had been found, the Bank of Nova Scotia, but the bank wanted indemnities against any bad loans over £100 million and late on Sunday evening the deal was off. Threadneedle Street now presented its own version of the type of crisis meeting popularised at Number 10 by Harold Wilson. Different groups met in different rooms, coffee, beer and sandwiches were passed round and at last bleary eyed bankers got a deal. The Bank of England had decided to buy JMB. The deal was done just in the nick of time. At 2 a.m. London time on Monday the Hong Kong markets opened and JMB's local office stayed shut. The Hong Kong market had already heard vague rumours on Saturday, that being a working day for the bullion markets there. Hong Kong reacted to the Monday morning shut down of JMB's local office by fanning more rumours and by 4 a.m. London time news was coming from the Far East and Australia that, fearing the worst, some American and international banks were refusing to do business with British banks.

It was 8.30 in the morning before the fine print of the JMB package was agreed allowing the doors of the silver and black offices of JMB next to Fenchurch Street station to open. All the public had was a bland Bank of England announcement that 'problems' in commercial lending had led to the rescue. Privately, the Bank briefed correspondents on the implications for London's bullion market and the effect a bust JMB might have had on the whole financial system. For a few days it seemed the Bank of England, which has never been a great exponent of *glasnost*, would be able to present it as yet another conjuring trick. The early press notices were full of praise in the way the lifeboat, in dry dock since the secondary banking crisis of the early 1970s, had been successfully floated. The Bank released no details about who JMB had lent money to, how much, or how it got itself into such a mess. Later that week we at *Financial Weekly* provided the first names of borrowers, a picture of the type of lending that had caused the problems and raised questions about fraud in the City. But this was still the great unmentionable in the City, though wider events soon made it clear that the Bank's bland announcement would not do.

At that stage the miners were on their long, fruitless strike, and towards the end of October Dennis Skinner, the charismatic left-wing Labour MP, asked the Chancellor Nigel Lawson whether it was right that public money should be used to rescue JMB. Lawson dealt easily with the question saying it would not cost a great deal. Later he would tell Dr David Owen that there was a £10 million contribution from the Bank. Lawson had been misinformed about the cost and by now Johnson Matthey Bankers, which was not much known as a bank outside the City, suddenly found itself in the limelight. Dr Owen, whose expertise had been in foreign affairs and the health service, focused on JMB's bullion operations alleging that it was the bullion business that had brought JMB down. Though Owen's allegations were proved wrong, the parliamentary focus never left and soon the Bank of England was fighting a rearguard action, every now and again conceding some scrap of information, or being ambushed by revelations in Parliament, while Lawson and the Treasury refused to concede to Opposition pressure for a public enquiry. Eventually it was decided to set up a committee to consider banking supervision under the chairmanship of the Governor of the Bank of England, Robin Leigh-Pemberton.

Over the summer of 1985, slowly, like a leak, the figures for JMB's bad debts were upped until finally it was announced that the bank had lent a total of £450 million and of that sum £248 million, or well over half, was bad and doubtful debt. By then the Bank of England had been shown to have been economical with the truth, in Sir Robert (now Lord) Armstrong's memorable phrase. It had injected £100 million of capital into JMB, £25 million of this as loan stock, and then misled the Chancellor and the public about it. It had first pretended it had not happened, then when a leak in the *New Statesman* forced its hand it tried to pass it off as a short-term deposit. When the truth emerged that it was an injection of capital it did nothing to stop the erosion of the Bank of England's standing.

The rescue of JMB did force a re-think of the Gordon Richardson-inspired Banking Act, and a new Banking Act has been brought in to replace the 1979 one with better supervisory powers, elimination of the two-tier system (the first division banks lightly regulated, the second strictly controlled), and introduced a relationship between the Bank of England and the auditors of individual banks. How effective this will prove remains to be seen, but for a period that lasted for almost two years after JMB's rescue we saw a steady decline in the Bank of England's standing, what has been called a drain of spiritual energy. Lawson publicly rebuked the Governor and admitted that JMB showed an 'appalling and bizarre record of incompetence and mismanagement'. Much of the drama was played in the House of Commons where dramatic revelations by Brian Sedgemore, Labour MP for Hackney, led to furious rows in parliament between Sedgemore and Lawson, with the Labour politician making the most of the Treasury's problems with the Bank. At last the question that had been nagging everyone burst into the open: surely JMB was a subject for the Fraud Squad? On 6 October 1984, five days after the rescue, the *Financial Times* had confidently declared, 'JMB's demise is not the stuff of a Paul Erdman novel or even a case for the City of London Police Fraud Squad. There is no evidence of fraud or malpractice.' But, as unlikely as it may seem, JMB's story was even more bizarre than a Paul Erdman novel and fraud was most definitely involved.

As it turned out the man whose loans had played a big part in causing JMB's problems had used the money to finance films, and he was busily involved in writing a business thriller in the Erdman mould. The JMB story was to turn out to be a lot stranger than fiction. The parent, Johnson Matthey, had been in the precious metals business in Hatton Garden since 1817 and the company name was known to the wider public because it was a bullion dealer. In the City it had a special position because as a bullion dealer it had a banking licence and was one of the five members of the group that meets twice a day at Rothschilds and fixes the price of gold. Banking proper came late to Johnson Matthey in 1965, and soon the banking offshoot, known as JMB, was lending from Fenchurch Street. Fenchurch Street may be no more than a couple of miles from Hatton Garden, but the two worlds could not be more different. The bullion business at the edge of Fleet Street and a stone's throw from the *Daily Mirror*'s headquarters at Holborn Circus, is a place where you expect wheeler-dealers to operate. Close by is Leather Lane, one of London's famous street markets, and just down the slope is Smithfield market. Fenchurch Street is the City of the brolly, the bowler and the striped suit writ large.

For a long time it was not so much that anything was amiss, but that nothing very much happened with the banking outfit. JMB might have been based in Siberia for all the difference it made to the parent company. In 1970 it had obtained exemption under the Protection of Depositors Act. In 1980, after the Banking Act with its two-tier regulatory system came into force, JMB, almost automatically, was placed in the first tier as a recognised bank that would escape the more rigorous scrutiny of the licensed depositors. But even now JMB formed a small part of Johnson Matthey. The 1980 accounts showed that of the total assets of £874 million, £678 million were bullion and customers' bullion-related accounts. The banking business was just £34 million and contributed only one million to Johnson Matthey's £14.4 million profits. The banking side, thought the directors, had some catching up to do.

Over the next few years JMB did catch up – and how. Between 1980 and 1984 its loans and overdrafts rose from £34 million to £309 million, a rise of nearly a thousand per cent. Over that period the holding of bullion and customer-related accounts rose more conventionally from £678 million to £1,359 million. Other bank lending also rose from £18 million in 1980 to £65 million in 1984. By 1983 the directors could take pride in the effect JMB was having on profits. The 1983 profits were £24.3 million, £20.8 million from dealing, including bullion, and £3.5 million from banking, a trebling of banking profits since 1980. But in 1984 when the furies caught up with JMB, profits declined to £9.4 million, of which banking contributed just £0.5 million, half of what it had done in 1980. Its great banking expansion had taken it no further than where it was when it had started back in 1980.

Crucially, JMB's 1980 decision to expand had come just as there were businessmen emerging who were eager to help JMB 'catch up'. These businessmen were mostly from the Indian sub-continent. For various reasons certain Indian communities have a marvellously developed business sense and are often dubbed the Jews of the East. In the days of Empire these business skills were deployed either in India or in East Africa. Indeed, Indian business enterprise did almost as much to open up Africa as any European exploration. Then, as the winds of change began to blow through Africa, casting Indian businesses to the far corners of the world, many Indian entrepreneurs decided to come to London. They were now no longer in awe of the Raj or the white man's mystique, and found in JMB the ideal bank to further their interests. The bank that could not say no had met businessmen who always knew when to say yes and the mixture was heady and, for a time, enchanting.

Inevitably, in such situations there were stories of great personal interest. One of these stories we have already looked at, that of Raj Sethia. Then there was Mahmud Sipra, Abdul Shamji and Ian Robert Fraser. Fraser was a Scots banker, Shamji a trader very much in the old Indian business mould, and Sipra a modern sub-continental businessman. Fraser was a director of JMB and one of the men largely responsible for its banking expansion in the 1980s. He quickly struck up a friendship with the growing list of Asian customers, enjoying their company both socially and during business hours and often chiding those who tried to warn them of their activities. One of the features of the Indian business scene is that the businessman draws the banker into his social circle, often inviting him home to his dinner parties, etc., and Fraser grew very friendly with many of JMB's clients, including Ummed Goleccha, a business friend of Sethia. Later, Brian Sedgemore was to allege in the House of Commons that an investigator in maritime fraud had tried to warn Fraser that Sipra was involved in a £3 million fraud but was brushed aside. It was Fraser who was involved in the futile attempts to rescue Raj Sethia's Esal group and had a meeting with him in New York while the businessman was on the run from the Fraud Squad. He later told creditors at a meeting that Sethia ought to be backed. While investigating Esal the Fraud Squad's Brian Cooper tried to get Fraser to act, but he was told to mind his own business.

Mahmud Sipra was JMB's biggest borrower and also the most colourful. In the midst of the crisis when Sipra published his novel *Pawn to King Three*, this is how the gushing blurb described him: 'Mahmud Sipra provides the contemporary definition for the word polymath. Copywriter, media man turned international entrepreneur, shipping magnate, polo player and now novelist – he straddles several disciplines and cultures with a lifestyle to match. Having lived in the fast lane for over two decades he has savoured both success and disappointment.' In the novel the protagonist, Adnan Walid, ends up fighting an election in Pakistan, Sipra's native country.

Sipra, himself, had political ambitions which were strangely revealed when he stepped in to help finance the film his Mayfair neighbour film producer Ben Fisz was making. 'The Jigsaw Man', a thriller, had a crucial scene which showed an ex-British Prime Minister being assassinated. Sipra cut the scene, claiming it was immoral. When

Fisz asked him for the basis for his morality, Sipra explained that he, himself, wanted to be Prime Minister of Pakistan. Sipra injected £5 million into the film and went, as Fisz says, 'completely Hollywood. He just took over the film. When you are a pro and you realise you have to deal with an amateur then it is the time to go. I completely lost heart and sold the film to him.' This only spurred Sipra's film ambitions and as JMB was collapsing Sipra kept announcing further movie plans.

Some of his flamboyance was well captured by a *Daily Express* reporter, in September 1985, just as he was being named as a 'fraud' by Sedgemore in the Commons. He was pictured in the house overlooking Regents Park he had bought from Sir Ralph Richardson having tea with his companion, former British model Elaine, the accoutrements of high living scattered about him and a servant hovering in the background. Sipra did not appear to be fazed by the fact that a few months earlier a district judge in New York had described his actions as 'old fashioned piracy on the high seas and overwhelming greed' during a $1 million law suit brought against his companies by Dow Chemical and Manual International, a steel wholesaler, over a cargo of steel which was not delivered to the people that owned it.

Certainly Sipra, with his good looks, his polished manner and his lavish lifestyle, had the making of a film magnate and it was little surprise when he featured in the American TV show the 'World of the Rich & Famous'.

Sipra's business empire was built round the El Saeed group, whose main activities were in shipping. Before JMB collapsed few knew about El Saeed; after that, the Liberian registered company became notorious. Sipra, the son of an army major from Pakistan, had gone into shipping in America in the 1970s. He had arrived there, as he would often say, with either $30 or $32 in his pockets – the figure varied in different interviews – and keen to break into films. He found his niche in marketing and realised that he was good at trading. A lucky break involving the shipment of scrap metal for Pakistan got him into shipping and by the late 1970s he was heading a growing shipping group which made money from transporting commodities from the US to Third World countries. Shipping, he soon discovered, ran in families and he dealt with fellow-Pakistanis who, like the Greeks, have established some reputation as great shippers. Sipra married a daughter of a Pakistani shipping family, the Imams, who were also clients of Johnson Matthey Bankers. For JMB, keen to expand its business, Sipra seemed an ideal customer. Soon he was one of JMB's biggest customers, and as the El Saeed Group grew and spawned other subsidiaries into steel-trading, oil, films and publishing, so did JMB's exposure. At one time Sipra's various companies had borrowed as much as £70 million from the bank without any offsetting credit balances. By the time the Bank of England stepped in, Sipra was the bank's biggest creditor with debts of nearly £70 million.

During the debate on the Queen's Speech in the winter of 1985, almost a year after JMB had been rescued, Sedgemore alleged in the House of Commons that 'the number of frauds that Sipra has perpetrated is infinite', adding for good measure that 'he does nothing else but commit fraud'. Despite this, Ian Fraser told the *Sunday Times* that he thought Sipra was a very talented entrepreneur. In October 1985 Sipra left the UK and at the time of writing had not returned. His companies are in liquidation, he is debarred from being a director of a UK company and in November 1986 was declared a bankrupt with debts of £42 million. The Assistant Official Receiver, Michael Bennett, then applied for a warrant for his arrest after he failed to appear at a bankruptcy hearing. Sipra, who is a US citizen, originally went to the States but attempts by the Fraud Squad, who had earlier searched his house in Regents Park, to interview him in New York failed. His subsequent move to Pakistan has frustrated Fraud Squad plans to bring criminal charges against him as the UK has no extradition treaty with Pakistan.

The story of Abdul Shamji, who along with Sethia, Sipra and the Imams was a major JMB client, makes an interesting contrast. If Sipra was the polished product, Abdul Shamji was more of a rough diamond whose style and manner were not quite as polished – for a start he spoke English with a thick Indian accent – and nobody would mistake him, as Fisz puts it, for the 'smooth Sipra. Shamji was a bruiser, a street-trader, Sipra was a smooth trader.' Shamji had become involved with Fisz and his business friends when he tried to buy Wembley Stadium, a complicated deal that eventually collapsed with Fisz and his friends still owed nearly £175,000. Bruiser Shamji's route to power and fame had been quite different to Sipra's. Having arrived in Britain as a refugee from Idi Amin's Uganda in 1972, Shamji successfully followed the pattern set up by other East African Asians.

Ten years after he fled Uganda, he had offices in Park Lane and, under the banner of the Gomba group, a diversified hotel, trading, handbag-making and vehicle assembly interests. When, in August 1982, the *Financial Times* wrote fairly fulsomely about him, he was shy about revealing his profits but told the story of how he had started with arranging a shipment of Johnny Walker whisky and cutlery to Zaire and had never looked back. His Gomba group built up an impressive list of assets, including, at one stage, Safe Deposit Centres, three London theatres – the Duchess, the Garrick and the Mermaid – and a controlling interest in London Leisure and Arts Centre, which had a major stake in Wembley. His Gomba group had assets of £100 million, but for much of the time Gomba rarely made money – though this did not prevent him from making friends and influencing people. A very remarkable collection of friends they were, too: Mrs Thatcher, who spoke at a Shamji dinner and whose photograph hung in his Park Lane office; Norman Tebbitt; a couple of Tory MPs as paid advisers and notable journalist contacts who generally wrote some very complimentary articles about him. In March 1981, when Shamji bought the Scottish Stonefield Vehicles from the Official Receiver, he was hailed in the press as a 'saviour' by the *Observer* and a 'miracle man' by the *Sunday Times*. Like many other Shamji ventures, the press billing proved to be way over the top. The Stonefield saga was to end in tears as the company eventually ended up with the receivers and the Scottish courts imposed a record fine on Shamji for failure to file the 1983 accounts of Gomba Stonefield.

Like Sipra, Shamji borrowed heavily from JMB to finance his various deals and found Ian Fraser and the bank a very willing lender. The money came through overdrafts, even to members of the Gomba group who did not have up to date accounts. Later Sedgemore was to allege in the House of Commons that Shamji had provided a flat for Fraser, who had used it for entertaining two mistresses. Sedgemore told the House of Commons, 'I have always understood that Victorian values were about respect for family life and a fear of God. But according to Mr Abdul Shamji they are also about bribery, corruption, fraud and tarts for bankers.' Shamji and Fraser indignantly denied the allegations.

Publicly Shamji was never very worried that his companies were highly geared – that, to him, was a function of trading. He was confident that he had a strong asset base and could trade his way out of trouble. But the collapse of JMB and the departure of Fraser changed the picture, and a year later Shamji's companies were in liquidation owing JMB £21 million and other banks some £40 million. In

December 1986 Shamji paid back his debts to JMB, but seven of his companies remained in liquidation, though he did assure a London bankruptcy court in March 1988 that he would pay back all his creditors in full. Shamji has since been charged with one count of perjury.

But if these names took the public limelight in the intense glare that followed the JMB collapse, the bedrock of the tremendous expansion in business was based on what has come to be known as the JMB Sindhi connection. JMB sought to become an important bank by an over rapid expansion of trade finance to the Sindhi trading house operating out of the UK and West Africa, the Middle East, India and Pakistan. These loosely connected trading groups relied heavily on bills of lading, ECGD guarantees and other trading paper as collateral. JMB, keener to get business than worry about the quality of the business, did not check the terms and continuing validity of enough of this collateral to have good security against the millions it loaned in this way. This was particularly so with respect to Nigerian trade. It did not matter as long as the remarkable political and economic systems then operating in Nigeria remained stable, but the coup of December 1983 changed all that and the traders were caught on the hop. For many JMB clients it meant borrowing more to try and trade out of trouble. But for JMB, without adequate systems to keep an accurate record of individual – let alone total – exposures, it meant over-extending itself into near oblivion.

Yet the irony is that JMB's fall should have been due to lending in a field considered rather boring by most bankers – trade finance. In banking circles lending money on letters of credit and bills of exchange is neither new nor exciting – nor very innovative. Old-time bankers recall it as dull business which involves a great deal of technicality. In the old colonial days, this was the way the wool and textiles business was financed. But those bankers then knew their clients, they had the right connections, and they were confident about lending, having made sure the wool trade they were financing actually had a market. JMB forgot or ignored these old-established rules and paid the price. So while Sipra and Shamji were a substantial part of JMB's total loan book of £400 million, a good £130 million was also owed on letters of credit and bills of exchange to a group of businessmen who mostly came from Sind in the Indian sub-continent. Their business activities cleverly exploited the poorly controlled JMB banking division.

These Sindhi businessmen operated mainly from London's Grosvenor Square. Long before JMB's problems forced the Bank of England rescue, Indian banking circles were already talking about the Sindhi connection that was said to be leading JMB a merry paper-chase. In this case, very like the one Sethia led the other banks, letters of credit followed bills of exchange, which followed supposed sales of sugar and commodities to Nigeria and other, mostly West African countries.

We have seen how Sipra and Shamji built up their JMB connections, but how did these Sindhi loans arise? Why did so many Sindhis build up such a cosy relationship with a small banking subsidiary of one of London's biggest bullion names?

Some clues can be found in the nature of the operations set up by the Sindhis. Even more than the Jews or the Poles, the Sindhis are a lost people. Jutting out on the western edge of India, Sind has been conquered frequently, falling to the Muslims in the seventh century and wrenched from India and given to Pakistan in the partition devised by the Raj before the withdrawal from India in 1947. For the Hindus of this province this meant exile – first to India, then to East Africa and England. With these moves came a sharpening of the business skills that had already made them feared and respected. It also fostered a communal spirit with one Sindhi easily identifying another by the fact that all Sindhi names end in 'ani' (pronounced annie).

But such subtleties were lost on JMB, where banking supervision was so lax that there was not even an index of drawees to check that bills of exchange were not being drawn on connected companies or individuals. Old-fashioned trade finance always made sure of such boring details for its success in this complex field.

This made borrowing from JMB remarkably easy. When the Bank of England stepped in with its rescue it was discovered that some £90 million of its bad loans resulted from reconfirming letters of credit to Sindhi business houses incorporated in the UK as exporters and confirming agents, dealing with Nigeria. A Sindhi trader would arrive from Nigeria with a letter of credit endorsed on a Nigerian bank to import a commodity – sugar, for example. A Sindhi businessman in London would approach JMB to re-confirm the letter of credit – which would only acquire value in this country and be used to buy goods once so re-confirmed. In the late 1970s and early 1980s, most of the major UK clearers shied away from such business, partly because it was dull, partly because of the technical complexities. But JMB, small and hungry to make its mark, was eager for it. It also found it could charge a lot more for such business than other banks.

Normally the commission on re-confirming letters of credit is about a quarter per cent above the London Inter Bank Offer Rate (Libor). But as the early 1983 dip in oil prices affected Nigeria's economy and balance of payments, JMB found it had the field to itself and could charge as much as 2% above Libor – a colossal profit given the volumes involved. Or so it would have been had the business gone according to plan. Instead JMB found itself dragged into a paper pyramid where letters of credit seeking payment chased bills of exchange, which, in turn, chased yet more letters of credit, and more bills of exchange. Not all the companies borrowing the sums had the capital to meet the loans. JMB's monitoring was so inadequate that the information it had on these companies was several years out of date.

This state of affairs was compounded by the fact that while JMB had four computers at work, the systems were incompatible. An integrated system might have revealed that of the 400 borrowing groups and 3,000 accounts, one or two groups appeared regularly in many transactions. With transactions having to be put on all four systems, mistakes were easily made. Worse still, there was no procedures manual to guide the banking staff, many of whom were relatively junior, promoted from within the organisation, and without the wider experience that might have alerted them to the dangers of the transactions. They were also overworked. All this may appear mundane but proves crucial when suddenly millions of pounds turn out to be bad loans.

Neither JMB's capital base nor staff numbers had increased despite the mushrooming of the commercial loan department since 1981. Indeed, such was the state of confusion that when the Bank of England took over, Ian Fraser, who had left within a few days of the rescue, had to be brought back as consultant to help sort out the rescue. Contrary to normal banking practice, loan conversations with customers had not been minuted by the banking staff, and customers' claims after the collapse did not match the books – where the records were available. Fraser was used until February 1985 almost as a human computer to check the veracity of customers' claims. Only when the fees he was paid for this work were revealed was there an outcry and some realisation of the mess JMB had been in.

But it was not merely that JMB's systems were inadequate, or that

JMB's directors were not aware of what they were up to. There is the role of the auditors, Arthur Young. It did not qualify the March 1984 accounts. The accounts had carried a note saying, 'Provision is made for all known doubtful debts.' This satisfied the auditors and it was only under pressure from the Bank of England that in August 1984 the company asked the auditors to examine the loan books in more detail. It was this that provided a glimpse of the can of worms that was festering there. Later, the Bank of England sued the auditors for negligence and the auditors, in turn, sued the Chancellor, and BBC radio and television, ITN and Channel 4 for remarks made by Nigel Lawson outside the Commons. In October 1988, Arthur Young agreed to pay the Bank of England £25 million in an out-of-court settlement, which is believed to be the largest such settlement by an accountancy firm in the UK. They also agreed to withdraw their actions against Lawson, BBC radio and television, ITN and Channel 4.

Then there is the matter of the Bank of England's supervision of JMB. Since it belonged to the first tier, in the two-tier system devised by the former Governor Sir Gordon Richardson, its supervision was somewhat lighter. The Leigh-Pemberton Committee report which looked at banking supervision in the light of the JMB scandal, though not the scandal itself, conceded that, 'JMB's position as a recognised bank was a factor in the delay in the supervisors becoming aware of, and reacting to, its growing problems.' In other words, JMB who were probably not entitled to be in the first division, was treated as such, and by the time it dawned that it was really second division on a par with licensed deposit-takers it was too late.

It has since emerged that the lady who handled JMB's supervision at the Bank of England was overworked. She also had Continental Illinois to deal with and allowed JMB to get away with reporting inaccurate statistics about the loan exposures of clients like Sethia and Sipra. Since then at least one senior official has revealed his sexist inclinations by saying that such an important job should never have been left to a woman. The more prosaic truth is that the banking supervision department was not adequately staffed nor properly led, with the Assistant Director Brian Quinn, who had been promoted in 1982 and asked to sort the department, distracted by the Third World debt crisis. For a good part of 1982 and 1983 Quinn was a regular passenger on Concorde shuttling between London and New York. As Roy Shuttleworth, the Bank of England Staff Organisation's secretary, says,

'If you run an organisation on a shoestring with insufficient control, its inevitable that from time to time there's going to be an almighty cock-up.'

A graver charge against the Bank of England is that after it had discovered the cock-up in full bloom, as it were, that weekend in September 1984, it did not realise that something more than lapse of banking supervision was involved. For months it resisted any thought that there might be fraud when the Sethia affair was already public knowledge and Sethia was known to be a prominent customer of JMB, having borrowed 39% of JMB's capital. Sethia had already decamped from England. Here was the man who had acquired a building opposite the Bank of England to try to become the greatest Indian; now he was being sought by the Fraud Squad. Should this not have rung some alarm bells? Perhaps it did not because JMB's whole banking growth, and the client base it had acquired, must have seemed so extraordinary to the bank. This is revealed in the strange feeling that came over Michael Hawkes, Chairman of Kleinwort Benson, when he was summoned to the Bank of England on that last weekend in September. As he went through the JMB books there was not a single name he could recognise, yet they had large amounts of borrowings against their names: £60 million to one name, £30 million to another. It was unbelievable. But while Hawkes could not recognise the names, these were people doing business in the new City. They were part of the new generation of immigrants maintaining the tradition of the City as a welcoming home for foreign businessmen, banks and institutions.

The existence of foreign banks in London is nothing new. Indeed, banking was brought to what we now call the Square Mile by goldsmiths and silversmiths from the Lombardy region of Italy. Historically, mankind has not only searched for gold but used it as security and it was trading in gold and silver that had begun the development of banking. Wealthy clients, aware of the risks of storing gold under their beds, used the safes of smart gold- and silversmiths in exchange for receipts. This guaranteed their right to the gold and were the first banknotes. In the early Middle Ages this practice had developed best in Lombardy and when the smiths were granted land – one of them being the area round Lombard Street, hence the name – by Edward I, the Italian banking practices spread to London. Even the word, 'bank', and the historical symbols for English money, '£.s.d.' are corruptions of Italian words. In Lombardy, the Italian moneylenders conducted their work from a banco – a wooden bench in the market place – and this in English became bank, while £.s.d. were Italian symbols for lire, soldi and denarii.

As Britain acquired an empire, and sterling became the language of the men of money, there were many other immigrants who came to London to set up their banks. Examine the history of the great British merchant banks of today and behind nearly all of them you will find a story of immigrant success: Charterhouse Japhet, Hambros, Kleinwort Benson, Lazard, Morgan Grenfell, N.M. Rothschild, J. Henry Schroder Wagg, and perhaps the most amazing of all, Warburg, illustrating as it does Europe's horrendous mid-twentieth-century history. But these were immigrants wanting to become part of the greatest Empire the world had seen, as the Imperial propaganda would have us believe. After the Second World War as Britain lost an empire and, in Dean Acheson's cruel phrase, struggled to find a role, this view of the City changed. Foreign bankers still came to London but now they set up branch offices in London rather than acquire British banks.

This process accelerated in the 1960s and 1970s. In the 1960s it was through the growth of what is called the Euromarket – a whole gamut of financial activities based upon the offshore use of currencies, principally the dollar. In the 1970s the catalyst was the oil price revolution that not only made life for the motorists a nightmare but also produced vast revenues in the hands of oil-producing countries. These countries did not have the financial systems to cope with such huge amounts and did not want to keep all their loot in dollars in New York, worried by the leverage this would give the US government. Their decision to spread their cash around various European countries gave a big boost to London as an international banking centre.

There were many things going for London. Nearly everybody spoke English, or at least everybody that mattered. Also the practical English with their practical English commercial laws were considered by lawyers to be superior to the legalistic continentals with their more theoretical and general formulations. Above all, the financial authorities in London welcomed this sudden influx of rich foreigners. The Bank of England, the guardian of the City, produced a regime that in the words of Otto Schoeppler, former Chairman of the Chase Manhattan Bank, 'was a very warm place for doing business' – a warmth that not only brought Arab money but also Arab and other banks. Between 1970 and 1980 the number of foreign banks with offices in London doubled from 163 to 353. By the end of 1984 there were 470 foreign banks in London with a further 97 foreign security houses. In popular myth Switzerland was still the place for bankers, but in reality it was London that was becoming the Mecca of the international banker.

Publicly, many of the new banks were motivated by lofty ideals as can be gauged from this explanation of its emblem in one of the early annual reports of the Allied Arab Bank. The emblem showed two outer circles enclosing two geometric shapes which, in turn, had pictograms of a horse and a palm tree. The bank's report explained that the two outer circles represented the alliance of the Arab and Western worlds, the geometric shapes the participation of both the Western and Eastern Arab worlds, the horse was a symbol of nobility of action and reverence for the word as bond, and the palm tree a symbol of Arab continuity. Allied Arab, set up in 1977 with a 20% Barclays Bank holding and the rest from two principal Arab interests, was just one of the banks hit by Sethia. A whole host of others who were charmed by Sethia also arrived in London at about the same time: Middle East Bank (1976), Oriental Bank of Credit and Commerce (1980), Punjab National Bank (1976), Union Bank (1981). Today these banks, apart from the Middle East Bank and Allied Arab, have had to close their London operations.

The JMB story has ended more happily. The bullion banking business was sold to the Australian bullion company Mase-Westpac for a sum of £17.5 million over net asset value. The original estimate of nearly £250 million of bad loans was whittled down to £41.5 million by December 1986, and after all the disposals the total cost of JMB to the Bank had been £30 million.

But the fraud story rumbles on. Michael Flawn, a JMB assistant manager, and Amjad Iman, a customer, were tried at the Old Bailey on corruption and theft charges. Flawn was found not guilty of corruption, but received nine months' imprisonment for theft. Iman was acquitted. Ummed Goleccha's Berg & Sons went into liquidation owing JMB £6 million. In May 1988 Geeta Lakhiani faced trial on charges of false accounting and forgery, and was found not guilty. Lakhiani was a director of two companies which were customers of JMB. In June 1988, Harsh Melwani, the London manager of a confirming house, faced trial on charges of false accounting and theft, and was sentenced to eighteen months in prison. In September 1988, Manchester businessmen John Ashton and Jeffrey Boardman appeared at the Old Bailey and received six months' imprisonment, suspended for two years. Ian Fraser was arrested, but no charges were pressed on the advice of the DPP and the Serious Fraud Office.

At one stage, there were thirty-seven officers combined from the Metropolitan and City police forces investigating the affair, and while this number has reduced the investigators carry on. The Bank of England may have washed its hands of JMB, but the Fraud Squad has not.

5

That Sinking Feeling

I: Trouble at Sea: the *Salem*

Christmas came a little late to three anxious men in the Swiss town of Zug in 1979. Three days late, to be exact: but it was worth the wait. For on that day US $32 million arrived as if by magic in the bank account of a little company owned by one of the trio: Beets Trading AG. Before the day was out, the three had divided the windfall and spirited their unequal shares of it away. The biggest oil fraud of the century had come to an apparently successful conclusion.

But while the three conspirators celebrated the coming year and their new fortunes, nemesis in the form of a 213,928 tonne deadweight oil tanker called the *Salem* and flying the Liberian flag was lumbering her way round the Cape of Good Hope. The tanker was heading towards a watery grave of the deepest sort: a patch of ocean off the coast of Senegal, West Africa, above a deep geological crack in the Continental Shelf.

On 16 January 1980 the *Salem* reached the spot — her final destination, but only the start of her notoriety. Her Greek captain, Dimitrios Georgoulis, summoned his crew of twenty-five and told them a fantastic story. Of the 193,000 tonnes of light crude oil worth some $62 million the *Salem* had been carrying and which belonged to the Shell group of oil companies, the bulk had been offloaded illegally at the South African port of Durban where she had called three weeks before. It had been an unscheduled stop (and had been carried out under a brief change of name to the *Lema*).

Georgoulis apparently told his crew that he only discovered that the unloading was illegal, meaning that the cargo was being stolen, after it had been completed. At any rate, the deed was done, and could not be undone. The tanks had been filled with seawater to make the *Salem* look fully loaded, and he had now been told to scuttle her. For the crew, extra bonuses in Swiss Francs were on offer in return for their silence over the scuttling. What, in the circumstances, did they wish to do?

Georgoulis was later – much later – to repeat this story in an Athens court and testify that, after some discussion, the crew had decided to go along with the plan to sink the *Salem*. A small amount of oil – 15,840 tonnes – had been left in her tanks to provide enough of an oil slick to convince the outside world that she had gone down fully loaded. The depth of the spot chosen, wind, and currents would be held accountable for the rapid break-up of the larger slick that a genuine disaster should have left . . . and no one would be any the wiser.

But the best-laid plans have a nasty habit of going awry and the *Salem* cover-up went wrong almost from the start. As the crew packed their baggage and a snack to keep body and soul together, rummaged out their passports, and donned their best clothes rather than lose all to the salt sea, another tanker was travelling towards the doomed *Salem*.

The *British Trident*, managed by the oil group British Petroleum, was in the same area – and next day chanced upon an unusual scene off the Senegalese coast, just forty-six minutes before the *Salem* vanished forever. The *British Trident*'s presence changed everything. Without it, the *Salem* affair might never have hit the world's headlines.

As it was, on 17 January 1980, at 10.50 a.m., the *British Trident* reported sighting the *Salem* with 'an unusual list and trim'. Some twenty minutes later, a distress signal was received on the radio from the listing tanker. At 11.15, the *British Trident* recorded orange smoke pouring from the stricken vessel.

By 11.29, two lifeboats had been spotted in the water. Just seven minutes after that, the *Salem* sank. She was out of sight; but by no means out of mind.

By 12.35, all the neatly dressed 'survivors' were safely on board the *British Trident* en route to Dakar in Senegal, just a day away. Not one man had been lost in the explosion and fire which the crew told everyone on board had caused the disaster. The adventure at sea was over.

But the adventure on dry land was only just beginning for most concerned – not least the Captain and his senior crewmen, who were to face five years of investigations, and stop-start court cases, before the full story was unravelled, the major conspirators traced, some of the participants sentenced, and the world made wiser about how easy it was even for the inefficient to perpetrate a multi-million pound shipping fraud.

The crew told their rescuers on the *British Trident* that an explosion at 5 a.m. in the pump rooms on 16 January had been followed by fires, and resulted in the flooding of the parts of the laden oil tanker. Fear of further explosions led to the decision to abandon ship – more than thirty hours later – and take to the lifeboats.

But right from the start, the crew of the *British Trident*, and soon the rest of the shipping world (no stranger to funny business and smaller scuttlings at sea), were suspicious about the sequence of events reported. Quite apart from the neatly packed cases and obvious preparedness of the rescued seamen, there was something odd about the *Salem*'s entire journey, and even odder about her demise. As one investigator later put it, 'Everybody knows tankers don't explode with full tanks. You need a mixture of oil and air to have a fire.'

On board the *British Trident*, meticulous notes were taken of what the *Salem*'s master and crew said about her demise and her travels. This was to prove a piece of bad luck for the conspirators meeting in Zug.

The *Salem* had loaded her oil at Mina al Ahmadi in Kuwait on 9 and 10 December 1979, and left the Gulf on 10 December. How had it taken her until 16–17 January to reach the Senegalese coast? The Captain later claimed that she had developed engine trouble off Port Elizabeth, which had taken some time to repair.

But that was still pretty slow going, even under a captain who was suspected of not even having a proper master's ticket. That in itself was curious. Moreover, Georgoulis had been the master on the *Alessandros K*, which had disappeared the previous May while technically under arrest at Piraeus. The ship had been arrested there in late 1978 *en route* from the Bulgarian port of Bourgas in the Black Sea, with $2 million of steel reinforcing bars aboard. In addition, the *Salem*'s first mate, Andreas Annivas, had previously been chief officer of the *Alexandra*, another ship that had come to grief – leading to a total loss claim for the value of the hull with the Lloyd's of London underwriters of the insurance cover.

The gossip mounted. The *Salem* was just ten years old and had been bought only six weeks before she sank by the Oxford Shipping Co. of Monrovia (the capital of Liberia) for $12.3 million. Yet she had promptly been insured for $24 million. Just what had made her founder and sink? If fire and explosions had started at 5 a.m. on 16

January, as the crew said, why had it taken until 11.36 a.m. the following day, more than thirty hours, for the tanker to go under? That too was slow going.

As these and other questions mounted, pressure on the crew to answer them also grew. Georgoulis stuck to his story for over five years. But before the month of January was out, a Tunisian seaman from the *Salem* on his way home from Dakar spilled the beans, first to a journalist, and then in Paris to the British Embassy when the French authorities showed little interest.

The first confirmed reports that the *Salem*'s cargo had been sold off illegally to South Africa, at the heart of an embargo by the Organisation of Petroleum Exporting Countries (OPEC) against that nation – and that the tanker had been scuttled to cover up the deal – hit the shipping press on 31 January. By then, the hunt for the men behind the scam was underway.

Piecing together the story proved difficult and time-consuming. Investigators working for the insurers of the cargo had a lucky break within the first few minutes of their inquiries, establishing very quickly indeed that the *Salem* had been spotted, and even photographed, tied up at Durban. But it took five years, involved investigators from at least eight different countries, thousands of documents, court hearings in Liberia, trials in Greece, Holland, and the USA, before an accurate picture of the *Salem* affair emerged. It was a very big scam, described even by one of the conspirator's defence counsel as 'the biggest oil fraud of this century'.

The background to the *Salem* affair was a political one. Back in 1973, OPEC had declared an oil embargo against South Africa in an attempt to force her to abandon her apartheid policy. South Africa was heavily dependent upon imported oil in those days. She managed to continue getting 96% of her oil supplies from Iran through the mid 1970s, but with the overthrow of the Shah in 1978 all that changed. Iran's troubles led to a fall in world oil production of about six million barrels per day, and anxiety over the shortage forced world oil prices up dramatically. Meanwhile, the South African Government was having to buy its oil secretly on the world markets wherever it could find brokers willing to break the OPEC embargo.

This combination of rising world oil prices and the OPEC embargo created the perfect conditions for fraud: high stakes, and maximum secrecy. For a small group of Greek shipping men who were no strangers to the industry's bane of 'diverted' cargoes and quiet scuttlings for cover-ups and fraudulent insurance claims, it was a golden opportunity – and they seized it. Amongst themselves it was nicknamed 'the Pension Job': a really big fraud, to retire on in luxury. The *Salem* affair was just what had been done with other cargoes, and other vessels, but on a monumental scale. For the scapegoats and conspirators alike, it had repercussions to match.

The Greeks' Mr Fixit was Piraeus shipping agent Nicolas Mittakis. Piraeus is Greece's major port, berthed cheek by jowl with the city of Athens. Mittakis seemed to be in with three shipowning families who were widely believed to be past masters at losing old ships and diverting their cargoes. For the Pension Job, he cast around for someone to front the whole deal. He needed a suitable oil cargo, an oil-broker who would find a buyer for it, and a system that would mask the true ownership of the cargo that was to be diverted and sold off before the rightful owner knew it was missing.

Here the conspirators were a bit out of their depth and the whole scam was a bit leaky. Mittakis seems to have talked to quite a few people before he found the team that set up the *Salem* affair. Most backed off, suspecting trouble. A New Orleans businessman was later to testify in a Houston, Texas, court that he, for one, had been approached to find a buyer for the oil and had even lined up the Romanians at one point. Others also said they had been approached. But by mid-1979, Mittakis had contacted Dutchman Anton Reidel, managing director of a ships' chandlery firm in Rotterdam, and asked him for help to find buyers for crude oil in boycotted destinations. Reidel was in turn introduced by an American oilman to his future partner: Lebanese-born US citizen Frederick Soudan. From Missouri City, he styled himself President of American Polomax International of Houston.

These three – Mittakis, Reidel, Soudan – were the men waiting in Zug just after Christmas 1979 to collect their shares of the *Salem* scam. (Mittakis collected most, to share out again later with his shadowy masters in Athens.) Beets Trading AG, into whose bank account the $32 million profit flowed, was a Swiss subsidiary of Anton Reidel's Rotterdam business.

Soudan had found Mittakis his oil buyer that autumn: the oil-hungry South African Strategic Fuel Fund, or SFF. Soudan was as smooth a talker as he was smooth looking. He convinced South African commodities trader Daniel Fourie of Johannesburg that he was a wealthy man, busy putting up a big new office tower in Houston for American Polomax. Fourie was to introduce him to the South African bank, Mercabank – a vital if unwitting link in the scam. Meanwhile, two other South African businessmen, James Shorrock and his partner John Austin, arranged a meeting for Soudan with officials of the SFF in October 1979. Soudan said he owned $200 million of Saudi Arabian oil which he could deliver in four shipments to the SFF.

A deal was agreed, on 20 October, for Soudan to supply 6 million barrels of crude, the first shipment to be 1.4 million barrels for which SFF would pay $44 million. With this deal under his belt, Soudan needed a ship, a cargo of oil, and a charter for the ship. And he needed financial channels. Now he turned to Mercabank's international division manager, Hermanus (Manie) Du Plessis, and asked him to fund the purchase of a tanker. Du Plessis also believed that Soudan's American Polomax was in the big league of businesses – and there was the SFF deal to prove it. So he agreed a deal in which Mercabank would put up the $12.3 million needed to buy the tanker, and would also receive for Soudan and his team the $44 million that SFF was due to pay for the cargo on its arrival in Durban.

It was agreed that Mercabank would deduct its $12.3 million outlay on the tanker, and send the balance – about $32 million – on to the Swiss bank account of Reidel's Zug subsidiary. In this way Mercabank was conned into putting up the money for the *Salem* itself, and enabling the whole affair to get up steam.

Fourie's Mon Repos company was paid $100,000 for acting as the intermediary between Soudan and the bank. He was later to testify in court in the USA about all these events.

The *Salem* was duly bought – from Pimmerton Shipping of Monrovia, a Liberian company – at the close of November 1979 with the money borrowed from Mercabank. The purchase was supervised by a London shipbroker, John Masters; and the buyer was the Oxford Shipping Co., also of Monrovia: director, Frederick Soudan. The tanker was ten years old and named the *South Sea*; Soudan renamed her the *Salem*. Meanwhile, Mittakis had approached Greek shipping agent George Ristos, and asked if he could find a charter for the *Salem*. Ristos later claimed that it was he who first suggested Pontoil, a Genoa-based oil-broker with offices in Lausanne, Switzerland – though the actual charterer was one Bert Stein of Liberian-registered agency Shipomex, also with offices in Switzerland.

Pontoil bought around four million barrels of oil a year from Kuwait, acting as a middleman by taking responsibility for large quantities of oil and selling it on to others in a variety of smaller quantities. Kuwait is a member of OPEC, and therefore one of the countries operating the oil sales embargo against South Africa at the time.

Pontoil's presumably unsuspecting Lausanne office provided the *Salem* with her cargo. On 9 and 10 December, she loaded 193,000 tonnes of light crude oil at Mina al Ahmadi in Kuwait and set sail for Italy. On 14 December, Pontoil found a new purchaser for the oil, selling it on while it was still at sea, to Shell International Trading for around $60 million. Shell insured its new cargo for $56.3 million with Lloyd's of London, and waited for it to arrive.

Cargoes often change hands like that while still at sea, and this was a normal brokering deal. The date set for Shell to hand over the purchase price was 23 January. By that time, though neither company knew it, the *Salem* would already have sunk. But under the terms of the contract, Shell still had to pay Pontoil.

Even when news of the loss of the *Salem* broke, Shell expected to be able to claim for the lost cargo under the $56.3 million insurance cover. No one, however, had reckoned with the cargo having already been spirited away. As the *Salem* affair broke, so did the legal wrangle over who was liable for what. It lasted almost as long as the investigations into the rest of the affair, and went all the way to the House of Lords for a final ruling.

Eventually the insurers paid only for the oil lost in the scuttling – about $5 million worth. South Africa gave $30.5 million compensation to the oil group, however.

For the scam to work, it was important for the conspirators that the South Africans did not realise that the oil to be unloaded at Durban already belonged to someone else. Reidel took care of that. When Mittakis passed him the original bill of lading – effectively the title deed to the crude oil cargo – which named Pontoil as the original consignee of the oil, Reidel simply created another one. He was later to argue in court that he was entitled to do this, having the original bill of lading, and that such procedures were common during the oil embargo to protect suppliers.

Instead of going straight to its northern European destination, the *Salem* sailed secretly for Durban, changed its name again, offloaded most of the cargo there into tanks at the quayside, filled its own tanks with seawater, and quietly departed for its final voyage.

The SFF duly paid $44 million over to Mercabank, which fulfilled its part of the bargain. The $32 million balance, less the *Salem*'s purchase price, arrived in Zug in the account of Beets Trading AG on 28 December. Nicolas Mittakis and his masters took $20 million of it, collected from the Central Union Bank of Switzerland under two false names. Mittakis' was Nicolaos Trilizas. Later he was to claim that he had only kept $385,000 of the loot for himself, in the form of a brokerage fee, plus an extra 2–2.5% commission per barrel of oil for breaking the embargo. Anton Reidel later confirmed that Mittakis had given at least $1.4 million to two Greek companions that day – who had stuffed the money into a suitcase and left.

Fred Soudan took one cheque for $3 million and another five for $250,000 each. His share, at $4.25 million the smallest of that day's division of the spoils, went into a numbered Swiss bank account. Of that, about $2 million went towards paying various fees and expenses incurred in setting up the *Salem* purchase. But investigators think he might have also expected a share of any claim on the hull insurance. It was not to be, however. The *Salem* affair was getting too hot for the conspirators to risk making a claim for double what had been paid for the ship, and stirring up more enquiries.

The arrival and division of all this money in Zug puzzled Beets Trading's finance director Paul Bertsch. He had major reservations about its origins, but was told it was the proceeds of a large oil deal the three men had just completed – as indeed it was. This explanation was probably the most truthful thing any of them had said about the deal so far.

Soudan and Reidel were in London when news broke of the *Salem*'s sinking. The reports horrified John Masters, the shipbroker who had just supervised the *Salem*'s purchase by Oxford Shipping, particularly when coupled with rumours that her cargo had been offloaded first. Feeling 'very stirred up', he confronted Soudan and Reidel at the London Hilton. Reidel did most of the talking, Masters later said, but both men denied reports that the *Salem* had discharged oil in Durban before she sank. Masters simply did not believe them.

He was not alone. As the rumours spread, the investigations began. By the end of January, the Liberian Bureau of Maritime Affairs was questioning members of the crew – since the *Salem* had sailed under the

Liberian flag. Greece also began a preliminary enquiry. On 1 February came news that Shell had been to the Director of Public Prosecutions in London, and called in Scotland Yard. Soudan checked out of the London Hilton the same day, and with a friend, John Haddad, set off on a spending spree round Europe and the Middle East. Scotland Yard officers' investigations soon took them abroad too: first to Switzerland. Later on they sought West German help in tracing 'Bert Stein' of Shipomex. Meanwhile, Lloyd's of London underwriters, who were faced with Shell's insurance claim for the lost oil cargo, also began an investigation through their solicitors, Clyde & Co. – a firm well versed in the antics of Greek shipowners and able to spot dubious connections that others might have taken longer to unravel.

The legal profession was in for a busy – and no doubt lucrative – time. The men at Lloyd's decided to contest Shell's insurance claim in the British courts – on the basis that the cover had not extended to unscheduled trips to Durban. Shell decided to sue Oxford Shipping and Soudan for the $56.3 million-worth of missing oil. In the USA, Southern Texas Federal Prosecutor Tony Canales asked the FBI to look into whether there were grounds to investigate Soudan in America, for possible wire or mail fraud (using the US mail or other communication systems to plan a fraud). In South Africa, tight-lipped officials were refusing to say what had happened to the oil at Durban – but then in April 1980 the country did offer Shell $30.5 million compensation. This was accepted but had to be held to one side while the insurance wrangle went on.

The last thing South Africa wanted was to be suspected of stealing a major oil company's cargo – and she did eventually decide to co-operate with Greek and US investigators to nail the conspirators. Pontoil was in hot water too. Kuwait, suspecting it of deliberately busting the OPEC oil embargo, quickly suspended sales of its crude oil to the broker. For Pontoil's managing director, Paulo Mantovani, it was not a very agreeable start to 1980. South African investigators later also raised questions about the extent of Pontoil's role in a report into the fraud, though nothing came of their remarks.

The various investigations made steady progress at first. Liberia sent its Solicitor-General, Mr E. Winfred Smallwood, to London to discuss the situation. He was 'satisfied that criminal offences had been involved'. Prevented from leaving Dakar, in Senegal, the *Salem*'s Captain Georgoulis and his chief engineer Antonio Kalomiropoulos were being questioned by Dakar police. In early February, Liberia and Senegal struck a deal – with creative use, in the absence of any modern extradition treaty between them, of a 115-year-old agreement between Liberia and the then French colony – to extradite the two men to the Liberian capital of Monrovia. They arrived a month later. In April they were formally charged – first with offences under a section of Liberian Maritime Law covering the licensing of ships' officers, and later, with the theft of the *Salem*'s cargo.

But history had other plans for Georgoulis and Kalomiropoulos. In April 1980 a military coup installed a new Liberian leader: Master-Sargeant Samuel Doe. Ten weeks later, Doe suddenly released the two men, saying there was insufficient evidence against them. Liberian officials were stunned. Word was that the Athenian conspirators had offered hefty bribes – $500,000 say some – to the previous Justice Minister to free the men for fear that they would become restless and talk. Did new leader Samuel Doe decide to accept the offer for himself, the gossips wondered? He went in person to free the men from jail.

Georgoulis promptly gave a press conference at which he repeated the story of explosions, fire and the decision to abandon ship. The Liberian report into the affair went on ice until February 1984, when Liberia finally announced that Greece would be charging the two. By then Georgoulis had melted away, and was not arrested by the Greeks until 1985 – nearly six years after the *Salem* sank (and six months after Mittakis had been jailed).

At his trial, Georgoulis told a very different story: of fraud, scuttling and of threats to his family to ensure his silence for so long. In fact the police had already decided to prosecute Georgoulis, Kalmiropoulos and the first mate Andreas Annivas and other crew members, in August 1981. The investigations carried out by Clyde & Co. had thrown up enough disturbing details for the Lloyd's underwriters to feel that it was time something was done to curb shipping fraud. After setting out to find out who was behind the *Salem* scam, they wanted to see them brought to book.

'One thing you do not want in international trade is an increase in documentation and bureaucracy which will increase the potential for fraud – but you don't want changes in trading proceedings to eliminate fraud if it kills off trade. If over-regulation stifles trade, you need effective general prosecution of those who beat the system in a fraudulent way: effective sanctions. Policing a system is an important part of the effectiveness of the system,' went the argument.

So, as one of the investigators later phrased it, 'Steps were taken to encourage countries where the fraudsters were known to come from, to take action against them.'

Various hitches and delays in the trials followed – caused by anything from a 300-page South African report having to be translated at the last minute, to an interlude spent finding out whether sinking a ship in Senegalese waters was actually illegal under Senegalese law. At one point the court even had to establish whether crew members released by Liberia could be charged again in Greece.

But the delaying tactics eventually came to nothing. The Greeks redrafted their maritime laws to close loopholes. Mittakis was found guilty, and in April 1985 was sentenced to a combination of eleven years in jail for a mixture of cargo embezzlement, moral complicity in causing a shipwreck, and maritime fraud against the insurers. He appealed, arguing that he had not known that cargo fraud was involved though he had realised that the oil was 'marginal', and in May 1986, his sentence was reduced to eight years.

Also 'sacrificed' to the wheels of justice were the *Salem*'s chief engineer, who got four years, later reduced to three; the second engineer, who got three years, reduced to two years and two months; and the third engineer, whose three years were cut to two years and six months on appeal. Radio operator Vassilis Evangelides got two years and two months. All the rest of the crew in court were acquitted.

The Greek court also passed sentences, in absentia, of three years for moral complicity in an insurance fraud on Frederick Soudan, Anton Reidel, Attar Wahib (Soudan's cousin) and Johannes Lock, also known as 'Bert Stein' of Shipomex. The missing Georgoulis and first mate Annivas faced charges that could not be heard in absentia. But Georgoulis' turn was coming.

Scotland Yard (called in by Shell) had also issued warrants for Soudan, Reidel, Lock and Georgoulis in August 1980. Unable to extradite any of them to the UK, the Yard had sent its own fifty-page report to Interpol the following February for circulation around the police forces of the world, also in the hope that other jurisdictions would move against the men.

In February 1981 Holland had re-opened its enquiries, as had Greece. Anton Reidel was arrested in Rotterdam in March that year, and faced criminal charges including fraud and forgery. He was finally acquitted in Holland in 1988.

But Soudan's hash was settled by then. He was arrested in the USA by the FBI in May 1984, and charged with defrauding Shell International Trading, the SFF, Mercabank, Pontoil, and Lloyd's of London syndicates. He faced, in all, twenty-two counts of fraud, conspiracy, income tax evasion (on his $4.25 million share of the scam's proceeds) and perjury.

His brother-in-law, Syrian Abdul Wahab Al-Ghazou, was charged with conspiracy to defraud the US, to obstruct justice, and commit perjury. James Shorrock, the businessman who had introduced Soudan to SFF officials in Johannesburg, also faced charges of trying to thwart US justice, but was later put on probation on condition he returned to testify at Soudan's trial. Shorrock duly testified, and was eventually given a sentence equivalent to the time he had already spent in custody, plus five years' probation.

The US District Court in Houston refused to allow plea-bargaining by Soudan or Ghazou. They were well and truly in the dock. British investigators were later fulsome in their praise of the US Department of Justice's investigatory and prosecuting style.

The trial started early in 1985, lasted eleven weeks, and involved seventy witnesses from around the world and 1,500 documents. Soudan had denied knowing the oil had been stolen from Shell, though he admitted misrepresenting himself to the South Africans, and charges of tax fraud and obstructing justice. But, on 27 March 1985, he was found guilty on seventeen counts, and led from the courthouse in chains. Eight counts of wire fraud, three of perjury, one each of conspiracy to defraud the USA, to obstruct justice, to commit perjury, to make false statements to the Internal Revenue Service, and to file a false tax return, plus the international transportation of his fraud proceeds, made up the tally. He was sentenced to thirty-five years on 30 April 1985, having already been inside for nearly a year. What little cash remained in his account, was to be divided between SFF and Shell.

A shocked Al Ghazou got five years for perjury, obstructing justice and helping Soudan to evade tax on his $4.5 million.

One of the men who came to the USA to testify at Soudan's trial was Anton Reidel. Still awaiting the outcome of his own trial in Holland, he came to Soudan's on the understanding that he had 'safe passage' and would not himself be arrested in the US.

He told the Houston court that the oil deal had been offered to several other brokers before Soudan came into it. He confirmed that Soudan had fixed up the sale of the oil to South Africa – in secret because of the embargo. He denied that either of them had known the oil had been fraudulently diverted from its correct destination and its true owner. The Greeks, he and Soudan's defence argued, were to blame for that. Mittakis, said Reidel, had appeared to be the man in charge – until a meeting in Athens on 14 January, three days before the *Salem* sank and two-and-a-half weeks after the spoils had been divided in Zug. At that point, Reidel claimed, he realised Mittakis was not the boss of the Greek contingent.

So the two conspirators' story was that Reidel and Soudan were innocent middlemen, acting for and duped by dubious Greeks. (Even Mittakis pleaded innocence of the oil's theft.) True or false? The US court did not believe it.

Reidel's and Georgoulis' turns came last. Reidel's Rotterdam trial began in early February 1986. It was then more than six years since the *Salem* sank off Senegal. The verdict was due on 19 February, and the prosecution wanted a three-year sentence for his part in the *Salem* affair. But on that date the court instead ordered investigations to be re-opened into Reidel's involvement with the South Africans.

He was being accused of having misled South Africa by forging a new bill of lading for the oil cargo. But if, as his defence argued, the SFF knew that these documents were forged and that the oil was stolen, then Reidel had committed no crime against them.

In Athens, meanwhile, Reidel was acquitted on appeal in May 1986 on a technicality from his conviction in absentia and three-year sentence there: the Greek court had not had Reidel's correct address and thus the trial in absentia was ruled invalid. Case dismissed. But the government still wanted to try him for cargo embezzlement and fraud, if he could be arrested.

It was in the interim between a repentant Soudan being found guilty in March 1985 and sentenced at the end of April, that Mittakis, the man whom Bertsch of Beets Trading had thought was the top dog of the three conspirators, was sentenced in Greece. But what of 'Captain' Georgoulis? He was finally arrested at his home in the Kolnaki district of Athens in October 1985. His trial began on 12 February 1986 – and he finally broke his silence, giving the Athens court a detailed account of the scuttling. Yet previously sentenced crew all stuck to their story that there had been no deliberate sinking. Georgoulis, like everyone else, did, however, maintain that he had not known that the oil had been sold illegally to South Africa.

Even so, as well as being found guilty of causing a shipwreck and endangering the lives of crew members, he was sentenced for being an accomplice to embezzlement of the cargo. He was given a total of twelve years' imprisonment; reduced on appeal in May 1986 to seven years.

All these cases reflected a successful co-ordination of investigative effort by the various authorities and other investigators at work behind the scenes. But it was chiefly South Africa's decision in August 1984 to lift the veil on its own secrecy over the *Salem* affair that made successful prosecutions possible. Dr D.F. Mostert, director of South Africa's Strategic Fuel Fund at the time of the *Salem* affair (and later senior general manager of SASOL, South Africa's oil-from-coal operation) made full disclosure to the Johannesburg Chamber of Commerce. Two things had gone wrong for the conspirators early on, he said: the *British Trident*'s unexpected arrival, and South Africa's not being prepared to aid and abet a fraud. That was why she had confirmed back in 1980 that she had bought the *Salem*'s cargo.

The *Salem* affair broke on a maritime world already increasingly worried about levels of crime and fraud against shipping and cargoes. But no one agency has the facts and figures at its fingertips to point to the total amounts that might be involved. And while cargo and shipowners were worried, national governments were loath to advertise the problem.

The *Salem* affair did help to concentrate the mind, however. The scale of the scam shook even hardened observers of the shipping world. It also raised questions of when and whether maritime fraud is an extraditable offence; and of jurisdiction: in an internationally planned crime, who investigates, who prosecutes and in the courts of which country? What constitutes an offence under different countries' laws? Contrasting Soudan's thirty-five-year sentence with Mittakis' original eleven years also highlighted the issue of differences in sentencing policy, and differing national assessments of the severity of a particular kind of crime. No doubt Soudan wished he had faced the music in Greece, instead, and served the three years handed out to him by the Greek court in his absence.

One man who took a close interest in these events was Eric Ellen, a burly former chief constable of the Port of London Authority and an expert in maritime fraud. He had first suggested setting up a central agency to combat the rising tide of maritime crime – notably, scuttlings – back in 1978. At first no one took him very seriously or seemed keen: many insurers, though worried, preferred to pay up on borderline cases rather than launch costly and possibly inconclusive enquiries that could drag on for years. National governments found the topic embarrassing, and most countries' police forces already had enough on their plates coping with ordinary crime, and were unenthusiastic about the idea. But then came the *Salem* affair, of which Ellen later said: 'The most significant thing . . . was that it made people sit up and take notice.'

Ellen wheeled out his proposal again, this time to the International Chambers of Commerce (ICC) at a Paris conference into the problem of maritime fraud. The time was ripe: and this time he was taken seriously. In January 1981 the International Maritime Bureau, or IMB, was established under the aegis of the ICC and with support from the International Maritime Organisation (IMO), whose secretary-general went on to the IMB board.

The IMO is a United Nations agency set up to foster co-operation between countries on technical regulations and other practices in international shipping. It is also concerned with safety standards and trade practices in the shipping world.

So: the IMB was established, and respectable. Its brief was to act as an information service designed to prevent maritime fraud. But it was a very tiny outfit to begin with. Notwithstanding, in the first nine months of operation Eric Ellen's slender team calculated that they had already saved their early members a staggering US $75 million that had been at risk from fraud attempts of one sort or another.

Over the years the IMB's range has extended to tracing lost containers on land or at sea, air-freight frauds, and, through a younger, sister organisation, the Counterfeiting Intelligence Bureau, into the field of tracing and countering illegal and often dangerous counterfeited goods.

In 1985, the IMB foiled 110 separate cases of fraud, worth close on $170 million. But Eric Ellen reckoned this was merely the tip of a vast iceberg of fraud on the world's oceans. 'We estimate that our cases were not more than 2% of the maritime fraud which takes place around the world,' he said then.

INTERNATIONAL MARITIME BUREAU: COSTS AND
ESTIMATED VALUES OF FRAUD PREVENTION

	1985	1984
Documentary fraud	26 cases,	15 cases,
	$ 60.5m	$105m
Charter party fraud/	18 cases,	13 cases,
disputes	$ 26m	$ 25m
Sinkings	3 cases,	2 cases,
	$ 8m	$ 2.5m
Deviation of cargo	15 cases,	15 cases,
	$ 20m	$ 12m
Insurance fraud	21 cases,	23 cases,
	$ 38.5m	$110m
Others	16 cases,	33 cases,
	$ 10m	$ 6m
Negotiations	8 cases,	2 cases,
	$ 6.5m	$ 1.5m
Voyage/container monitoring	3 cases	6 cases
TOTAL	110 cases,	109 cases,
	$169.5m	$262m

Investigating particular instances of fraud and tracking lost cargoes is part of the IMB's work. But it is essentially a preventative organisation – 'proactive not reactive' in the jargon – and the backbone of its operation is its information service. Members can ring the bureau to check the probity or otherwise and what is known of potential business partners, shippers, charterers, customers, etc. One might expect this to give the bureau legal problems: is it slander to point out that Bloggins is a well-known, or widely suspected, fraudster? The answer, for the IMB at least, is 'no'.

In 1981 the question was thoroughly aired in the British Appeal Court after businessman Harilaos Kleomentis Harakas, running a Greek shipping line for a Panamanian company that he apparently also owned, briefly gained an injunction to stop the Baltic Exchange in London and the IMB from warning Harakas' potential clients that behind his business appeared to be one Kostas Komentaro, described in the Appeal Court as 'notorious as a maritime fraudster'. Lord Denning set the injunction aside. The IMB was responsible for gathering information and warning members of the dangers of fraud, he ruled, and therefore should be able to give information 'to those interested and in good faith'. No one has tried to sue the bureau since then.

It now has several hundred members – insurers, bankers, ship-owners, multinational corporations, government agencies, and many others involved in international trade – who get IMB Confidential Bulletins every fortnight, listing what funny goings-on there have been and who was involved; followed up by an International Cargo Crime report every month giving cargo losses in more detail. Regular, longer reports – sometimes book length – explore larger worries, like piracy and armed robbery at sea, fire at sea, cargo thefts that abused legal loopholes (in the Greek legal system), port security and container crime.

In the 1980s, piracy – unprovoked attacks on shipping and the theft of cargoes – was once again rife on the high seas. From the suffering of Vietnamese boat people seized, robbed, and raped by pirates, to attacks on commercial shipping, it has become a very grave problem.

Under international law, pirates are given no quarter. Any country may arrest and charge them. Since the dramatic hijacking of the cruise ship *Achille Lauro*, combating terrorism at sea has also become a top priority for agencies like the IMB, and the maritime trading nations. But it was not a new problem: one agency counted 263 incidents of terrorism at sea between January 1961 and February 1986, many of them in war zones.

On 1 October 1986, the IMB opened a Technical Services Department to train ships' officers in protecting their vessels from possible terrorist attacks. The new division also advises on, and supervises the provision of, equipment designed to reduce the risk of terrorist attacks (and took on the IMB's existing one-off service to members of supervising goods right the way through a journey to their final destination).

Consultants on preventing terrorism at sea recommend the use of modern technology to make access to vulnerable areas of a ship more difficult; to warn of intruders in restricted areas; to allow visual and audio surveillance within the ship, possibly to a command centre somewhere on board, and allowing shore or even airborne stations to keep an eye on what is going on aboard. Additional benefits would be the use of technology to send a steady stream of data on whether the ship is on course, where and how fast she is going. Courses could even be set in advance, automatically. And if there were an attack, doors could be automatically locked, areas flooded with water or gases. Sounds a bit James Bond-ish? All this is being seriously discussed at high levels in different countries and agencies. The technology would not, however, be cheap. So only very valuable or high-risk cargoes or targets may get it. Passenger liners, since the *Achille Lauro*, are one area of concern. But so is commercial shipping.

There are other moves afoot to deal with maritime crime, under the aegis of the United Nations Conference on Trade and Development: UNCTAD. This was established in 1964 to study the trade problems of developing nations but its brief also extends to shipping, insurance and commodities trading. UNCTAD set up an *ad hoc* inter-governmental group 'to consider means of combating all aspects of maritime fraud including piracy', in 1986, which reported back on the possibility of an international convention on extradition for maritime fraud along the lines of the 1970 Hague Convention on hijacking, or the 1971 Montreal Convention on dealing with the saboteurs of aircraft. It was time to establish a set of international principles designed to make combating international maritime fraud easier.

The *ad hoc* group shied away, however, from making maritime fraudsters 'enemies of the human race' in law in the way that pirates are regarded. This definition brings pirates under the tenets of inter-national law, and means any state can take criminal proceedings against pirates regardless of whose flag they might be sailing under.

For maritime fraud, the normal rule is that jurisdiction follows the flag of the country under which the ship sailed, which is why Liberia was the first country whose authorities started investigating the *Salem*. Where a very grave crime is committed in someone's territorial waters, however, that coastal country may be able to take action as well. The UNCTAD ad hoc group suggested that this proviso should be extended to include maritime fraud too.

The group's general feeling was that maritime crooks should be punished in the country in whose jurisdiction the offence was commit-ted. And to make that work, easier extradition of maritime criminals is a must. So some sort of international convention on that looked desirable.

Also suggested was that all countries party to any convention that followed should report to an international organisation 'as promptly as possible any relevant information in its possession' so that maritime frauds could be recorded and the working of the convention monitored.

In December 1986, another UNCTAD meeting was due to hear more about plans to set up an international information centre – from Lloyd's of London, the ship charterers' organisation BIMCO, and the IMB, who have been looking into how best such a centre might be established. Eventually plans for a Maritime Advisory Exchange were agreed, with a start date of 1 November 1988. The IMB, Lloyd's of London and BIMCO were the main participants, with the International Chamber of Shipping doing the legwork to run the exchange.

Another very serious concern facing the maritime law enforcers is the presence of organised crime in the shipping world. 'Organised' crime means just that: not just the Mafia with whom the term is so often associated. Anyone who conspires with a friend to set up a clever scam along business-like lines is creating 'organised' crime.

But the Mafia and associated racketeers are a problem in that they have traditionally controlled the US labour unions that man America's eastern ports. And from there, it has spread. As a top US investigator George Havens told the IMB annual lecture in 1986, 'Organised crime . . . is a problem wherever goods and commodities are shipped in international commerce.' And where the Mafia runs the port, the incidence of cargo theft is high. So are the costs of labour and the port charges. The consumer – you and I – pays in the end for pricier goods.

The whistle was blown on what goes on in these US ports when Miami businessman Joe Teitelbaum was persuaded to help the police put a stop to mobsters who, thrown out of New York, were moving in on the South Florida seaport. Teitelbaum, like others who ran a business in the port, had agreed under duress to pay union officials weekly sums in return for peace on his dock, undamaged goods, and other 'favours' after the mobsters moved in and took control of the local labour-force. His co-operation with the police revealed that payoffs, kickbacks, extortion and ghost payrolls (naming men who did not work there, but whose salary went somewhere) were rampant.

Teitelbaum's story sparked the formation of a combined Federal, State and local investigations, Operation UNIRAC (Union Investigation of Racketeering and Corruption). In 1978, after three years of work, a Federal Grand Jury in Miami indicted twenty-two people on seventy counts of extortion, embezzlement, bribery, theft and labour racketeering. The convicted included known mobsters, some with previous criminal records. Rather than start a new life, Teitelbaum returned to run his dock – with round-the-clock protection.

To counter the sort of rackets taking over US ports and airports, Havens also recommended preventive or 'proactive' moves: from intelligence networks and greater co-ordination of different investigations' efforts, to legislation to control who comes and goes in high-value cargo areas, and licensing to stop people with criminal backgrounds from taking key positions in labour unions.

But cargo loss continues around the world. In the face of all this, the IMB opened the world's first cargo loss reporting system in September 1986 to log any cargo lost anywhere, to see if there is a pattern and to improve the chances of recovery. Not all missing cargoes are stolen by crooks, mobsters or racketeers – some simply go astray and get lost, and can be traced and recovered. Others get caught up in charter party fraud, in which the charterer arranges early part-payment for his services and the ship, and then disappears, without ever paying the shipowner in full and leaving him with a cargo he has an obligation to deliver but no payment for doing so.

In such cases, the cargo may just be dumped and abandoned somewhere, or the shipowner may be in cahoots with the charterer, and the goods are quietly sold off illegally to a third party. Fraudsters have devised a host of clever tricks that make full use of the intricacies of local legal systems to run their scams and avoid retribution: there have even been instances of rightful owners coming near to arrest for trying to repossess their own goods.

Frauds encountered in the shipping world vary from complex schemes to much simpler variants. Easily forged bills of lading have been deposited with banks to borrow money against non-existent (or someone else's) goods as collateral; or have been presented to claim another's goods before the true owner appears at the dock to collect them. Again, the fraudster will sell the cargo on very fast and vanish – leaving the third party to argue over ownership when the true consignee arrives to find them. Sometimes a false bill of lading is used to intercept and steal a cargo somewhere en route – and the same rapid sale follows by the fraudster. He may even replace the missing goods with worthless items, which sail on towards the stolen cargo's true owner.

Another scam crops up when a cargo – like the *Salem*'s oil – changes hands during the journey. A new bill of lading is issued with each change of ownership, showing who the new consignee is. The more times the cargo is sold in transit, the more perfectly genuine bills of lading are kicking around with its details. If a fraudster can lay his hands on one of these and moves fast enough, he can collect the cargo and spirit it away or sell it on. Or he might use the bill of lading simply to gain access to the line of credit arranged by the real purchaser with his bank to pay for the cargo on its arrival, and just have the money released to him instead. It has been done. Ownership of the bill of lading amounts to title to the goods but it can also be used, in conjunction with documentary credits arranged by the buyer with a bank, to claim payment for them. Using a faked bill of lading filled in on a real form – they are easy to get hold of – to cash a genuine documentary credit, has also been a popular fraud, once described as 'the boom crime of the maritime world' by one investigator, who pointed out that 'one good documentary fraud could pull $50 million'.

The men behind the *Salem* affair cut their teeth on a racket that ran successfully for a time by abusing the complexities of local Greek law. It went like this. A shipper, preferably on the verge of bankruptcy, collects a valuable cargo. Instead of sailing straight to its destination – which the bill of lading requires him to do – he makes for a small Greek island or a remote bay. Then, not telling the cargo-owner where he is, he contacts a firm of lawyers who will usually be in on the scam. He claims to be in financial difficulties, and gives them a blanket power of attorney over his interests. Now it gets complicated. A second lawyer, usually associated with the first legal firm, is instructed to act for the crew. They have not yet been paid and, in return for their silence, an inflated wage bill is prepared.

The second lawyer applies to the local court to seize the shipowner's assets to pay the crew's wages. The shipowner does not dispute the court petition so there is a judgment by consent that they can be sold. But when the bailiff comes to seize the ship, he is told the cargo also belongs to the shipper and can therefore be sold instead of the vessel. The bailiff will go to the local Justice of the Peace – who will have little or no knowledge of maritime law, it not being his patch – for permission to take and auction the cargo instead.

Auctions in Greece are held on Sunday mornings. These scams are timed so that the bailiff's application to sell the cargo at the next auction will go in on a Friday. It is too short notice for many people to notice that the cargo will be auctioned in this out-of-the-way place on the Sunday – so a nominee of the corrupt law firm is able to bid for it at a very low price. Then it is sold on for far more, with legal title because it was bought at the auction. It has not officially been stolen. A neat trick;

and, meanwhile, the true consignee of the cargo knows nothing. If the legalities take time and the true owner does become aware that there is a problem, all sorts of little tricks are used to delay him while the cargo is sold on. In one case, instead of sending legal notification of the hearing to seize the ship's assets to an Indonesian cargo-owner's Athens lawyer, a telegram was sent in Greek to Indonesia just the day beforehand.

Once the cargo has been semi-legally spirited away, the vessel can be used again, under another name perhaps, or – if she is an old rust-bucket – may mysteriously sink on a subsequent voyage and become the subject of an insurance claim. When stealing cargoes through unscheduled stops in Greece became harder as victims became more aware of the legal-loophole scam, the fraudsters would seek to sell the goods in Lebanon under the order of the Greek magistrate.

Getting involved in legal wrangles over ownership of cargoes is no fun. But it is not always the buyer or consignee who gets stung in freight frauds. One case the IMB investigated was of an importer stinging his supplier. A Korean knitwear manufacturer happily sent off a consignment of goods in exchange for a letter of credit given him by the importer. So far, all quite normal. But the importer went to the airport and flew back home, arriving before the Korean could cash the letter of credit. It was well-timed. Having the genuine airweighbill showing him as the consignee, the importer collected his goods. Then, as he knew it would, his bank alerted him to certain discrepancies in the letter of credit. 'Don't pay it,' was his instruction. When the out-of-pocket supplier took legal action to get his money, the importer simply went into liquidation. End of story.

So freight fraud can work both ways, and either way it is costly for the business left without its goods or its cash. Whole projects can be held up: construction groups can run into expensive penalty if they go over time on a contract because vital items have vanished; and small companies can even go bust if goods and payments are diverted, with all the job losses that implies. Maritime and freight fraud are part of the wider field of commercial crime – and they cost countries dearly.

Dramatic evidence of that came when Johnson Matthey Bankers collapsed into the rescuing arms of the Bank of England in October 1984, with debts of £248 million. JMB was one of the five pukka banks fixing the London gold price twice daily, and thus occupied a place right at the heart of the British financial establishment. But it was also a trading bank that had grown rather too fast. Many of the bills of lading and other documentation it had lent money against turned out to be fakes, fraudulent or unrealisable. Its largest debtor was shipper and trader Mahmoud Sipra. Ironically, Eric Ellen had previously tried to warn JMB that Sipra's reputation in the shipping world left much to be desired. But he had been shown unceremoniously, even rudely, out of JMB's City of London offices a stone's throw from the famous insurance market, Lloyd's of London.

II: Trouble at Lloyd's

One of the ironies of the *Salem* scam was that the lead underwriter of the cargo was a Lloyd's of London syndicate set up by a man called Peter Cameron-Webb, who at the time said he felt something should be done to curb shipping fraud. Yet even as he voiced this view, he was himself quietly and cleverly defrauding the members of his syndicate of many millions of pounds in what was to be exposed as the greatest fraud ever to be committed within Lloyd's of London itself. The PCW affair was to trigger a major rewriting of the rules of the world's grandest insurance market.

It was in late 1981 that the first whispers of a scandal within Lloyd's reached the ears of the British financial press – in the shape of journalist John Moore, at that time the *Financial Times* man in the insurance field.

Moore's discovery that there was something fishy going on over reinsurance placed by syndicates owned by the insurance broker Minet Holdings led first to the discovery of a fraudulent scheme (Unimar), set up by Cameron-Webb and his friend and colleague Peter Dixon, and then to the PCW scandal itself, in which they had defrauded wealthy individuals to the tune of at least £38 million. Ultimately their activities, coupled with some very bad underwriting, left a gaping £235 million hole in the PCW syndicates' finances.

Here a quick sketch of how Lloyd's operates is in order. It is essentially a market in which only members of the club can operate. The world's most famous insurance market, as happens with old institutions that have first profited in one sense, and then learned by their mistakes, it has known several periods of infamy in its long history. Each has led to a burst of more stringent new rules and greater efficiency in the aftermath of, and reaction to, the scandal breaking.

None has led the club to change its motto – 'utmost good faith' – though its accuracy has been severely tested on several occasions.

It began life as a coffee house in seventeenth-century London – named after the man who ran it, Edward Lloyd. All forms of business and broking in those days went on *ad hoc* in the new and congenial coffee houses-cum-gathering places of the day in the old City of London. In the late 1600s, if it was maritime insurance you wanted for your goods or your ship, or news of how they fared, Edward Lloyd's rapidly became the place to go. Here, ships' captains, owners and men with interests in burgeoning overseas trade would meet and discuss the latest shipping news and gossip. (The Stock Exchange had its beginnings in another coffee house – Jonathan's – where men of business would also congregate and negotiate shares in business ventures.)

Insurance against shipwreck and loss at sea became important business as Britain's great seafaring and trading days dawned. A merchant who wanted to insure his ship or cargo would go to one of the new insurance offices, whose proprietor would then trot round to Lloyd's coffee house (if not already *in situ*) and try to find enough other wealthy merchants and businessmen amongst the throng ready to accept the risk of paying out if the ship and cargo were lost at sea, in return for a share of the insurance premium that the insured party would pay now.

It was up to the broker – the man arranging the cover – to ensure that the people who put their names down to share a risk were wealthy enough to meet their share of any claim, even to the full extent of their personal fortunes if need be.

Over the years this system was formalised. The shippers, insurers and traders moved from the coffee house into the first of a series of their club's own premises, but retained the name of Lloyd's – and rules and regulations about the conduct of business became established. As time went on, other types of risk as well as shipping were given insurance cover, starting with cover against burglary and fire.

Today, almost any contingency can be insured against through Lloyd's – at a price. The wealthy backers, or 'Names', are carefully vetted before being accepted into the club, having to prove that they are worth a substantial amount of money. They must also deposit with Lloyd's assets worth an agreed sum to meet their share of liabilities that could arise when insurance claims are made. Names are grouped into syndicates, who are looked after by a members' agent – someone who can act for them and look after their interests at Lloyd's – and by managing agents who manage the syndicate's money and arrange for it to underwrite insurance deals. Managing agents could double up as members' agents, before the post-PCW changes in the rules brought in 'single' capacity to reduce conflicts of interest.

Syndicates tend to concentrate on certain types of insurance business, and the agent appoints underwriters to specialise in each main type. Underwriters sit at work stations – known as boxes – in the main trading room of Lloyd's. To them come the insurance brokers acting for the companies and people who want insurance cover. The broker shows him a 'slip' on which are spelt out the terms of the risk involved. If the underwriter agrees to accept all or part of the risk, he stamps his syndicate's mark on the slip and signs or initials it on the syndicate's behalf, indicating what proportion of the risk's cover it will provide.

The assured pays a premium – a price – for his insurance cover and that money belongs to the syndicate and its members (the Names) who bear the risk and will pay up if a claim is made. The broker is paid a commission – brokerage – for his trouble, out of that, for supplying the business.

Because it takes time to know whether a claim is likely or not, Lloyd's syndicates' accounts are kept 'open' for three years. At the end of each set of three years, the amounts received and claims paid out are totted up for the last time and the syndicate's remaining money is transferred to a new open year of account, which takes over both the right to receive the net annual batch of premiums and the liability to pay any claims that arise over the coming three years. Thus business rolls over, and new business flows in, and the Names are able to share out the profits – or losses – of each year, three years later.

In this way the profits on the cover underwritten in 1983 were finally calculated at the end of 1985: 1983, 1984, and 1985 being the three open years. Then 1984's profits were finalised at the end of 1986, and so on.

Now come some of the complexities. Once an underwriter has accepted a risk on behalf of his syndicate, he may decide to spread that risk by reinsuring part of it – that is, by passing a share of it on to someone else, for an equivalent part of the premium, less an agreed percentage which remains with the syndicate to cover its costs – such as the brokerage for the broker that places the reinsurance business.

It was in this world of reinsurance that Cameron-Webb and Dixon spotted their chance to siphon off millions from the syndicates they managed, robbing the Names they represented by secretly taking a slice of the reinsurance premiums and salting them away for themselves.

How this was done was best illustrated in the scandal that John Moore found out about. This was known as the Unimar affair. Basically, the two syndicates run by Peter Cameron-Webb – the PCW syndicates – were reinsuring some of their risks through a broker called Seascope, run by David d'Abrumenil, and an outfit set up in Monte Carlo, called Unimar.

It was arranged that a 5% quota of the two PCW syndicates' total business would be reinsured, and that 2.5% commission would be paid to Seascope, 1% to Unimar, and a staggering 10% (2.5–5.0% was the usual range) would be the discount left with the syndicate by the reinsurers. The wording of the 5% 'quota reinsurance' agreement was left sufficiently vague to leave the reinsurers with the impression that the large 10% discount was staying in the syndicates, credited to the Names who backed them; whereas the syndicates' and Seascope's own documents indicated that the 10% was a commission paid, almost on account, to Unimar for chasing up future high-rolling takers in Europe of the quota reinsurance. In fact, Unimar actually produced no reinsurance business, though Seascope did find some takers. But, meanwhile, the money was steadily paid over by Seascope to Unimar's little Panamanian subsidiary.

In the three years from 1978, about £1 million was siphoned off in this way. Some of the money was used to set up and invest in a highly speculative insurance venture, supposed to provide information on government policies around the world, so that the political risk insurance market could assess situations more readily. Called International Reporting Information Systems, or IRIS, this outfit never really got off the ground despite drawing heavily on former Prime Minister Ted Heath's name at the time, and finally went into liquidation in September 1983.

The founders – amongst them Peter Cameron-Webb, using the Unimar cache – lost least money though other backers lost millions. Minimal losses were just as well for Cameron-Webb when the Unimar pot of money was discovered, as we shall see.

Cameron-Webb and d'Abrumenil were able to put up quite a smokescreen when the Unimar affair came to light, which at first made it look as though the continued payment of 10% of the PCW syndicates' reinsurance premiums to Unimar was just an administrative cock-up that had already seen one attempt to sort out. Unimar ended up repaying most – not all – of the money; and an enquiry led by the then chairman of Lloyd's, Sir Peter Green, concluded eventually that no dishonesty had been intended or involved. He did not know about the involvement in IRIS, however.

Had IRIS flourished, the plan was for the PCW syndicates to benefit from the insurance business that could be drummed up from it: giving the syndicates yet more reinsurance to lay off – and from which Unimar could cream off more cash.

It was partly the disproportionate size of Unimar's 10% 'commission', and partly a Seascope employee's surprise that it was paid direct to Unimar's Panama arm, that first led to rumours circulating in Lloyd's about the affair, and so to John Moore's hearing of it.

That also coincided with Peter Cameron-Webb's retiring from the syndicates in January 1982, and Peter Dixon becoming their chairman instead, while a man called Adrian Hardman became the principal underwriter. It looked as though Cameron-Webb might have been forced to go because of something fishy about Unimar – and that was how the gossip went at first. In fact, it was worse than that, though it was 1986 before the whole picture became clear.

Sir Peter Green's conclusion that there had been no dishonesty over Unimar only added fuel to the flaming tongues of the gossips, who now suggested he had mounted a cover-up. Cameron-Webb and Dixon had left Sir Peter's father's old firm in 1967 to set up on their own as underwriting agents, and people thought they were old friends of Sir Peter's. In fact he had not been at all pleased by their departure at the time, feeling they had left his firm in the lurch. But anyway the rumours spread, and led to a full Lloyd's Committee of Enquiry into the affair. It found no evidence of any cover-up by Sir Peter, and that he had 'rightly' found there was no dishonesty involved; and that 'although Mr d'Abrumenil and to a lesser extent Mr Cameron-Webb behaved at times in an overbearing and unnecessarily secretive manner, no criticism can be made of anyone else arising out of the Unimar affair'.

But it did not end there either. No one is 'unnecessarily secretive': they always have a reason, however bizarre, and in this case the reason was fraud. Finally in 1986, a Department of Trade and Industry investigation concluded, in an interim report, that there had indeed been dishonesty at work – though no cover-up by Sir Peter.

The inspectors found that he 'had insufficient evidence to make a finding of dishonesty against anyone connected with the transactions'. The DTI inspectors' scope to interview was, as their report pointed out, much wider than Sir Peter's since it extended beyond the membership of Lloyd's and had the backing of the law behind it. They even took some evidence on oath, for example, and most people preferred to answer the inspectors' enquiries than face public censure in the report for being obstructive.

By the time these conclusions were reached, however, the real PCW scandal had broken. Early in 1982, a British insurance broking firm, Alexander Howden, had been bought by the world's second largest insurance group, the American business Alexander & Alexander. Going through their new acquisition, Alexander & Alexander stumbled across quota share insurance schemes going back to 1974 that looked dubious. Also involved were the two PCW syndicates. Alexander & Alexander alerted Lloyd's.

Right back in 1973, Cameron-Webb and Dixon had sold the holding company that owned their underwriting agency, to insurance broker Minet Holdings for around £2 million – and then continued to work as employees of Minet, in effect. The deal had one condition: that Minet did not interfere in how they ran the agency. The main contact between the two outfits was through John Wallrock, who was Minet's chairman and a friend of Cameron-Webb. The same year, a new agency called WMD was set up as a joint venture between the existing PCW agency, and an agency then owned by the Sedgwick Insurance broking group. Both WMD and the syndicates looked after by PCW were involved in the new scandal.

When Alexander & Alexander, furious at finding that money had been misappropriated, reported its findings to Lloyd's, the insurance club appointed two top lawyers to look into reinsurance, and purported reinsurance, business transacted by Lloyd's syndicates through the PCW agency and WMD.

That November (1982), Peter Dixon voluntarily suspended himself from his duties as chairman and director of PCW and was replaced – briefly as it turned out – by John Wallrock. Another underwriting agency, T.R. Miller, took out an injunction on behalf of some of the defrauded Lloyd's Names, and with the DTI was able to impound many of PCW's remaining books and records. (It later emerged that some had been destroyed.) The investigations were underway. In December Dixon, Hardman and a colleague called Hill, marine underwriter for PCW, were fired for benefiting from the reinsurance scheme. The scandal spread outwards, implicating John Wallrock himself who suddenly admitted to having had a personal interest in the group reinsurance programme, which he should have realised was in conflict with his responsibilities. He resigned just three weeks after assuming charge of the PCW agency.

At the end of 1983, Cameron-Webb finally resigned from Lloyd's itself. He and Dixon sloped off overseas to evade the consequences – arrest and trial for fraud – of their scam. In London, work had begun on calculating how much had been siphoned off, tracing the missing millions, and trying to get them back for the Names. The affair spawned a monster made up of investigations (Alexander & Alexander's, one by Minet, one by the DTI, one by Lloyd's itself), conflicting interests, and legal difficulties. Who had been defrauded? The Names, certainly – but what about Howden and Alexander & Alexander, and other brokers who had placed the reinsurance in good faith? And what about Minet? Who should reimburse the Names? Had the auditors really done their job properly?

By July 1983, Minet had established that £38.7 million had been misappropriated – of which £25 million had been traced to trusts set up in Gibraltar. There was also £4.25 million invested in a curious mixture of ventures, from two films – called 'Let's Do It' and 'The Last Horror Show' – to US oil and gas interests, a French orange juice company, and two Kentucky bloodstock syndicates. There was also the yacht once used by Cameron-Webb and Dixon for get-away-from-it-all breaks. That was impounded.

Luckily for Lloyd's, as the Unimar and then PCW affairs hit the headlines, legislation was already on its way to tighten up the insurance market's rules and regulations, and give it the power to police its members more thoroughly – which it now does. This was the 1982 Lloyd's Act. An independent chief executive of Lloyd's was appointed to ensure that the rules are kept; and in late 1986 the Council of Lloyd's granted him the right to demand to see all members' records, either by prior request or in a 'dawn raid' without warning, if he has reason to suspect that something fishy is going on. To avoid in-house conflicts of interest, insurance brokers are no longer allowed to own underwriting agencies, and were given until July 1987 to divest themselves of these businesses, and re-register them. Meanwhile Sir Peter Green had retired from Lloyd's. The new chairman was Peter Miller.

Changes in the law and tougher new rules within the club were small comfort for the Names whose PCW-run syndicates had lost even more money than they had been milked of, through poor underwriting and mistakes made even after the scandal broke as efforts were made to keep the syndicates going under new managements. Several changes of agent (and name) followed in the efforts to bring things under control and stem the tide of loss.

By the time the 1982 Lloyd's accounts were closed, three years on, the PCW syndicates had lost £73.2 million – and with the closing of the 1983 account, there was another, far larger, £143.3 million loss to take into account, knocking Lloyd's of London's combined global profits back to just £35.8 million instead of the £179 million the insurance market had earned before subtracting the PCW losses.

The total PCW losses were finally projected to be a net £235 million. While negotiations wore on about how the PCW Names were to be compensated, and by whom (Names are liable for losses made on underwriting but they made it plain that fraud is another matter altogether) it was agreed in July 1986 that PCW Names should be enabled to meet the Lloyd's solvency test 'on a collective basis'. So the Lloyd's Central Fund, with net assets of £260 million, earmarked £235 million of that to cover the 1983 and 1984 losses.

Eventually in mid 1987 agreement was struck with the 3,000 Names involved that they would only have to find £34 million between them towards the losses that the syndicates probably would have made anyway without the fraud committed by Dixon and Cameron-Webb. Lloyd's itself would put in £45 million (and a separate £2.9 million towards the tax liabilities facing the syndicate) and all the potential defendants to any litigation the PCW Names might bring (other insurance outfits) would put in £55 million. The £134 million raised should be enough, if invested, to pay off the £235 million future liability.

The scandal was damaging to Lloyd's of London's prestige and its (previously considerable) self-esteem. But, under the Lloyd's Act 1982, it made a series of efforts to put its house in order. The post of chief executive, created by the Lloyd's Act to help administer the club, was first filled by Ian Hay Davison, a tall, thin, dedicated man who ran into opposition, even obstruction, from the old guard even under Peter

114

Miller. But his successor, former Dunlop chief Alan Lord, had better luck. As a top civil servant, mostly with the Inland Revenue, he had learned the tactful ways of Whitehall before plunging into the hurly-burly of industry.

The City of London was changing, with the prime aim of improving regulation and ensuring greater protection of investors if the Stock Exchange and Britain's financial industry was going to keep pace with the burgeoning New York and Tokyo markets. The Financial Services Act was drafted to establish the new structures. But what about Lloyd's? It had its own 1982 Act. Was this going to be sufficient or did more need to be done? In January 1986 a committee was set up by the government, chaired by Sir Patrick Neill, QC, to look into how the insurance club's regulatory system compared with new rules being drafted for the securities markets in the Financial Services Bill. His brief was to find out whether Lloyd's, adjusting after the PCW affair, provided the same degree of protection as other investors in British markets were now to have. His answer was that it did not, though he praised efforts it had begun to make towards improvement: praise that smoothed the path of change.

Lord had already persuaded the Council of Lloyd's that it had to keep pace with the rest of the City, and now worked closely with it to implement the long list of recommendations in the Neill Committee report, including drawing eight (instead of four) Council members from the world outside as 'nominated' members approved by the Governor of the Bank of England.

There is still no shortage of wealthy individuals willing to become Names and take their chances in the risky world of underwriting insurance. Membership had risen from 21,601 Names in 1983 to 31,484 at the start of 1987.

The *Salem*, Unimar, and the PCW affair had all focused attention on the world of shipping and insurance, tarring it with a poor reputation in the public mind. Lloyd's troubles began when the rest of the City was enjoying a complacent period. But by the time the PCW affair was settled the old clubby atmosphere of the Stock Exchange had gone, rent by changes needed to keep up with the thrusting commercialism of the competition in New York and Tokyo, and by scandals of its own. The regulatory changes will be explored in more depth in Chapter 11. But let us have the juicy scandal next. Like Lloyd's troubles, it broke just as new rules were being brought in to prevent bad faith in high places.

115

6

Insider Dealing

Moby Dick

In the spring of 1985 an anonymous letter arrived at the New York offices of America's biggest investment and securities house, Merrill Lynch. It was to trigger the most dramatic detective story Wall Street has ever known, and expose a trail of greed and deceit that branched across the Atlantic to the City of London's most embarrassing scandal of modern times. Dashing reputations would be destroyed, careers ruined, markets shaken and millions of pounds and dollars called to account. In America, the dizziest fall from grace would be suffered by Ivan Boesky, king of the Wall Street 'arbitrageurs'. In London it was Ernest Saunders, the brilliant, ambitious executive head of the famous Guinness company, whose star would fall furthest. Other names would attract shocked attention, but ultimately these two reputations were destined to burn up in the greatest blazes of publicity.

Posted in Caracas, Venezuela, the letter on which so much turned intimated that two employees in Merrill's Caracas office had a share-trading record that foreshadowed with remarkable accuracy a good many recent major corporate mergers and acquisitions. The implication was that the two had advance, inside information about these deals and were buying shares in the target companies cheaply before the public announcement of a bid jacked up the market price further. This gave them a handsome profit.

Unfortunately, dealing on privileged inside information is illegal in the USA. In New York, Merrill Lynch passed the letter to its in-house lawyers and compliance officers; the people whose task it was to see that Merrill staff obeyed the rules of the New York Stock Exchange and of the powerful US Securities and Exchange Commission (the SEC) – which, only the year before, had been granted a dramatic, threefold increase in the fines and financial surrenders it could impose on insider dealers and their firms.

The Merrill lawmen began to investigate. The letter's allegations soon led them to brokers Carlos Zubillaga and Max Hofer in the Caracas office, whose history of well-timed share purchases in US companies, just before a bid, was indeed remarkable. Zubillaga and Hofer were summoned to New York to explain.

What they revealed had Merrill Lynch calling in the SEC, which in turn mounted a major – but secret – investigation code-named operation Moby Dick: so-dubbed because the enforcers realised they were in pursuit of 'a very big fish'. What they could not at this stage realise was the extent of the network that catching him was to expose.

The 1980s saw an explosion of bid and merger activities in the USA and then in Britain. A bid for one company by another should involve an offer price greater than the previous market price of the shares, reflecting the value of the business assets and the goodwill of its customers and suppliers. If other suitors decide to counterbid for the target company, the effect on the offer price is rather like an auction – it keeps on going up until no one will offer the shareholders a higher bid for their stock. The stock market price of the shares will respond, either rising above the latest bid if hopes of an increased or counter-offer are high; matching it; or sliding below it if the bid is expected to succeed and there is little interest in dealing in the shares in the market.

Smart investors who best-guess correctly who might bid for whom next, and buy shares in anticipation ahead of the field, could make a great deal of money from their hunches. But woe betide anyone with prior, confidential information about a deal who nips into the market and buys shares before the official announcement. That constitutes insider trading and is a crime on both sides of the Atlantic.

It does not matter whether the information is acted on directly by the original recipient, such as an investment adviser or banker whose client has informed him in confidence of plans to bid for another company; or whether he passes it on to an eager friend who buys the target company's shares; or whether the banker's clerk or secretary tells her boyfriend's father and he buys the shares. All of them are guilty of involvement in 'secondary', insider trading.

Alternatively, perhaps the banker's client tells him a new business contract is about to be announced, and any or all of these people 'in the know' buy shares in the client company itself before the news is made public. Or someone may know that unexpectedly dreadful trading news is about to be revealed, and recipients of a tip-off to that effect may sell the shares before the company tells all and the market price slides. All these actions are forms of insider trading.

Or they used to be. While this is true in the USA, a controversial legal ruling in 1988 in the UK, hinging on the definition of 'to obtain', concluded that the recipient has actively to solicit the information to be guilty of insider dealing. The Attorney-General disagreed with the judge's interpretation of 'obtain' and applied to the Appeal Court for a ruling. It asked the Law Lords for a final opinion.

Since the information has been acted on, or passed on, in breach of confidence or of fiduciary duty, civil court actions may also follow on behalf of the company whose shares were dealt in. Also, its other shareholders may have a case for compensation if they feel defrauded by the insider trading. Moreover, the bank or securities house to whom the information was orginally given, may find itself implicated in any insider trading or other actions based on leaks from its staff.

Quite a hornet's nest of potential litigation awaits the insider dealer who gets caught, then. But why all the fuss? The answer is that dealing on inside information is considered to be seizing an unfair advantage over the rest of the investing public, and ultimately to make the stock exchanges less, rather than more, efficient – both for investors and for the market-makers and specialists whose task is maintaining an orderly market in individual stocks and shares – not to mention also making a nonsense of the confidential relationship a company expects to have with its handsomely remunerated financial advisers. It is to protect all these players that trading on inside, unpublished information is banned in America, in the UK and, increasingly, in other financial centres.

Put crudely, Stock Exchange theory has it that markets' stock and share prices reflect the total amount of information known about any one stock; and that therefore the more rapid the flow of information and the greater disclosure there is, the more efficient the total market in securities becomes. Anyone dealing on the basis of secret information in advance of its wider publication is therefore detracting from the market's efficiency. The market may notice the unusual activity and the price may move up (or down if it is unusual selling) in response. But the true reason for the trading remains obscure so the market is unable to react correctly to it. Guesses that something

dramatic is about to happen may make the shares fluctuate exagger-
atedly while waiting for news and developments.

The idea is also that someone with inside knowledge of a company's
affairs that will be material to the share price when made public, and
who deals on the back of it, is really cheating other shareholders.
Suppose I actually know that Bloggins Co. has hit a sudden rough patch
and is about to announce that it expects this year's trading profits to
halve. If I sell my shares to you at the current market price, a price that
still reflects hope of a reasonable outturn to the year, I am really
defrauding you by dumping stock on you at a price I secretly know is
way above the true value of the shares. When the bad news is
announced and the price tumbles back, you will bear the loss.

Equally, if I hear from a secret source that Bloggins Co. is about to be
bid for by a larger group and I come back in and buy the shares off you
at their present, pre-bid level, I am cheating you of the full value that
the bidder is willing to pay.

'Insider trading undermines investors' expectations of fairness in the
securities markets. Investors will be less willing to place their money at
risk in securities if they believe insiders, who have access to material,
non-public information, utilise it to take advantage of them,' John
Shad, Chairman of the Securities Exchange Commission (the SEC) at
the time, told the Subcommittee on Oversight and Investigations, of
the House Committee on Energy and Commerce concerning insider
trading, in Washington on 11 December 1986. 'Some commentators
contend that insider trading should be legalised because it increases
market efficiency by causing stock prices to move in the "right"
direction. Most commentators, including members of the financial
community, institutional and individual investors, the Commission,
and members of this Subcommittee, disagree with this contention.
Capital formation and our nation's economic growth depend on investor confidence in the fairness and integrity of the securities markets.'
He went on 'Furthermore, the SEC is a law enforcement agency. Insider
trading is illegal. The Commission will continue to enforce the law.'

So much for theory. In practice insider dealing has gone on since
securities trading – or any trading – began and has only relatively
recently become an illegal act. In certain forms it has been outlawed in
the US since the 1930s. But it was 1980 before Britain made it a
criminal offence; and in some countries there are still no rules against it
nor penalties attached to it.

119

Maximum and speedy disclosure of material facts is one way a quoted company can reduce the temptation for others to trade on inside information. But some key people will of necessity be aware of confidential plans in advance. Some of the scandals that rocked Wall Street and later London followed from breaches of faith by top advisers whose greed got the better of their ethical obligations. For, on Wall Street, investment ethics were changing – for the worse. The spate of huge mergers and the passionate battles for control of companies that they brought led some corporate clients of investment banking houses to demand success at almost any price – including, behind closed doors, the cost to their integrity. The work ethic was rapidly being subverted into a notable absence of any ethics.

The hothouse atmosphere led to the rapid rise of bright young investment managers and bankers who seemed able to perform under considerable pressure and did well for their firms. These exotics were, however, still subject to the ruthless Wall Street hire-and-fire culture, that paid well but made flops clear their desks and leave at a moment's notice.

The combination of all these elements began to blur the distinction between the client's profit motive and corporate and personal greed. Obeying the rules became secondary to success achieved: for the client, for one's firm, and for oneself in the form of a reputation as a terrific Wall Street operator. And, once the rules were blurred or breached for the firm's or client's purposes, the temptation to make some extra money on the side for oneself on the back of confidential inside knowledge of the client's gameplan (as a sort of insurance policy for the future) became easier to succumb to – and a little harder to admit as just plain wrong.

And once everyone seems to be doing it, the next person begins to think there is no great harm in indulging in it himself. Why lose out by being honest when others make a mint from being sly?

'In 1981, well-known publications were reporting that insider trading was so pervasive nothing could be done about it. Unfortunately some took such articles as a licence to engage in such illegal activities,' Shad sumarised in December 1986.

Equally unfortunately – for the SEC – insider trading is not always easy to prove. Take dealing on hunch alone. There is no unfair advantage lurking behind that, just remarkably efficient (or lucky) reading of the signs by the investor. But there may be a fine line between expert knowledge of an industry that helps a perceptive investor to spot an interesting situation developing, and stumbling across or otherwise acquiring inside information that you then act on.

Since, for obvious reasons, inside information is generally passed on by word-of-mouth rather than in written form, how do the authorities distinguish between a brilliant record at apparently best-guessing the market in certain stocks, and the use of a stream of inside information where the investor's art may simply lie in not getting caught?

Clues may lie in how elaborate the investor's dealing vehicle is. Despite a brief fashion in the markets in the mid-1980s for arguing that a little insider dealing did no great harm to anyone, insider traders usually suspect it does – or, at any rate, do know that they are probably breaking the rules, and fear exposure. Nothing signals this awareness so strongly as the tendency to salt illegal profits away in secret, offshore accounts. If it is not wrong, why hide it in a tax haven?

At the SEC John Shad and his team had a valuable ally in their search for the hidden insider dealer. Modern technology in this instance, is on the side of the surveillance teams. While mergers boomed and insider traders basked in the opportunities they offered, during the 1980s, the technology that could trap the illegal trader was also developing rapidly. Now that all New York Stock Exchange (the NYSE) and the London Stock Exchange market transactions are logged electronically, any unusual or suspicious trading patterns that would once have taken weeks to unearth manually and might have passed unexamined, are now automatically 'flagged' and brought to the surveillance departments' attention.

Once an unusual price movement is spotted by the computers, and if the company and its brokers can offer no adequate explanation for it (such as recent announcement of news), checks will be run through the computer data on all bargains to see who was dealing, through what agency, when, and in what 'size'. The patterns that are revealed by the electronic data can be checked against the records kept by exchange member firms about their clients and where their dealing profits are sent. It is a requirement of membership of the NYSE and of the London Exchange, that when the inspectors call and ask to see a firm's records in the course of an investigation, the books and computer files and other records must be opened to them.

All the information collated can be measured against other 'coincidences' (the NYSE will use publicly available information to check trading patterns against whose spouse, lover, flatmate, friend or parent works where). An individual's trading can then be monitored and investigated. So it is much easier for the authorities to fill in the picture today.

They will also fight the insider dealer with his own weapons. Just as he (or she) will act on tip-offs from others that something is about to happen, so the investigators are happy to make good use of tips from informants that something fishy is afoot.

So it was that the letter from Caracas was taken seriously enough in the spring of 1985 by Merrill Lynch to check it out, leading to Zubillaga and Hofer being told to hotfoot it to New York to explain the nature of their remarkable share-dealing success. Was it genuine investment talent, or a talent to defraud?

Zubillaga supplied the answer – and passed the buck, giving the investigators the next point of interest in the trail. He had been acting on investment tips supplied by one Brian Campbell a twenty-six-year-old, who had worked at Merrill's New York office. Zubillaga told the investigators that he had got to know Campbell first on a training course. By now Campbell had moved on from Merrill, but the record of his own trading was still available to the compliance men. Put through the computer, it did reveal a close parallel with the dealing patterns of the men from the Caracas office. But there was more to know.

Looking into Campbell led to a more dramatic discovery. He executed large investment orders for an account in Nassau, in the Bahamas, opened in the local branch of the international division of an old-established Swiss bank called Bank Leu. The share dealings for this account followed much the same pattern as the Caracas dealings and Campbell's own, but this time very large sums of money were involved. Campbell himself had only been 'piggy-backing' the remarkably successful and now suspicious-looking trades of a much bigger fish, and the men in the Venezuelan office were mere minnows following in his wake.

But for Merrill, this discovery meant it was time to call in the SEC – where a new head of enforcement had just been appointed. Gary Lynch was thirty-three, a lawyer, and a man determined to put a stop to the insider trading that was so widely believed to have become the shadowy rule, rather than the shocking exception, on Wall Street. At the time, Wall Street's high-flyers were not unduly disturbed by Lynch's declaration of this mission. Received wisdom had it that the SEC had not the resources to carry out the clean-up he envisaged as being necessary.

This sort of complacency almost certainly encouraged newcomers to the securities game to think they could get away with using inside information to feather their own nests – either by trading on the back of it themselves or by selling it to someone else in return for a cash share of the profits. Suspicions that well-regarded, rising Wall Street stars were modestly supplementing their handsome salaries this way probably moved smaller players to do likewise on the quiet. Nobody expected Lynch and his mob of investigators to call – let alone to prove anything.

But Gary Lynch now had Bank Leu's name from Merrill Lynch, and Bank Leu had been attracting the attention of the New York Stock Exchange surveillance system for some time.

The convenient timing of Bank Leu's purchases, just before a corporate bid, had begun to show up on the NYSE's computer surveillance system five or six years earlier. By the third or fourth well-timed purchase the NYSE had started to pass on the Nassau branch of Bank Leu's name to the SEC as one to watch. But being a branch of a Swiss bank, protected by Swiss banking secrecy laws, not to mention Bahamian ones, and being beyond the SEC's jurisdiction, the Bank Leu account's dealing had continued unhindered and uninvestigated.

But the international climate was changing. In 1982, the SEC had signed a memorandum of understanding with the Swiss, known as the Swiss Accord, to allow the SEC to seek help from members of the Swiss Bankers' Association in cases of insider dealing. (This accord supplemented a 1977 treaty between the Swiss and the USA on mutual assistance in criminal matters. Insider dealing was not a violation of Swiss law at the time and so was not covered by the earlier agreement.) In May 1986, the SEC was to sign another Memorandum, this one with the Securities Bureau of the Japanese Ministry of Finance, concerning the exchange of information relating to securities regulation and enforcement. This was followed by a similar agreement with the British Department of Trade and Industry in September of that year – and very timely it proved.

British Commonwealth member countries were also making greater efforts to combat fraud including insider dealing offences, and were growing willing to co-operate with other jurisdictions.

In the Bahamas, the SEC sought the help of the islands' local

Attorney-General over the Bank Leu account and its trading history. He assured a by now anxious Bank Leu International that Bahamian secrecy laws would not be breached if it handed over to the American SEC documents it wanted that might reveal the identity of the person behind the mystery account without that person's knowledge or permission. The bank was reluctant but gave way in the face of these written assurances, and some strong-arm tactics by Lynch's team. They had pointed out that Bank Leu's New York branch might face difficulties from US regulators if its Bahamian branch was unco-operative over a matter that concerned suspected breaches of US securities laws. After four months' wrangling, Bank Leu supplied the documents in return for assurances that no prosecutions of its US branch would be necessary. Operation Moby Dick now had the evidence it needed to identify and land its fish.

Bank Leu had initially argued that the smart trading record of its mystery customer reflected the expertise of an equally smart Bank Leu securities analyst who did his homework thoroughly. But the SEC was not convinced. When Bernard Meier, the bank's securities analyst in Nassau who acted for Moby Dick – passing on his trading instructions for execution to executives like Campbell at Merrill, and others – went to New York to see his client's lawyers in an effort to cover up the scam by claiming to be the brilliant analytical brain behind Moby Dick's trading successes, the SEC pounced and subpoenaed him. Though rattled, Meier ultimately refused to co-operate and ended up having the SEC's book thrown at him too. He had also been piggy-backing Moby Dick's trades. But Meier did not return from Switzerland, where he had retreated, to face the civil charges of violating US securities laws though his lawyers did start settlement discusions. He no longer works for Bank Leu.

Meanwhile, the SEC turned instead to Meier's boss, Bruno Plet-scher, general manager of the Bahamian branch of Bank Leu, at a rendezvous held in London on 14 April, 1986. Pletscher refused to name the mystery client (pleading Swiss banking secrecy rules). But eventually enough information was extracted to work out that Moby Dick was behind two Panamanian registered companies using accounts with Bank Leu in Nassau. One, Diamond Holdings, used Moby Dick's own code name – Mr Diamond.

In May, Bank Leu agreed to seek, and got, permission from the serving Bahamian Attorney-General, Paul Adderly, to reveal the client's name. A top Bank Leu man flew from Switzerland to the Bahamas for a meeting with the governor of the Central Bank, Pletscher, the SEC men, and Moby Dick's lawyer. When the letter came late that afternoon from Adderly giving official permission to reveal the client's identity, it was not a moment too soon. Moby Dick, aware of the SEC investigations and now becoming sufficiently rattled to be unsure of carrying off his Bahamian cover-up, had given firm instructions that very day to move his money out of the Bahamas. Bank Leu told the SEC men what those instructions were.

The fish was hooked on Monday 12 May 1986 when Dennis B. Levine, an investment broker and expert adviser on corporate mergers at the large Wall Street firm of Drexel Burnham Lambert, was invited to call in at the offices of US Attorney Rudolph Giuliani. He went and was promptly reeled in. Much to his surprise, he was arrested, and spent that night in a Manhattan cell. Moby Dick had been landed.

Bruno Pletscher, despite his key if somewhat anxious assistance in netting Moby Dick, was ultimately forced out of Bank Leu, at the insistence of the Bahamian authorities, for his role in the Diamond affair. Advised by Meier from time-to-time, he had also dabbled in securities trading – generally on the back of Moby Dick/Mr Diamond's track record, and that was seen as a breach of trust. Out of favour in the banking community, Pletscher subsequently became a computer salesman in Switzerland.

The SEC's investigations led Lynch to conclude that Dennis Levine had made a staggering $12.6 million over six years trading in at least fifty-four different group's securities, 'using information learned through his employment about actual or proposed tender offers, leveraged buyouts, mergers and other business combinations'.

As Lynch's boss John Shad later described it, 'Levine allegedly learned of the impending transactions, in many cases, through his employment as an invesment banker with firms that had been retained to represent corporations involved in such transactions. The Commission alleged that Levine repeatedly placed orders for accounts in the name of his Panamanian corporations or in a codename through a Bahamian bank before the public announcements of these transactions.'

This was insider dealing on a scale never known before. Levine pleaded guilty on 5 June 1986 to one count of securities fraud, two counts of income tax evasion on the money stashed away in the

Bahamas, and one count of perjury (lying to the SEC). On 20 February 1987 he was sentenced to two years in prison and fined $362,000.

These were criminal prosecutions brought by Giuliani's office. But that was not the end of the matter – for Levine, nor for his associates.

The SEC's case aginst him was a civil action – it has no powers to bring criminal prosecutions, though it will work closely with the US Attorney and supply the necessary evidence for those – and here Levine was able to do a deal that was useful to both parties. Without admitting, or denying, the SEC's allegations, Levine agreed to 'disgorge' or hand over, $11.6 million – of which $10.6 million came from his Bahamian bank account. He also agreed to a permanent injunction from breaking any of the securities laws again, and to being permanently barred from the securities business. So he lost his illegal profits and his livelihood.

The money Levine disgorged went into an escrow account to which investors who felt that his secret dealing might have defrauded them could apply for restitution. For example, an investor who sold stock to Levine unaware that he had inside knowledge of a bid or merger deal planned for that company, might feel he had been defrauded of the premium that the stock went to once the plan had been announced – a premium which Levine had pocketed as a dealing profit and hidden in Nassau behind the façade of his Panamanian corporations' account. The US taxman – the Internal Revenue Service – would also have a claim on some of it.

His deal with the SEC meant the authorities could wrap up the Levine case without long court battles that might have lasted several years. It freed the investigators to look into the activities of some of Levine's associates; and it extricated the maximum possible amounts of money, undepleted by large legal fees, for wronged investors. By depriving Levine of the fruits of his insider dealing, it also serves as a far greater deterrent to future would-be insider dealers than had Levine been able to finish his two-year sentence and retire on ill-gotten millions.

None of this would have been possible without the 1984 Insider Trading Sanctions Act (ITSA) which revolutionised the penalties the SEC could ask the courts to levy on insider dealers. In the past the SEC was only empowered to ask the courts to order insider traders to hand over their profits, or the equivalent of any losses their activities had enabled them to avoid, and to ban them permanently from repeating the violations of the securities laws under threat of a contempt action if they did.

Now, ITSA allows the SEC 'to seek court-approved civil penalties of up to three times the profits gained or losses avoided by persons who illegally purchase or sell securities while in possession of material non-public information. The penalty may also be imposed upon persons who aid and abet violations by communicating non-public information, even if they do not trade' (John Shad in his 1987 testimony to the Subcommittee). Between ITSA's passage into US law in August 1984, and early December 1986, twenty-five defendants in fifteen insider dealing cases, including Levine's, paid penalties totalling $54.4 million. In some cases the penalties were twice their profits. In others, the defendants had not traded themselves but had passed on tips to others, and were forced to pay penalties based on the profits of their 'tipees'. ITSA punishes the illegal tipster as well as the insider trader who acts on the information. The hope is to deter those with inside knowledge from passing it on to others as well as from trading on the back of it themsleves.

Settling with Levine was not the end of the SEC's interest in his activities. It continued to look into his sources of inside information, for Levine had not simply acted on information he had come across through his own job. It emerged, over five months' of further investigation, that he had also had a variety of informants who, the SEC alleged, misappropriated information about intended corporate take-overs from their own firms and swapped it with Levine for the tips he could pass on to them.

Four were bright young merger experts working at other, well-known New York investment banking firms, and one was from a law firm. The miscreants included Robert Wilkis, an investment banker at Lazard Freres until May 1985 when he had moved to E. F. Hutton as a First Vice-President; David S. Brown, an investment broker at Goldman Sachs; and Ira B. Sokolow, an investment banker at Shearson Lehman (as it later abbreviated its name). Randall Cecola, another Lazard Freres man at the time, who passed tips on to his *confrere*, Wilkis, and Levine's own contact, lawyer Ilan Reich of Wachtell, Lipton, were the other two. As these people were rounded up, the ramifications of the Levine case rapidly became known as the 'Yuppie Scam', and seasoned Wall Street men shook their heads over the apparent greed and lack of ethical sense of the younger generation. (In

1987 a book was published titled *The Complete Book of Wall Street Ethics*, by Jay L. Walker. Every page was blank. Wall Streeters loved the joke, and bought the book).

Challenged by the SEC, the yuppie five 'consented to a permanent injunction against future violations of the securities laws, and the four individuals associated with investment banking firms also agreed to be permanently barred from the securities industry. The defendants also agreed to pay a total of $3.7 million in disgorgement and $875,000 in civil penalties. Each of the defendants also pleaded guilty to criminal charges arising from the insider trading scheme. Three of the defendants received sentences of 366 days in prison, one defendant received a thirty-day sentence and was fined $10,000, and the remaining defendant was sentenced to six years probation,' as Gary Lynch reported back to US Senate's Committee on Banking, Housing and Urban Affairs in April 1987. He had a good deal more to report about the previous year's events.

When Levine was first arrested, and began to confess all, rumours went round Wall Street that he might even incriminate Ivan F. Boesky, a mighty arbitrageur and financial guru who had made a vast fortune from speculating on takeover deals – amongst them, some Levine's firm Drexel Burnham Lambert had been involved in. So skilful did Boesky appear to be at spotting companies ripe for takeover and taking a position in their shares ahead of a predatory bid, that he became a cult figure and even wrote a book about his peculiar talent to enrich, *Merger Mania* – flying over to London in the spring of 1986 to promote it in the UK and, as one reviewer described it, 'holding court' at the Savoy hotel. In 1984, Boesky had reportedly once offered to buy a 70% stake in the Savoy from the British company Trusthouse Forte – itself then anxious to gain voting control of the reluctant Savoy group as its stake carried only 42.3% of the shareholders' votes. The British newspaper the *Observer* wryly quoted the Savoy's managing director Giles Shepard's disdainful comment at the time on Boesky's reported interest: 'People who can't afford newspapers, want hotels.'

Though it transpired by mid-November 1986 that Levine had indeed fingered Boesky soon after his own arrest in May 1986, the SEC had chosen to pounce first on the smaller fry with whom Levine had traded inside information. Boesky, an even bigger catch than 'Moby Dick', was left to lord it a little longer before being trapped in his own network of informants and hauled in.

Nicknamed variously Ivan the Terrible, the Rambo of Wall Street, and the Shark of the NYSE – and, later, after his exposure, King Rat and Mr Piggy – Ivan Boesky only sprang to fame with the rise in merger and takeover activity of the 1980s. His career before then had been chequered. His first attempt at running his own business devoted to securities arbitrageing, Ivan F. Boesky & Co., began in 1975 on $700,000 of capital that some versions of his story was said to have been raised from his mother-in-law and others. It ran into problems in 1980. He relaunched his activities in 1981 under the banner of the Ivan F. Boesky Corporation – and built it into one of the biggest arbitrage outfits on Wall Street. He also turned his attentions to the British stock market, using as his investment vehicle there a business called Cambrian & General Securities.

An arbitrageur seeks to spot a company whose shares are undervalued but whose potential should shortly be recognised by other investors, who will buy the share and fuel a sharp rise in the market price – and make a handsome profit for those who bought in early. Various factors may liven up the price but few are as dramatic as a bid by another company. The bidder may be intent on merging the businesses, or wish to break up the acquisition and auction off parts of it later. Once an arbitrageur, or 'arb' as Wall Street dubbed them, has a high success-rate and a reputation for being quick to spot takeover situations, he will acquire a following. The mere fact that he is buying a stock will fuel speculation that a bid of some sort is likely, and will send the share price up. Boesky acquired an almost magical ability to spot interesting situations – if you believe in magic. It turned out that he put his faith more in buying inside information.

Boesky was born in Detroit in 1937 to Russian emigré parents William, who had arrived in the US aged twelve, and Helen Boesky. His father established three Russian delicatessens-cum-restaurants in Detroit (the proceeds of whose eventual sale are said in another variation of Ivan Boesky's story, to have formed the start-up capital of his first arbitrage business). Ivan Boesky later claimed to be unable to stand the smell of the Russian delicacies he grew up amongst – 'surrounded by piroshky and kolbasa', he was quoted as saying in *You*, the magazine section of British newspaper the *Mail on Sunday*. 'I can still taste the cucumbers in brine and mountains of roulades and salami, all made strictly to the Russian recipe. And I'm still trying to get away from all that.'

The youthful Ivan fled to the University of Michigan in 1958 but switched a year later to the Detroit College of Law. While there he married, in 1962, Seema Silberstein, the daughter of a wealthy real estate (property) magnate who owned the Beverly Hills Hotel, and, according to gossip, thought Boesky was marrying above his station in winning Seema.

Boesky graduated from law college in 1964, becoming first a clerk to a federal judge, and then a tax accountant with Touche, Ross, before joining the securities analysts firm of L. F. Rothschild in 1966. In 1972 he moved on to become the general manager of the arbitrage unit of Edwards Hanley and then in 1975 set up his own partnership. Between then and 1977 he also taught part-time at New York University and was a Fellow of Brandeis University. He even tried to buy a magazine, *US News & World Report*.

He was ambitious, reportedly wanting (according to one associate) to build one of the richest families in America. He did not do badly. Even after his denouement on Wall Street courtesy of the SEC, and the substantial $100 million penalty imposed on him, he was still believed to retain financial and real estate 'guesstimated' to be worth about $200 million in late 1986.

As an arbitrageur, Boesky was not always content just to 'spot' a takeover target and then sell out to the highest bidder if a battle for the company emerged. Once a company is bid for, it does influential holders of its shares no harm to encourage other contestants into the field. So an active arbitrageur might be tempted to pledge the support of his own substantial shareholding in the target company to a rival bidder prepared to offer a higher price than the first contestant's opening shot. From there it is but a short step to shuttling discreetly between contestants, murmuring words of support to each on condition that they outbid the other. Thus the 'takeout' price for the company is massaged upwards, to the apparent benefit of all shareholders in the bid-for company. Having to pay an inflated price may not, however, be in the best interests of the bidder in the long run, if its aim is simply to merge the two businesses. Nor is it ideal for the target company which will almost certainly be asked to find the cost savings necessary to temper the price. That probably means job losses, in senior management as well as on the shop floor.

However, if the succesful bidder is a 'white knight', a company persuaded by the bid victim's board of directors to enter the fray as a preferable or more appropriate new master than the original bidder, the outcome may be felt to be relatively satisfactory all round.

But there are bidders who specialise in mounting tough takeover bids for companies in whom their commercial interest lies at most in only one or two of the divisions, if any. These are corporations whose real interest lies in auctioning off the different parts of the company for more than has to be paid for the whole. This is how it works. The target company is made up of several different operating divisions each in unrelated business areas. It has no plans to sell off any divisions though there are other specialist companies who might be able to make some of these interests work harder and earn more. None of these, however, can afford the cash or the management time to buy the whole thing and split it up. Enter the corporation that is more than happy to do the job, and invite subsequent bids for the constituent parts. Its profit will be the premium that specialist companies are prepared to pay for the individual divisions.

British company Hanson Trust, active on both sides of the Atlantic, is a prime example of a company that has been able to sell off, as going concerns and over a period of time, major divisions of taken-over groups at a combined and handsome premium to the total outlay for the entire group, retaining those operations that do slot into the Hanson corporate empire, and which it has in this way effectively got for nothing. In the US it did it with SCM, for whom it fought a long and bitter battle. In London, it had a similar, successful but bloody battle to win control of the Imperial Group, which it then broke up.

A refinement of this activity was for a corporate raider like Boesky to attract the attention of groups like Hanson Trust to a suitable situation – having first bought his own stake in it. The harder they battled to buy it, the greater this profit was likely to be on selling out to the victor. Accepting a bid, or selling a stake directly on either to a corporate raider or to a generous white knight, is also a surer way of coming out with a 'full' price than selling a stake in the market. A large stake coming out through the market will take the edge off the price; and once the market-makers know the 'arbs' are selling, the price could slide a bit too fast for comfort.

But Boesky did not stop there. An even better bet was to know in advance that one company was preparing to bid for another and buy a stake. Once the bid was announced, the corporate raiders and counter-bidders should need little encouragement to join the fray; and even if they did not materialise, Boesky could still be sure of the gain between the purchase price and the bid price. By the same token, any advance information about trading news or developments good or bad would enable him to buy or sell shares for almost certain gain. To get the inside track on what bids were definitely in the offing, he established a remarkable network of informants – among them, Dennis Levine.

This group included merchant bankers, industrialists, waiters who overheard lunchtime and bar-room gossip, a Kennedy airport official who passed on details of whose private jet was going where, and – rumour has it – high-class prostitutes whose high-ranking clients were indiscreet or could have information charmed out of them.

His telephone system had 300 hotlines to such informants, each one's number accessed by a private code. James Bond could not have hoped for a better network of spies. But Boesky lacked Bond's romantic side as well as his licence. In an oft-repeated quote, he once rebuked his wife for waxing lyrical about a moonlit night in Paris. 'What good is the moon if you can't buy it or sell it?' he demanded. He knew his own star might wane, however, once saying in an interview: 'I do not know when my demise will come but when it does, I know it will be abrupt.' It was, to a Wall Street which was beginning to think he had survived the Yuppie Scam. But – ever the insider – Ivan Boesky did know just when his number was up, and took his profits on $400 million worth of stocks sold before news of his own arrest could undermine the share prices of all the quoted companies in which he held an 'arb's' stake. Fellow-arbitrageurs got a nasty shock on Friday 14 November 1986 when they realised what he had done, and Wall Street mythology quickly dubbed the day Boesky was exposed, 'Black Friday'.

That was the day the SEC announced to a stunned financial world that Boesky had agreed to pay a $100 million penalty in cash and assets for alleged insider trading offences – '$50,000,000 representing disgorgement of profits allegedly obtained by his illegal trading, and $50,000,000 representing a civil penalty to be paid to the Treasury of the United States under the Insider Trading Sanctions Act.' Without admitting or denying any offences, he also agreed to a permanent ban from violating various sections of the Securities Exchange Act of 1934 and was banned from having anything further to do with the securities markets – though that order was stayed for a period to allow him and a compliance officer to keep his assets intact.

He met the $100 million penalties by agreeing to hand over to the

US Treasury 5,786,712 ordinary shares of his UK vehicle Cambrian & General Securities; 8,482,371 capital shares in Cambrian & General Securities and 193,827 common stock in US outfit Northview Corporation. An escrow agent was appointed to handle and reinvest the funds in approved securities. The money had to come from Boesky's private investment vehicles so as not to damage innocent parties who had invested money in special funds to be administered by Boesky and who remained temporarily locked into those situations. They included the British company Guinness, which had secretly invested $100 million (about £70 million) in a Boesky fund after he had supported its successful takeover bid for the Distillers Co. – of which more anon.

Meanwhile, Cambrian's shares were suspended from dealings in the UK by the London Stock Exchange (only returning to the list in June 1987); and various legal wrangles over who could claim compensation from the escrow agent meant the assets Boesky handed over were frozen pending agreements anyway.

For Boesky the whole deal hinged upon his keeping his word to co-operate with the SEC's further investigations. The *quid pro quo* would be facing just one criminal charge from Giuliani's office, carrying a maximum five-year sentence, instead of a barrage of them. But if he lied to the SEC or withheld any information, then Giuliani would throw the book at him. This degree of co-operation between the SEC and the US Attorney's office was new and very effective, and very much part of Gary Lynch's style. Being 'lynched' took on a whole new meaning on Wall Street.

Boesky therefore pleaded guilty to just one count of criminal violation of the Federal securities laws, of conspiracy to evade the requirement to disclose holdings of over 5% of a company's shares by 'parking' securities with someone else. (He was due to be sentenced on 21 August 1987). In March 1988 he began an eighteen month sentence in California's Lompoc jail.

Boesky apparently collaborated with the SEC with gusto. After 14 November word swept Wall Street that he had even taped conversations with informants, between first being reeled in by the SEC and the announcement of his unmasking. Moby Dick's big brother had been used as bait. It was a nerve-racking time on the Street.

The SEC's complaint against Ivan F. Boesky alleges that Boesky's insider trading links with Dennis Levine began in February 1985 with Levine supplying him with 'material non-public information concerning tender offers, mergers, or other business combinations or extraordinary corporate transactions relating to companies the securities of which are registered with the Commission pursuant to the Exchange Act and traded in the US securities markets. This information was obtained under circumstances in which Boesky knew or had reason to know, or acted in reckless disregard of the fact, that the information was confidential and had been obtained through misappropriation or a breach of a fiduciary duty or other relationship of trust and confidence. During the period from February 1985 through February 1986, the Defendant caused to be effected, through certain of the affiliated entities, certain transactions in certain securities while in possession of said information.'

Levine had been promised payment for his information in the form of 5% of the profits accruing from any purchases made solely on the back of Levine's information, less any trading losses; and 1% of the profits from trading in securities that Boesky vehicles were already in, and which Levine supplied information about, that led to increases or reductions in those stakes. By April 1986 Boesky and Levine had agreed that Levine was due $2.4 million under these arrangements. None of it had been paid by the time Levine was arrested on 12 May, however, and he never received any of it.

Some of the information Levine passed on to Boesky came from his own informants, Robert Wilkis and Ira Sokolow. Boesky made $4 million profit from shares in Nabisco Brands, bought after Levine passed on a tip for Sokolow at Shearson that its merger with R.J. Reynolds Inc. was being planned. He made $4.1 million from a tip that came to Levine from Wilkis (at Lazard Freres) in April 1985 that InterNorth was considering making a tender offer for Houston Natural Gas. David Brown at Goldman Sachs supplied the tip that led Boesky to make $975,000 from shares in FMC's plans for a recapitalisation. Levine supplied information himself about plans afoot at American Natural Resources, Boise Cascade Corp., General Foods Corporation, and Union Carbide. Net of a loss on Boise Cascade, the SEC reckoned Boesky had made $50 million profit from acting on these tips.

All these people had been shopped by Levine. Now it was Boesky's turn to yield up his secrets. In the USA he led the SEC to Martin Siegel, co-head of the mergers and acquisitions department of Levine's old firm Drexel Burnham Lambert, which he had joined in February 1986 having been previously an investment banker at Kidder Peabody. This was another jolt for Wall Street, and by no means the last reverberation from Levine's and Boesky's fall. But Boesky had news for Britain too.

Thanks to the memorandum of understanding signed with the British Department of Trade and Industry in September 1986, to exchange information on investigations into securities trading and share manipulation, that November the SEC was able to pass on to the DTI information from Boesky about his role in British takeover battles including his interest in the Guinness bid for the Distillers Co. in the early part of 1986. Without this tip it is questionable whether the subsequent DTI investigation into share dealings before and after that bid battle, an investigation that culminated in the arrest of former Guinness supremo Ernest Saunders on 6 May 1987, would ever have got underway.

Back in the US, Martin Siegel was exposed as a Boesky informant on 13 February 1987. The SEC alleged he had been feeding information to him since August 1982 while at Kidder Peabody (where he had been a director from 1977), in return for a percentage of the profits. He had received about $700,000 in cash handed over to him in a series of meetings by 'agents of Boesky' who 'met Siegel in a pre-arranged conspicuous public location, identified themselves by the use of a password and delivered to Siegel a briefcase containing a substantial cash payment'. It was real *Boys' Own* stuff. Siegel allegedly supplied Boesky with tips on Carnation Company, Natomas Inc., the Bendix Corporation and Getty Oil, from which Boesky made some $33.4 million profits.

Siegel, like the others before him, was banned from further breaches of the securities laws and agreed to surrender his interests in Drexel Burnham Lambert where he then worked, and its subsidiaries; and to disgorge $4.25 million reflecting his profits and some of Boesky's.

The investigations continued in the US, where Giuliani's office arrested four men in their Wall Street offices (shaking the yuppie brigade) only to drop charges later for lack of evidence. The SEC moved against Boyd Jefferies of Jefferies & Co., accused of 'parking' securities for Boesky. Another on the Boesky roll-call was trader Michael Davidoff, formerly of the Seemala Corporation which had links with Jefferies. And there was bad news in London for Merrill Lynch where, in March 1987, the thirty-six-year-old head of its mergers and acquisitions department in the UK, Nahum Vaskevitch, was accused of pocketing $2.5 million in insider profits in a scam organised with

Israeli businessman David Sofer. They made $4 million between them, the SEC alleged, filing civil charges for insider trading against both men. Israeli citizens, neither returned to the US.

II : The British Tale

In the UK, meanwhile, all eyes were fixed on the Guinness affair. This began in late 1985 as a battle for control of the Distillers Co., whose famous spirits brands include whiskies Johnnie Walker and Dewars, and Gordon's Gin.

The fight was between the old, Irish family brewing group Guinness, and the Argyll Group, a food retailer built by three-man team James Gulliver, Alistair Grant and David Webster from a capital base of just £850,000 in 1979, into the fourth largest British supermarket group by mid-1987 – with a stock market value of £1,750 million. That was shortly after the purchase of the UK interests of the Safeway foodstores group earlier that year. Before the chance to buy Safeway arose, however, the Argyll team felt that to compete with the giants of the food and drink industry it should have a strong drinks manufacturing division, and set its sights on acquiring Distillers to this end.

But in August 1985, when Argyll was almost ready to pounce, rumours began to circulate that a bid might be in the offing for the company, and the Distillers share price began to race upwards, gaining 47p to 360p inside one trading week. Argyll was regarded as a likely predator, but because of misunderstandings over who was going to underwrite the ambitious bid (vast UK electronics group GEC was expected to participate but did not follow through in time), it had to be postponed. At the request of the British Takeover Panel, Argyll issued a denial of imminent bid plans to take the steam out of the Distillers price and let things calm down to a sensible pace again. The Takeover Panel told Argyll it must hold its fire for three or four months before launching any takover offer for Distillers.

By early December Argyll was again ready to bid and launched a huge, £1.87 billion share offer for Distillers. But the sleepily managed, old-fashioned Distillers Co. did not care to mix its portfolio of drinks with Argyll's low-priced supermarket image. Once it realised that neither the City nor the Scottish institutions, who might have saved the whisky business from falling into Argyll's hands, were going to rally to the cause of keeping Distillers independent, the directors sought a white knight. They thought they had found one in Guinness, the brewing group that had already swallowed up a smaller distiller, the Bells whisky group, in a fiercely fought and rather acrimonious bid earlier in the summer of 1985. On 20 January 1986, Guinness, whose chief executive was the able and highly ambitious Ernest Saunders, put in a rival bid, offering £2.2 billion worth of its shares in exchange for Distillers. Battle had begun.

It quickly emerged that, with some reluctance, Distillers had agreed a deal to pay up to £80 million of Guinness' bid expenses incurred in rescuing it from the unwelcome embrace of Argyll. The Takeover Panel somewhat feebly rejected Argyll's complaint about this and Argyll then issued a writ alleging that the plan breached Section 151 of the 1985 Companies Act. Argyll got no help from this action, though in March the Stock Exchange (under pressure from the Bank of England, watching this scrap with some concern) issued new rules limiting cost-sharing in takeover bids under which the Distillers/Guinness deal would not have been allowed. But the rules were not retroactive.

Ivan Boesky was on the sidelines almost from day one. Indeed, not content with just watching the action, he was playing a telling part in the fight. Not long after Argyll mounted its bid, a Boesky henchman was in touch with James Gulliver, indicating that Boesky was thinking of building up a stake in Distillers and probing to find out what sort of price Argyll was willing to pay if a rival bid came along. This was before Guinness stepped into the fray.

Also in touch with Argyll was Meshulam Riklis, husband of starlet Pia Zadora and, through his Rapid-American Corporation, the ulti-mate boss of US drinks distributor Schenley — which had looked after Distillers' products in America for many years. He wanted to know what might happen to the Dewars whisky brand in the US if Argyll won Distillers.

Gulliver and Argyll never fully followed Boesky's approach through, not entirely clear just how he proposed to help them but far from happy with the implication that to secure his support they might have to pitch their offer price at the level he wanted. Riklis' approach they understood even less clearly. 'We were too naïve,' Alistair Grant was to say later, 'to realise what he was hinting at.' Guinness, however, was less slow on the uptake for, after winning control of Distillers, it passed the coveted Dewars trademark over to Schenley — of which more, later.

At Guinness, Boesky and Riklis seemed to have more luck. After Guinness had finally won control of Distillers, not only was Schenley given the rights to the valuable Dewars trademark, but a new fund set up by Ivan Boesky to work the investment magic for others that he had already wrought for himself, received a secret $100 million (near £70 million) investment of Guinness cash, tied up for a year. By a curious coincidence, he is believed to have spent a similar amount on purchases of Guinness shares around the time of the bid when it was important to Guinness that the value of its own shares, and therefore of its sharepaper bid, stayed high.

Once the bid battle was in its final weeks and days, both parties knew that the highest bidder would win. Since each one was offering its own shares in exchange for Distillers shares, the name of the game was keeping up the value of its own sharepaper so that their own bid would hold or increase its value. By the same token, both parties wanted the rival's share price to weaken, eroding the value of the other bid.

British takeover rules lay down a strict timetable for bids, which may be extended up to a point by developments such as the bidder deciding to increase the value of his original offer, but which nevertheless is limited to a final closing date, that is established as the situation develops. The bidder will offer his own ordinary shares or other 'paper' (preference shares, perhaps) and/or cash, in exchange for the shares of the company it is pursuing. It is illegal for a UK company bidding for another to buy any of the victim's shares at a price above the current value per share of his latest offer. This rule also applies to its close advisers and anyone who may be acting in concert with it.

But if the stock market price of the bidder's shares rises, that will increase the value of its sharepaper offer to the victim's shareholders – and the bidder can make more purchases up to that price level. The market price of the victim's shares will tend to reflect the highest current offer and, possibly, any hopes of a better one arising either from the original bidder or a rival entering the fray.

If I am offering two of my shares, market price 20p, for each share of another outfit, I am valuing its shares at 40p. If they were traded in the market at 30p, say, they will almost certainly rise to 40p on my bid. But if the market feels the company is worth nearer 50p to a rival bidder, its shares may rise to around that level even before another contender actually counterbids. If a counterbidder comes in with a 50p offer – let us say, of five of his 10p shares for every one of the victim's – I may have to raise my offer. Or I may be lucky and see some other factor lift the value of *my* company's shares in the market to 30p each. That makes my existing bid worth 60p per each of my target's shares, and outclasses my rival too. But if *his* shares rise – say to 15p each – then his bid is worth five times 15p – i.e., 75p – to the target's shareholders. If mine fall to 25p, my bid is only worth 50p. And so on. So if two rivals are slugging it out for control of the shares, it is an advantage if your shares rise more, or the opponent's fall, to a level where, either way, your rival can no longer buy more of the prey's shares in the market without breaking the rules.

Argyll was struck a telling blow on 17 April when a large 3% block of Distillers shares was bought by Guinness broker Cazenove at 700p, a price above the level Argyll's own share price permitted it to buy Distillers at. There were rumours in the market that Argyll shares were being sold 'short' – a device whereby you agree to sell shares that you do not yet own on an agreed date. Large sell orders force the price down to below the level you agreed on, so you buy in the market and are able to make a profit on the agreement. But if the shares rise before you have made your cheap purchases, you still have to honour the agreement, buying the shares in at the higher rate to do so – and you can lose a lot of money. Being 'caught short' is expensive. But suspicions surfaced at Argyll that Guinness supporters were selling Argyll shares short in the crucial closing days of the bid in order to weaken the value of Argyll's offer.

At the same time there was a sudden surge of support for the Guinness share price near the end of the bid battle. The net effect was that Argyll's price was depressed, falling 23p to 345p in the final stages of the fight, while Guinness' price enjoyed a sharp rise that placed a total value of £2.8 billion on its final and victorious offer for the Distillers Co.

It is illegal for a company to buy its own shares except in highly specialised circumstances requiring other shareholders' prior approval. But it is all right for supporters and even advisers to spend their own money on buying your shares. However, after the bid fight was over, the value of Guinness shares dropped back sharply; leaving those who had bought its shares with substantial losses on their investments, and about 20% of Guinness stock in the hands of supporters who now wanted to get out, and to get their money back.

That was later. While battle raged, Guinness had other problems to overcome. One was the Office of Fair Trading, which in the UK looks at mergers and bids to check whether the combination of the businesses concerned is going to be in the public interest. If the enlarged group ends up with a very big chunk of a particular industry, for example, the result could be less competition and higher prices charged to the consumer. If the OFT's director-general reports to the Secretary of State for Trade and Industry that a merger may not be in the public interest, the Trade Secretary may refer it on for detailed reports to the Monopolies and Mergers Commission.

Argyll had very few drinks manufacturing interests when it bid for Distillers. But with the purchase of Bell's, Guinness had become a force in the UK whisky market, and now it was after Distillers the OFT was concerned that it might end up with too large a slug of the whisky industry for everyone else's good. The Guinness bid was referred to the Monopolies Commission. That meant it automatically lapsed until the Commission reported, and traditionally the Commission has six months (and often takes longer) to look into these things. Meanwhile, Argyll's offer, not referred, was still live and in sole possession of the field. Guinness protested that this gave Argyll an unfair advantage. Either both bids should be referred, or neither. Matters were complicated by the then Secretary of State for the DTI, Paul Channon, being a member of the Guinness family, and a junior Minister, Geoffrey Pattie, had to handle the case.

After a week of frantic activity it was agreed with the Monopolies Commission chairman Sir Godfray Le Quesne that the referral could be set aside if Guinness undertook to reduce its total whisky interests with the sale of five of the Distillers brands should it win control of the group. The list was agreed, and Guinness was able to re-enter the battle with a new and higher bid of £2.35 billion for Distillers. Once Guinness had found a firm buyer in the form of Lonrho subsidiary Whyte & Mackay – who got the Mackenzie, John Barr, Buchanan Blend and Haig Gold Label brands at a knockdown £3.5 million – the question of Monopolies referral was finally set aside, on 21 March. Argyll hit back with an increase in the value of its offer for Distillers, to £2.5 billion.

Argyll had also rushed to the courts – ultimately unsuccessfully – to challenge the brands agreement. Both sides did a lot of running to and from the courts to complain about each other, but to little avail in most instances.

Meanwhile, the advertisements placed in the press, and the circulars sent to shareholders, by Argyll, Distillers itself, and Guinness, got more and more vitriolic. The Takeover Panel introduced new rules about the type of pro- and anti-bid advertisements that companies could run in the national press during a bid campaign. The protagonists' bitter tactics were making the City rewrite its rules.

Allegations also flew of a 'dirty tricks' campaign to spy on each other, and to smear the Argyll camp. Private detectives were said to be following and burgling key individuals' houses and trying to rake up embarrassing scandals that might scupper each side's bid chances. Things took a savage turn when James Gulliver's *Who's Who* entry, which implied that he was a Harvard graduate, was exposed as only referring to a brief three-four week marketing course there.

It was all getting very nasty.

The closing date for Argyll's final offer, under takeover rules, was set for 18 April. During April there was massive turnover in the shares of all three companies, with reports of heavy US buying of Guinness and selling of Argyll. Argyll's shares slipped while Guinness' rose, increasing the final value of the latter's sharepaper bid to £2.8 billion. Boesky was rumoured to be active in the market. 18 April dawned – and closed with Argyll holding acceptances of its bid totalling just 27.4% of Distillers' shares. It conceded defeat and sold out to its arch rival Guinness. The bid battle was over but the scandal was only about to begin.

First, Guinness reneged on its battle promise to make Bank of Scotland's chairman Sir Thomas Risk the new chairman of the enlarged Guinness/Distillers group. This had been promised to win the support of Distillers' substantial Scottish investors. Sir Thomas was spurned and the job given instead to Ernest Saunders, combining the roles of chairman and chief executive. Lord Iveagh, the head of the Guinness family and grandson of the firm's founder, was bumped up to President but had very little real say in what went on. The City was not entirely happy, and the Scottish financial community was furious, but no serious resistance was made to this cavalier act. Too many big investing institutions had backed Saunders thus far to rock the boat now.

But Saunders' own increasingly autocratic behaviour was causing waves. At Distillers, management soon realised that their white knight wielded a savage pruning knife and most of the old guard felt its cut as they were thrust overboard. The 'Risk Affair' was getting Saunders and

Guinness a less favourable press than Saunders liked to read. Under pressure from City advisers, Guinness appointed four new, non-executive directors in August 1986: Tesco chairman Ian Maclaurin, Vickers boss Sir David Plastow, Anthony Greener of Dunhill Holdings, and Sir Norman Macfarlane of Macfarlanes and the Clansmen companies.

Meanwhile, Olivier Roux, the finance director of Guinness who was really a management consultant from the mighty firm of Bain & Co. on secondment to Guinness – as were whole teams of 'Bainies' – was looking into what to do about the one-fifth of Guinness shares left in friendly but now somewhat impatient hands. The problem was how to persuade them not to sell out all at once and depress the Guinness price further. An orderly release of Guinness shares, without publicity, was required.

Then, in November, Ivan Boesky confessed all to the SEC. Telephone lines buzzed across the Atlantic. On 1 December, the British DTI sent inspectors into Guinness to look into the share dealings that went on during the Distillers bid.

Riklis' business Schenley rapidly admitted, on 11 December, to having had an undeclared stake of over 5% in Guinness during the final stages of the bid. The UK rules required any shareholding of more than 5% to be made known to the company and published. Schenley had only just been given the conveted Dewars trademark, which later became the subject of legal action by the new Guinness board to get it back. The matter was finally resolved by Guinness buying Schenley in its entirety in September 1987, for £320 million. This widened its own international drinks distribution network and nullified the original gift of the Dewars trademark, now safely back in the Guinness drinks cabinet.

A week later, on 18 December, came the news that Guinness had invested $100 million in Boesky's US fund in May 1986, just a few weeks after winning Distillers. So had others – the Imperial Group's pension fund had put in £3.5 million, Riklis had put in around £5 million and Heron Corporation, run by Gerald Ronson, had invested £5 million, but the Guinness involvement outweighed all others and had been kept secret from its shareholders, and most of its directors too. A stream of revelations about the conduct of Guinness friends and advisers during the bid now began to flow in the financial and front pages of the UK press.

The next major news was that merchant bank Henry Ansbacher, run by Patrick (by then, Lord) Spens, which had bought 2m Guinness shares during the support operation, appeared to have sold them back to Guinness for just over £7.6 million. This looked like an illegal purchase of its own shares by Guinness though it was clouded by confusion over the role of Guinness adviser, merchant bank Morgan Grenfell. Morgan's Roger Seelig, the brilliant senior banker most closely involved with Guinness throughout the Distillers bid, and Olivier Roux, claimed that the curiously precise sum of £7,614,682.10 involved was only a deposit put with Ansbacher in May 1986 to provide it with liquidity so that it did not need to sell the Guinness stake just yet. But Ansbacher said it thought the cheque amounted to a purchase of the shares for a Morgan Grenfell nominee – complete with dealing costs – with the money being deposited at Ansbacher by Guinness for a Morgan Grenfell account. Nobody wanted to claim ownership of the 2m shares involved, and heads soon rolled. Olivier Roux had already thrown in the towel and cleared his desk at Guinness. He resigned in mid-January as a director and was later to become the Fraud Squad's chief prosecution witness in cases to be brought against the members of the former Guinness 'war cabinet'.

On 30 November Roger Seelig succumbed to pressure to resign from Morgan Grenfell for getting the merchant bank into a mess. Nearly two months later, his bosses, Morgan's chief Christopher Reeves and the corporate finance head Graham Walsh, had to go too, this time under pressure from the Bank of England. Ansbacher's Lord Spens also caved in and resigned in January 1987. Meanwhile the new Guinness board had come across enough unsettling evidence of the way the bid battle had been conducted, to decide to sack the chairman and chief executive, Ernest Saunders himself.

But he, ever a fighter, only agreed to step down from his executive posts for the duration of the DTI investigation. Since only shareholders can remove a director from the board entirely, the Guinness board had to wait until the annual general meeting in May to move a motion to sack him completely. By then he had been arrested; and resigned as a director on the eve of the AGM.

Arthur Fürer, brought on to the Guinness board by Saunders (who had worked under him at Nestlé in the past) and who chaired a Swiss bank – Bank Leu – that turned out to have played an interesting role warehousing Guinness shares for supporters who wanted out, did resign from the board when requested on 14 January – and later, decided to leave Bank Leu too. Thomas Ward, the American lawyer who had been Saunders' most loyal sidekick, carrying out unpleasant tasks such as sacking long-serving Distillers directors, and whose loud ways and bullying manners had irritated many, followed Saunders' lead and did not oblige the board's request for his resignation as a director at this point.

Two days after asking for these resignations, the Guinness board, now chaired by Sir Norman Macfarlane, announced that a series of invoices for a missing £25 million of Guinness cash, and evidence of a mystery £50 million deposit at Bank Leu, had been rooted out, and that it would be moving heaven and earth to get these monies back. (It was after this emerged that Reeves, Walsh and Spens resigned their posts.) It also wanted back the $100 million invested with Boesky, but that was tied up in the SEC proceedings.

The £50 million had been deposited at Bank Leu to balance the monies it was expending on buying in and warehousing Guinness shares bought by supporters during the bids. The deal allegedly was that supporters could sell their shares into the Bank Leu holding at no loss. That would involve Bank Leu paying much higher prices than Guinness shares were then traded at on the London Stock Exchange. But was this legal? Did it constitute Guinness effectively providing the money to buy up its own shares? If so, it would be a clear breach of the Companies Act.

Companies named on the £25 million invoice list that Guinness had managed to compile were embarrassed by publication of their names and the sums involved. Gerald Ronson's Heron Corporation promptly handed back a £5.8 million 'fee' received for support during the bid. So did Erlanger, the US subsidiary of UK commodity-trading company S. & W. Berisford run by Ephraim Margulies (£1.3 million). Others on the list were Viennese bank Zentralsparkasse und Kommerzbank (£250,000); Tony 'the Animal' Parnes (£3 million), a half-commission man previously associated with London broking house Alexanders, Laing & Cruikshank; and consultant, Sir Jack Lyons' firm J. Lyons Chamberlayne (£300,000); while Sir Jack himself was paid £2 million in advisory fees by the group.

Some £5.2 million had been paid to a Jersey registered company called Marketing and Acquisition Consultants. Guinness lawyers began legal proceedings to find out who was behind the company and where the money had gone on to. To their surprise, the man behind MAC turned out to be Thomas Ward who, after some prevaricating, said the £5.2 million constituted fees he had received for his advice and hard work during the Distillers bid (work he evidently felt was above and beyond the call of his normal duties as a director of the Guinness company).

On 25 March, Guinness went to the High Court in London to initiate proceedings against Ward and Saunders to trace and recover this money. It said the payment was illegally authorised, being without the approval (or indeed the knowledge) of the full board. It was even alleged that over £3 million of the money had passed through Saunders' own Swiss bank account. His lawyers argued that he had lent the account to Ward as a temporary repository for the money, but that Saunders himself had never had any beneficial interest in the money. (If he had done it would have looked very like theft from his own employer.) The Court granted an injuction freezing Ward's and Saunders' assets, including Saunders' family home – the mansion he had bought in Penn, Buckinghamshire. Saunders' and Ward's lawyers tried to get the injunctions lifted but on 15 April in the High Court Britain's Vice-Chancellor Sir Nicholas Browne-Wilkinson ruled that the payments of £5.2 million could not have been legally authorised, and upheld the big freeze.

Ward appealed the case right through to the House of Lords where it was due to be heard some time after the House resumed sitting in the autumn of 1988. Actions against him personally for the recovery of that money also continued in the USA. Meanwhile, it took until the summer of 1988 for Guinness to reach a settlement with Ward's law firm, Ward, Lazarus, in a dispute over fees charged to the UK brewer for US legal services. Eventually the fee was more than halved to approximately $1 million, and Guinness got its legal files back.

It also got back the apartment in the (infamous) Watergate building in Washington, of which Ward had had the use.

Olivier Roux had okayed the payment of the £5.2 million. In an affidavit he now said Saunders knew about every payment on the now notorious invoice list – where Saunders claimed only to know about the Ronson/Heron one, and that Ward had submitted the invoice for consultancy costs in the US. Roux had paid it in the belief that no director had a personal interest in the money. But Saunders claimed that Roux had known to whom the fee was going – Ward. In the High

Court, Sir Nicholas did not mince his words. 'There is no possible halfway house; either Mr Roux or Mr Saunders is lying,' he pronounced, before ruling that the injunction freezing Saunders' assets could stay in place.

Saunders was in Switzerland during all this, where his wife Carole was now seriously ill. But on 4 May he returned to Britain to go into a huddle with his lawyers at Payne, Hicks Beach, in their offices behind the Law Courts in the Strand, before a meeting with the DTI inspectors on 6 May. After seeing them as arranged, he went back to his lawyers' offices where, at 6.10 p.m., two men from the Metropolitan Police Company Fraud Squad arrived, arrested him, and carted him off to their office at Holborn police station in Theobalds Road. It was widely assumed that DTI or DPP men had been in cahoots with the police and let them know of Saunders' presence. The DDP'S office had just called in the Fraud Squad to follow up some of the DTI inspectors' discoveries.

Saunders was charged with intent to pervert the course of justice and with destroying and falsifying documents. He appeared the following afternoon at Bow Street Magistrates Court, in a jumper and pinstriped suit, and was described as 'unemployed'. Granted bail of £500,000 until 7 July, he went to stay at his solicitor's home until his next appearance on 12 May to finalise the bail agreement. Tiny Rowland, chairman of the Lonrho group whose subsidiary had bought the Distillers brands that Guinness had to hive off, put up £250,000 and so did an old family friend called Herbert Heinzel. Afterwards Saunders held a press conference. Radiating controlled fury, he read out a statement saying, 'I am incensed at the allegations of dishonesty and wrongdoing made against me and make it clear that all such charges are strenuously denied and will be vigorously defended.' The man who had alternately charmed and intimidated the business community and the press was still battling. He followed this statement up on 26 May with a letter resigning from the Guinness board, reiterating his innocence and attacking his adversaries. He also planned to start proceedings for unfair dismissal. The letter was front page news on the morning of Guinness' 27 May annual general meeting.

The week before, Henry Ansbacher had quietly handed Guinness back £7.4 million after selling their Guinness shares (net of dealing costs and some losses on the disposal), and Bank Leu had sold 40m of their Guinness shares through broker James Capel in order to return the £50 million deposit which was received on 26 May. Meanwhile, the

DTI inspectors worked on, and at mid-June 1987 were believed to be drafting their report though one year later there was little sign of it. Word was that it might still be many months if not a year or two before the report would be published in full – not least because since its inception a serious fraud investigation was underway into the affair. This broadened into areas covered by the Theft Act, conspiracy to defraud, and even forgery. More arrests followed of senior City and business figures – like Gerald Ronson of Heron Corporation, Lord (Patrick) Spens of merchant bank Henry Ansbacher, Roger Seelig of Morgan Grenfell, and David Mayhew of top drawer broker, Cazenove. Argyll, still regretting the loss of Distillers, reiterated its intention to sue the Guinness company for damages. A two-pronged suit would seek firstly, damages for the £53.7 million gross costs (£48 million net of tax relief, dropping to £34.1 million net of a £13.9 million profit on the final sale of its Distillers stake) that the contested bid had put the group to – on the basis that if Guinness had not weighed in, using allegedly illegal tactics, Argyll would have been spared that degree of outlay in fighting the rival bid. Secondly, Argyll believed it might be entitled to claim damages for the difference between what its stock market value would have been had it won Distillers and put it to rights, and what it was without the Distillers presence. Alistair Grant and Jimmy Gulliver argued that, since Argyll would have bought Safeways even with Distillers in its portfolio, the group would have been worth as much as Hanson Trust. (It had sold all its existing drinks manufacturing interest in disgust after losing Distillers.)

Just after Argyll's annual pre-tax profits for the period to end-March 1987 were published in mid-June 1987, Hanson was worth nearly £4.7 billion while Argyll's stock market value was a mere £1.74 billion. Guinness' market capitalisation was £3.04 billion. It looked as if the food retailer might make British legal history with a damages claim worth almost as much as the entire stockmarket value of the business it wanted to sue. But Argyll was not planning to drive Guinness into the sea even if its lawyers decided it was possible. It was also waiting for the DTI inspectors' report before pouncing; and in mid 1988 that situation remained unchanged.

Meanwhile the new Guinness board was fighting a legal battle with the UK Takeover Panel over reimbursing Distillers shareholders who may have lost out thanks to the brewer's tactics in the bid battle. The Panel wanted it to make good to all such former Distillers holders the difference between the value of its paper bid and the sum paid for a controversial 3% stake bought at the last moment apparently on Guinness' behalf by Cazenove, from a company called Pipetec that Bank Leu had since admitted was effectively working in concert with it. In practice this ruling could cost the brewer about £100 million – a drop in the ocean beside its billion-pound-plus annual turnover – but Guinness sought a judicial review of the Panel's decision and its timing (ahead of all the fraud trials). Guinness lost, appealed, lost again and had to decide by the close of August 1988 if it would go to the House of Lords or pay up. If faced with paying up, it indicated that it would look to sue its former bid advisers Cazenove and Morgan Grenfell.

The Guinness investigation was to be just one of many started that autumn of 1986. Even before it got underway, a separate insider dealing scandal had burst on the City. In early November 1986, Geoffrey Collier, the thirty-five-year-old head of equities at merchant bank Morgan Grenfell had resigned after being exposed for insider dealing. He had bought shares in engineering company AE just minutes before Robert Maxwell, a larger-than-life publishing tycoon with interests in many businesses, launched a bid for AE through the Hollis Group, which Maxwell controlled. Hollis was Morgan Grenfell's client and Collier knew of the imminent bid.

Collier, like Dennis Levine and Martin Siegel, had risen fast and far. A graduate of Trinity College, Oxford, in 1972, he gained himself a reputation as shrewd, hardworking and blessed with commonsense: a gift that seemed to desert him latterly. He had a spell in the tough New York market – where he perhaps learnt rather more wheezes than his bosses reckoned on. Morgan Grenfell took him from the broking firm of Vickers da Costa for a salary reputed to be as high as £300,000 a year. He and his wife Barbara, a wealthy woman in her own right, were able to entertain in style in a £1 million mansion at Ightham in Kent, and continued to make good money for his new firm. Colleagues nicknamed the chubby-faced, bespectacled high-flyer 'Rambo'. But it was not quite enough, it seems, and young Rambo strayed into forbidden territory. Collier when caught out faced two charges of insider dealing – one on the AE deal – and another relating to shares of food and drinks group Cadbury-Schweppes when a Morgan Grenfell client, US group General Cinema Corporation, was sizing up the business with a view to making a bid. He had made elaborate plans to try and cover his tracks. He placed the business with his friend Michael Cassell at the Los

Angeles office of his old firm Vickers da Costa, now part of the enlarged outfit Scrimgeour Vickers. Cassell had been sent to run the LA office. The proceeds went to a Cayman Island bank account in the name of 'Pureve Investments'.

Collier fared badly on the Cadbury-Schweppes deal. He called Cassell and told him to buy £30,000 of the shares – but the price fell later and Collier lost £10,000. With AE things went more smoothly, at least to start with. Collier went to a business meeting on Sunday 2 November, 1986 after which he knew his firm's client, Hollis Group, was about to announce a bid for AE. He phoned Cassell in Los Angeles before 7 a.m. UK time on the Monday with an order for AE shares. Cassell bought at 239p. The bid was announced at 8.30 in the UK and the share price rose to 265p. Some fifteen minutes later Collier called with a 'sell' order, earning himself a £15,000 profit, all in a morning's work.

However, things went awry from here on. The International Stock Exchange of the UK and Republic of Ireland, as the London Stock Exchange is now officially named, had a large and growing surveillance department headed by Bob Wilkinson, a tall, handsome silver-haired man of great courtesy and stong views on wrong-doers. His department monitors all trades electronically, as does the NYSE. In addition, each Exchange member firm is expected to have a compliance department to keep an eye on its own firm's activities. Scrimgeour Vickers noticed the timing of the Collier trade in AE shares, and alerted Morgan Grenfell.

Collier confessed to his boss Christopher Reeves, 'I have made a terrible mistake,' when challenged, but he was forced to resign his job. It meant selling his mansion and moving to a more modest house in Sevenoaks. It also meant arrest and court appearances. The AE deal was unravelled, so he never saw the profits. The Stock Exchange referred his case to the DTI which mounted an investigation. DTI inspectors – usually a leading lawyer and a senior accountant per case – are appointed by the Secretary of State for the department, and nowadays they keep the Director of Public Prosecutions Office (now retitled the headquarters of the UK's enlarged Crown Prosecution Service) up to date with their findings, and he can bring in the police when appropriate. It is the CPS that decides whether to bring a criminal prosecution (though the Serious Fraud Office now also has that right) and the new closer links speed things up more than the old route of DTI investigation, then police investigation, then the DPP's decision.

Collier was soon arrested, and appeared first at Wimbledon Magistrates Court on 23 January. The trial proper was held on 1 July at the Old Bailey. Much to the City's surprise, he got off lightly – with a £25,000 fine and a two-year suspended sentence. His was the first widely publicised insider dealing case to come to trial under the provisions of the 1980 Companies Act. He was lucky in the timing. Far tougher sentences were laid down in a piece of legislation presented to the House of Commons just as he came to trial, in the Criminal Justice Bill. But for the intervention and delay of a British general election, they would already have been in force that July.

The wave of insider dealing scandals that was to sweep the City that autumn and winter began with the Collier case though the Guinness affair was soon to swamp it. The Collier scandal shook old City hands just as Levine's and Siegel's demise had startled and disturbed older Wall Streeters. It also triggered the first in a series of moves by Government to tighten the defences against insider traders.

On 15 November, the day after the DTI investigation into Collier was requested, the Secretary of State Paul Channon announced that from midnight, the DTI inspectors should have tougher new powers to gather their evidence. He brought forward Section 177 of the new Financial Services Act, due to come into force early in 1987, to give them the right to question witnesses under oath, with recourse to a judge to declare in contempt of court anyone who refused to co-operate.

Since the penalties for contempt include fines and possible periods in jail until the contempt is purged, this gave the inspectors considerable powers of persuasion. The old part of the 1980 Companies Act that covered insider trading and had been beefed up in 1981 and 1985, had seen only seven prosecutions (four successful).

It was all very embarrassing for Morgan Grenfell, where Collier had helped to set up the securities operations ready for the massive changes underway in the City at the time: changes that allowed banks like Morgan to have 100% ownership of Exchange member firms and participate in the securities markets. Morgan had itself only recently floated its own shares on the Exchange at a hefty (and criticised) £5 apiece. It was to see them fall below £3 during that winter and in its weakened state, to become the subject of recurring takeover gossip itself.

The Collier affair saw the City tightening up on insider trading across the board as companies woke up to the damaging effects all round. New DTI investigations seemed to begin almost every week as worried directors begged a check into any unusual or unaccountable share price movement around the time of an announcement.

Within a week of Collier's exposure there were more headlines. A clerk at British & Commonwealth – a former shipping company moving steadily into financial services – was caught insider dealing in the shares of Steel Brothers, an associate company of British & Commonwealth, that the parent had decided to bid for and buy in. The clerk saw the papers, and placed an order with the London offices of Scrimgeour Vickers for 2,500 shares at 595p, in someone else's name. Scrimgeour executed the order but then realised the name was not a client of theirs. When the 630p-a-share bid for Steel Brothers was announced a few hours later, Scrimgeour's compliance officer guessed that an insider dealer was at work. It did not take too long to track down the culprit. He would have made just £875 on the deal. Instead he lost his job and faced the grim prospect of a DTI investigation and criminal charges.

As the DTI investigations into share price movements and possible manipulations piled up, long-held City suspicions that tips on merger situations might have come from within the DTI itself were brought sharply into focus by the sudden announcement on 18 December by Paul Channon that he had appointed inspectors to investigate possible leaks of inside information from within the DTI, the Office of Fair Trading and the Monopolies and Mergers Commission. Civil servants in all three offices would have advance knowledge of any plans to refer, recommend, or ban, an existing bid; all of which would be extremely price sensitive information.

The latest DTI inspectors had plenty to look into. The US fashion for big mergers, corporate raids and fiercely contested bid battles had been taken up in Britain which had seen the largest successful bids in its history – including Hanson Trust's purchase of Imperial Group and of course the Guinness/Distillers/Argyll fight. GEC's disallowed bid for Plessey; food group Hillsdown Holdings' attempt to win S. & W. Berisford; McCorquodale's bid for security printer Norton Opax; Gulf Resources' bid for Calor Gas – these were just a few of the recent bids. In 1985, the OFT had looked into 192 mergers with a total value of £15 billion.

As the probe went on, reports broke in the press that a secretary at the OFT was suspected of allegedly passing on information to her brother, a share dealer in the City, that he and possibly a ring of others had 'dealt' on the back of. One report suggested £10 milllion-worth of shares might have been traded on tips about whether or not a deal was to be referred, or permitted to go ahead. The girl's brother was named as Jonathan Greenwood, who left for Israel shortly after the DTI probe was announced. He stayed there, failing to return to meet the DTI inspectors, but proclaiming his and his sister's innocence in an interview published in *The Times* on 14 March 1987. 'I was only dealing in those cases on my view of the market and how the bids would go,' he said of three deals the DTI probe had focused on already. He was eventually arrested in March 1988 and, with his sister, released on bail till 9 September, while police inquiries continued.

In late March the DTI inspectors also tried to use their new powers to force financial journalist Jeremy Warner of the *Independent* to reveal his sources on two stories correctly predicting the outcome of two takeover situations. After much argument and a firm stand on protecting sources taken by Warner and his boss, founder of the *Independent* and former *Daily Telegraph* City Editor Andreas Whittam-Smith, the courts sided with the newspaper. But the incident gave rise to speculation that there might have been two rings of insider dealers in the City acting on leaks from different sources within the DTI.

The New Year had dawned with no respite. Paul Channon announced on 18 January that maximum penalties for insider trading were to be increased from two to seven years in an amendment to the new Criminal Justice Bill the Tory Government was to put before Parliament. In the event the changes had to wait a bit longer: the timing and timetable of the British election on 11 June intervened and the Bill was dropped *pro tem* until after Mrs Thatcher's party was returned for a third term. When Parliament was opened again for business later that month, the Bill was high on the new agenda, finally gaining the Royal Assent on 29 July and becoming law in stages thereafter. Two major innovations were making insider dealing an extraditable offence; and provisions to take legal evidence by satellite link – which could make gathering and presenting evidence from around the world a great deal easier, and revolutionise fraud trials.

The changes in the London stock market's composition and structure wrought by London's Big Bang (allowing foreign corporations and British banks to take 100% ownership of Stock Exchange member firms) and the preparations to introduce the new regulatory framework devised in the Financial Services Act, reflected the rapid internationalisation of the world's securities markets. Technology allows rapid dealing across frontiers, with a telecommunications link and the press of a few buttons. London's special position straddling the time zones of the other two great markets, Wall Street and Tokyo, put it bang in the middle of twenty-four-hour dealing activities.

This – even without merger mania, the arrival of the 'arbs' in force, the corporate raiders' activities, the contested takover bids – meant long hours and high pressures. With Big Bang bringing big new players into London, demand for good dealers and analysts exploded. Salaries soared. In all, 10,000 new jobs were created in the mainstream UK securities industry between 1984 and 1987 – an 8.5% rise, making it Britain's fastest growing industry. Along with the big bucks, however, went greater pressure to perform especially for those rapidly promoted to high office: clever and ambitious young men and women whose attitudes to investment and business ethics were brasher than the old guard's. It was New York all over again; but in London the 'yuppie scam' was nipped in the bud – thanks in large part to the warnings sounded by the SEC in Washington and directed to the DTI in London. (The October 1987 crash completed the picture. 1,500 yuppie jobs – managers, dealers and securities salesmen – were shed between October 1987 and June 1988, and more job losses were expected.)

The warnings and the example of this co-operation were heeded further afield in Europe, where Britain was not alone in seeking tougher rules and punishments for insider trading. The European Economic Community announced on 28 April 1987 that it was bringing forward proposals to outlaw insider trading with uniform rules across the Community. Plans already in the pipeline to co-ordinate and make more uniform the safeguards of all the different European securities markets – ahead of the creation of the single European market free of internal trade barriers, at the end of 1992 – were being speeded up for adoption sometime in 1989 (at the earliest), in the light of the US and UK scandals and experience.

Within the EEC at that point only Britain, France and Denmark had made insider trading illegal though West Germany operated a voluntary code not to abuse privileged information. Belgium, Ireland and the Netherlands were planning to bring in legislation. Italy, Greece, Spain, Portugal and Luxembourg had no anti-insider trading rules.

The EEC was also planning to improve the exchange of information between governments and regulatory authorities on securities trading and market manipulations. Only six months had passed since Boesky's confession had been announced to a shocked and nervous Wall Street, six months that rocked the world's securities markets, and rewrote the rulebooks – for the better.

7

The Electronic
Roundabout

Everyone has heard the one about the company computer expert who diddled his firm of millions and, when discovered, traded the secret of how it was done for immunity from prosecution. One version which is truer than most concerns the boffin who relieved a major UK clearing bank of a great deal of money, and when the game was up was actually given a reference to enable him to get another job. The bank just could not face the adverse publicity and potential loss of business to its rivals, at a bad patch in its corporate history, that it feared prosecution and trial of the miscreant would bring. True or false, various versions of these stories have joined the catalogue of modern myths under the section headed Computer Crime – or Datatheft, as Hugo Cornwall describes it in his excellent recent book of that title.

The latter half of the twentieth century has seen the age of the computer develop at extraordinary speed. From the vast machines of the 1950s, with their then miraculous but now limited memory and capability, in the late 1980s we have already reached a point where business life, many jobs and most of the conveniences of modern life would be inconceivable without the workings and applications of the computer in all its manifestations. From the well-stocked supermarket whose check-out till tells the central computer every night how much of which goods has been sold and what must be dispatched to arrive first thing next day to keep the shelves full; to the travel agent tapping into an airline's efficient holiday booking system; or the robotics used to build your car; and even the programme of your washing machine – the computer is part of all our lives. So is computer fraud – estimated to cost British business alone about £40 million a year.

The computer is no longer a simple tool that stores information or relays instructions. Its capacity to collate, interpret and, from the information gathered, to model and extrapolate the future based upon the present, with a few assumptions thrown in courtesy of the appropriate software, has knitted the computer into the fabric of our world. It has become an integral part of any business planning for the future, as well as a provider of right up-to-date information and analysis of what is going on in the business this week – even this minute, depending on what it is set up to do, and how immediate the processed information is required to be. And such is the ingenuity of man that, for almost as long as there have been computers, there has also been computer crime.

Computer crime takes many forms. The most common cases involve employees who have access to the firm's computer systems, or to items that are later processed by the computer, and who take advantage of lax surveillance systems to siphon off cash or goods for themselves: good old-fashioned payroll frauds and warehouse rip-offs that the computer can make so much easier to carry out when insufficient checks and balances are built into the way it is used and there is insufficient control as to who has access to the various programmes it can run. 'In the old days it was bookkeepers who committed fraud. Now it is the people who input the information or run the machines,' says Bob Wilkinson, head of London's International Stock Exchange surveillance department.

Computer crime can also encompass:

1. Sabotage, by disgruntled staff, either of the software by inputting false data or erasing vital information; or straightforward physical assault on the computer itself. Cases reported by Cornwall range from orange juice poured into a machine, or deliberate scratching of the hard disks on which data is stored, to terrorist bombings of state, or multinational corporations' computer installations.

2. The unauthorised use of the firm's computer to run your own business on. Examples range from biorhythm charts for sale, to a complete publishing business, taking up valuable storage space to the detriment of the company's own business.

3. The theft of unused disks, or 'peripherals' like keyboards or add-on software, and even entire desktop computers, either to sell or to use at home.

4. The illicit copying of data disks with vital trade information or forecasting programmes compiled by the business, to sell to rival firms – entering the world of industrial espionage.

5. The bugging of the computer or of the room a desktop keyboard is in. Each key gives off a sound all its own and an expert who can record the sounds and run that through another computer giving it a pattern to look for, like the occurrence of most common vowel in the user's language, for example, can soon have exactly what the user typed appearing on his own screen.

The simple hacker who breaks into a computer system out of curiosity – and may do accidental damage in the meantime – is the most publicised but probably one of the least immediately dangerous, illegal rider on the modern electronic roundabout.

The computer and its software is as good and as protected as its owner permits it to be. Sloppy procedures over who has access – to a building, to a screen, to passwords, to the mainframe – and, once access is gained by fair means or foul, how easy it is to move around within the system without hitting barriers, are the faults of management and planners for being complacent about the mysteries of the machine.

The computer criminal who is one of the hardest to beat is the one who either breaks into the normal, computer traffic of the modern banking world or makes some outwardly legitimate use of it for highly illegitimate purposes – like the advance-fee fraudster who cons a 'client' into handing over cash in advance for services, never to be rendered, and then relies on the electronic wizardry that transfers funds around the globe faster than Shakespeare's Puck could circle it (he claimed forty minutes to 'put a girdle round about the earth').

The electronic transfer of funds (or 'EFT' in banking jargon) from one bank's set of computer records to another's, means that a clever crook can churn cheques 'cross-fired' from account to account at crucial times to make it look as if he, or his business, has more cash-in-hand than he actually does. He may withdraw cash from an account at this moment and melt away before a series of bouncing cheques finally comes to roost at the branch concerned. Or he may do this to make his business look healthier at the year-end than is the case, possibly to extract a higher price from a potential buyer . . . and so on. The truly professional conman can use EFT to make money move from financial centre to financial centre, cash it thousands of miles away in another jurisdiction, and vanish before anyone realises there has been a mistake. A dramatic illustration of this came in July 1988 when a computer hiccup in Zurich threw up a transfer of nearly Sw Fr 82 million *en route* from the London offices of the Union Bank of Switzerland to a branch of Credit Suisse First Boston in the Swiss town of Nyon. The money was in the process of being transferred on the back of a fradulent but convincing telex instruction. But its size may have rung alarm bells in the computer. The attempted fraud was stopped and arrests swiftly followed. Fraudulent transfers are all the easier if the true owner of the cash is made an unwitting accomplice to conning genuine banks into transferring the money.

Take, for example, a potentially very embarrassing fraud attempt in 1981. The Commonwealth Secretariat's Commercial Crime Unit, based in London, was asked by a senior official of a non-Commonwealth country to check out the circumstances surrounding a US $2.5 billion loan deal being arranged by the country's Vice-President. The President had already given his blessing to raising the finance, intended for various major projects that would do no harm to the two men's electoral prestige, but for various internal reasons the main political faction in the government was being kept in the dark about the funding and where it was coming from. So secrecy had seemed important to the borrowers.

The Vice-President was put in touch with a financier who claimed to act for wealthy Middle Eastern contacts who wanted to lend internationally but who, for various family or local political reasons – such as laws against usury – supposedly did not want their identities known either. Usually this type of proposal is accompanied by a temptingly low interest rate which the lender is said to be willing to accept in return for anonymity. But the loan is a lengthy one – and, of course, collateral is required, preferably in the form of government-issued securities or other easily 'negotiable' (i.e., easily sold for cash) instruments.

In this case, because everyone wanted to keep their identities secret from everyone else, the deal proposed was that the $2.5 billion would be provided through a Norwegian bank, but the loan arrangements would be managed and handled by two Hong Kong-based companies. A well-known Swiss bank operating in Geneva would be used to provide the necessary deposit and drawing facilities – and this three-layered arrangement would help to protect the identities of all concerned.

The Vice-President handed over a non-returnable 1% advance fee to the lenders' representatives for their assistance, and a large amount of suitable negotiable securities were deposited as security for the loan – which was due to be completed in two days time. At that point, caution prevailed over the desire for total secrecy, and the London-based Crime Unit was asked to do a little discreet checking to make sure all was well.

It was not. In fact, the whole deal was bogus. As the Unit's head, Dr Barry Rider, reported, it rapidly found out that the Norwegian bank was already suspected in Scandinavia of being a fake bank. The man behind it was also wanted for questioning in Hong Kong, and the two Hong Kong-based companies supposedly managing the loan were front organisations for a businessman with links to organised crime in the Far East and North America, and who had earlier been involved with a financial institution in Malaysia that had collapsed. Luckily for the would-be borrowers of the non-existent $2.5 billion, the Unit established most of this within twenty-four hours – gathering enough information to alert the banking and securities exchange authorities in Hong Kong and to stop any cash being raised there against the securities deposited. It warned the innocent Swiss bank and the Swiss authorities that their banking system was about to be abused, and alerted officials in the would-be borrowers' country. Everything was stopped, the negotiable instruments were recovered in time, and even the advance fee was salvaged, along with the political reputations of the leader of the country and his deputy – saved the hideous embarrassment of losing $2.5 million cash and billions in securities.

The would-be fraudsters were arrested. It turned out that an associate of the man behind the fake Norwegian bank had just been convicted in the USA under its RICO – Racketeer Influenced and Corrupt Organisations – Act.

The computer can be turned against the criminal to track him down. If you can follow the trail of the conman you can probably find the cash, or vice versa. Starting from the first transfer, it is possible – though not easy – to track the money down however many forms it assumes en route.

First take the case of a relatively straightforward scam that happened in Britain recently. It all began with a cheque that went astray. A company that owned a block of offices in London went into receivership. The accountant appointed to salvage what he could continued to collect the rents due from the various businesses in the block on behalf of the company's creditors. When he sent out the regular rent demand, however, he added an instuction to send the cheques not to the company's old address, but to make them payable to the accountancy firm he worked for and post them to its offices.

But the best laid plans of mice, men and even of accountants can go awry and inevitably one tenant sent a cheque to the wrong address, though correctly made out to the accountancy firm. The postman failed to spot the redirection instructions for the company's mail and, unable to find the company at its old address, simply abandoned the envelope on a radiator in the entrance hall of the building. Enter the villain, who spotted the envelope, opened it, and found a cheque for £5,000 which he promptly pocketed.

Back at his desk, the accountant eventually wrote to the tenant asking why he had not paid his rent. Back came the indignant reply that it had been paid and that the cheque had been banked. The accountant decided to get onto the trail of the money. His first step was to ask the tenant to let him have a photocopy of the cashed cheque, front and back, from his bank. The tenant obliged. The stamp on the front of the cheque revealed that it had been passed through the Strand, London, branch of a major bank. The back showed why the cheque had been accepted. At first glance it appeared to have been endorsed by the accountancy firm— which wishes to remain anonymous so we will call it Penny Wisemen Ltd – with a scrawl that on closer inspection actually read, Penny Wise. In the rush and tumble of a busy day the unfortunate bank clerk who had paid over the money had missed the forgery. Because the cheque was wrongly endorsed the bank was liable for the £5,000 owed to company's receiver – money that as far as the tenant was concerned, had been paid – and duly coughed up. But where was the missing £5,000 that the bank had, effectively, been defrauded of? This was now a matter for the police to follow up.

The cheque had been paid into the account of a business in Kent that sold Range Rovers to the well-to-do. When the police called round to ask what was going on, the trail widened out. The Kent motor firm had just sold a green Range Rover for £5,400 to someone claiming to be a newish car firm in South East London (for form's sake we have called them Carbashers) with a customer seeking one that colour.

The caller had asked the Kent firm to hang onto it for him, and had sent over a £400 goodwill deposit through the banking system. This meant the Kent firm had given its account details over the phone to the caller. In due course £400 turned up in a clutch of smaller cheques and assorted methods of payment. Carbashers phoned to check that the Kent firm had had the £400. It checked with its bank, which said yes.

At that point the Carbashers caller said he had received the remaining £5,000 from his client – and duly paid the tenant's stolen, falsely endorsed £5,000 cheque into the innocent Kent firm's account, through the bank in the Strand. As soon as the cheque should have been credited he called the firm again to confirm. Had the fake endorsement been spotted in the meantime and the cheque bounced, he could have blamed 'the client' and cancelled the deal. In fact, it had been credited. He shot down to collect the Range Rover straightaway and was given the keys, the guarantee document and everything he needed as legal title to the vehicle. A stolen cheque had been laundered into a legit Range Rover. But there was one more wheeze, to turn the Range Rover back into clean cash. And here is where the trail could continue. Carbashers did not exist and was untraceable, but the vehicle did exist and it could be tracked.

Where did the villain take the car off to? The police asked the makers of Range Rover if they had received the completed guarantee card for that vehicle. They had: from a Herr Schmidt of Zurich. The UK police contacted Herr Schmidt. He had indeed got the Range Rover, bought from a garage in Zurich – where it had arrived the day immediately after it was collected from the Kent dealer. The villain had simply driven the Range Rover straight from the town where he bought it to the nearest port and hopped over the Channel to deliver it to what turned out to be his regular contacts in Switzerland.

'It was the banking transaction that gave the game away. It left a trail even though the "newish" motor firm didn't exist,' the accountant explained. This was a relatively small fraud in itself, though the overall scam being run by the conman turned out to be quite a big operation.

What this story – and though the names are changed the events are true – illustrates, is how the investigators of fraud and financial crimes can follow the trail left by the crook's inescapable need at some stage in his crime to go through the banking system, either to cash, shift or launder his ill-gotten gains. Computer thieves also leave a trail that can be investigated, and leads to a money trail that can also be followed. The computer gumshoe's first moves are explained a little further on.

Once on the money trail, the investigator needs two things: the co-operation of the banks in yielding up valuable information, and good relations between the police or investigative agencies of different countries, to tip-off each other when they believe that funny money has briefly touched down in the banks of another jurisdiction and left another imprint in the trail. If it leaves one land as cash in a suitcase, sooner or later it will turn up in a bank somewhere else, as a cheque or a deposit of securities against which cash is drawn, possibly after several changes of shape in the meantime; rather as the £5,000 cheque became a Range Rover before it was sold for clean money in Switzerland.

Interpol helps to provide the link between the police forces (as described in the chapter on the investigators, Chapter 8). But just how co-operative are the banks? In the Carbashers case the tenant instructed his bank to co-operate so there was no problem. But when the investigator wants information about the bank account of a suspect, UK banks have traditionally refused to yield up information for fear of being sued for breach of confidence, unless the investigator has been able to come at them with a court order.

But in 1986 the first in a wave of new legislation came in that obliged British banks to be much more forthcoming, freeing them from the obligation to protect clients' secrets at all costs. This was the 1986 Drug Trafficking Offences Act, followed by other new rules, which put the banks in breach of the criminal law if they dragged their heels too much. Banks had already been given some leeway to co-operate with investigators after a legal decision in the early 1970s when the Midland Bank had been unwilling to give details of a client account to a sequestrator in an industrial relations case.

In the Drug Trafficking Offences Act and again in the Criminal Justice Act, based upon the researches of the fraud trials committee led by Lord Roskill (described in Chapter 11) the banks and anyone else suspecting a crime may have been committed came under a new legal obligation to alert the authorities or face prosecution themselves. These changes themselves followed international moves to try and reduce banking secrecy. The Drug Trafficking Offences Act was modelled on an international draft designed to produce similar legislation in different countries and aid investigation and prosecution across jurisdictions. Nine years earlier, in 1977, the US and Swiss authorities had signed a Mutual Assistance in Criminal Affairs Treaty which lifted the veil on the famous Swiss banking secrecy – allowing US investigators who were able to convince the Swiss authorities that a crime had been committed, to have enforceable legal and secret access to the numbered bank accounts and records of suspects hiding their loot behind rules originally designed to protect the assets of people fleeing Hitler's Germany decades before.

The crooked Italian financier Michele Sindona was convicted in the USA partly on evidence uncovered under this Treaty (see Chapter 9). Britain was offered a similar treaty by the Swiss in 1980, but turned it down in 1981 on the grounds that the system of criminal justice in the UK, and its rules of evidence, did not lend itself easily to the application of mutual assistance treaties with countries with very different legal systems. That was pre-Roskill and the latest Criminal Justice Act (see Chapter 11).

Many of the lessons learned in the UK about trailing money that has gone AWOL on an international scale came from the experience of chasing money belonging to the striking National Union of Mineworkers around the world after a sequestration order was placed upon its assets following a case brought against the union by some of its own members during the strike. The successful sequestrator – an accountant from accountancy firm Price Waterhouse – later advised the government during the drafting of the Drug Trafficking Offences Act on details such as extending the seizure of a suspect's assets, to any cash and objects hastily given away to other people in an attempt to salvage them.

A sequestrator is appointed by the court to freeze or even seize the assets of the party concerned. This may be for breach of a previous court ruling (as in the NUM case) or when, as permitted under the Drug Trafficking Offences Act or the 1987 Criminal Justice Act, the court wishes to freeze the assets of someone facing serious charges pending the outcome of the case.

Where the subject of a sequestration order refuses to co-operate or has moved money offshore through the banking system's electronic funds transfer arrangements (EFT) to escape seizure – as happened in the NUM case and again when the UK print union SOGAT was ruled to be in contempt of court and its assets were ordered to be seized – the sequestrator faces a similar problem to the fraud investigator: where is the money and how can it be traced?

Unlike the private investigator, the sequestrator's task is made a little easier by being able to ask the judge who appointed him for a court order to serve on bank officials, auditors and any others who show reluctance in supplying the information he seeks. Faced with a court order, they have little choice but to comply with the sequestrator's request, or be in contempt of court with the risk of being jailed for their trouble. Few bank managers are that committed to the shibboleth of client confidentiality. So the sequestrator's first move on a big operation is to write to all the banks enquiring about any accounts that might be there or have been there in the name(s) of those concerned. He will look at the last set of accounts, if it is a company whose assets he is trying to ascertain and trace, by going to Companies House where certain records must by law be kept (and there has been greater effort lately to make companies file their records on time), and may call on the company's auditors for a more detailed up-to-date picture. Auditors who refuse to co-operate will be presented with a court order in very short order indeed.

From the auditor, be he reluctant or keen, the sequestrator gets details of what and where the firm's bank accounts are, or were, and what investments, properties, buildings, leases and other assets and liabilities the business has. This gives him a starting point: he now knows which banks to go to directly and asks to see the account records – copies of statements, copies of paid cheques, explanations of transactions. If money has moved out of the account, where did it go? The bank will be able to say what the first stop, at least, was. If it is a big sequestration, linked, say, to the seizure of drug traffickers' assets, the money has probably flowed overseas, either electronically or in suitcases.

If one stop was a foreign bank that does not feel in the least inclined to co-operate with a sequestrator holding a British court order, the sequestrator may well turn to the UK police. They will ask Interpol to put them in touch with the local officer who will make the necessary moves in his jurisdiction to get the information or freeze the money, if it is still there, pending moves to seize it. (Once the money is frozen the account holder can no longer get to it or move it on.) Both legal and informal links of this sort are exercised to the full. Life is slightly more complicated when proceeds have been taken abroad as cash or gold bullion or in some other portable, saleable form. But even these, and any other stolen items, have to be turned back into anonymous cash fairly quickly, less whatever the costs and kickbacks of those trans-actions may be. Criminals will rarely use cheques to pay off such debts for fear of leaving a trace. But a suitcase or two full of money also rapidly becomes an embarrassment, which might itself be stolen. So sooner or later the proceeds will have to pop up as a cash deposit somewhere in the world. Whatever metamorphoses it goes through on the way, if the pursuer has any inkling or hunches about where the cash might touch down en route or at its journey's end, he may be able to pick up the trail again.

Interpol can be of further help here both in an official enquiry or even to private investigators – often ex-policemen who can exercise old contacts – if its records indicate the whereabouts of the rest of a known criminal enterprise's operations. 'By getting at the bank where the suspect's money may have been paid in, then you have a trail as to where the money went from there – which is where it is important for the police to help each other to follow up the movement. Because of international co-operation between many many police forces, transactions do get traced. And very long and tedious it can be, while the money can be moved around the world and back in twenty-four hours. A telex transfer of £25,000 – or £25 million – will only cost £50–100 and is very easily done,' explained one seasoned sequestrator.

Thus, just as banking secrecy had been abused, so the rapid rise of banks' computer technology to ease and speed the movement of money round the world helps the bent businessman – the crook – to speed up his transactions and deals. It also creates the new crime of electronically diverting funds away from their rightful owners. This can be anything from shifting cash around the world, to the theft and abuse of cash cards in a high street bank's branch's automatic teller machine, to an insider rounding down the odd pennies on customers' cash inflows and transferring them to a secret personal account that mounts up to large sums, or an outsider breaking into a sophisticated computer program and shifting someone else's funds through a series of EFT transfers to an offshore account in Panama.

All this has in turn has spawned a new breed of specialist investigators. 'Technology is growing tremendously and the type of system is changing. There are more terminals and therefore more people can get access to it. The push towards increased "user friendliness" and fourth generation languages, all make people much better educated about what they can do,' reports one expert in tracking down computer crime of all sorts, including bank frauds.

'Companies also have their forms of information technology – management and decision support systems and a lot more, to handle market information and to record and monitor the type of transactions going on. In our experience too, the banking industry tends to regard computer security still as a rather bolt-on goodie, rather than as part of the integral design.

'They still put their effort into getting the system to go having paid some lip-service to security on the way, but it is only when moving to the latter stage of system development that they handle the question of security, by which time it may be too late.

'We are finding now that the bias of the risks is tending to move towards greater potential use of technology in penetrating the system. It is more available generally and people are more aware: user friendliness and security do not co-exist comfortably. It is a paradox of computing that we try to move towards both.'

Worrying stuff. Computer users can do a lot to protect themselves from fraud by weaving sensible checks and balances into their system, and teaching staff to be more security conscious about their signing-on passwords; about not leaving screens open and unattended; querying unauthorised personnel or strangers entering a computer room, and so on.

They can also limit the effects of tampering, theft or damage, deliberate or accidental, by having an efficent emergency procedure to fall back on, and a good back-up computer arranged. Valuable records can be damaged by fire, flood, electricity failure and accident too. Users should make sure the back-up computer system is also protected sufficiently against manipulation, theft or hacking. There is little point in elaborate security for the main system if the back-up can be easily tampered with – or if your main telecommunications points can be easily accessed and bugged by strangers.

Finally, there are forms of insurance available through Lloyd's of London in the UK against damage, disaster, and costly down-time – though insuring against the theft of information that is not actually wiped off the original records in the process is harder to cover.

Remedies may vary from charging miscreants with simple conspiracy to defraud – a criminal act in the UK even if no cash or valuable information actually goes missing – to criminal damage. But many firms fear that the publicity surrounding prosecution of the computer criminal will draw customers' and suppliers' attention to its losses and may reduce confidence in the business. They prefer to investigate themselves or call in private consultants who will keep them briefed about the enquiry's progress. Only later will most firms decide whether to call in the police. But few do – and how they solve the problem of what to do with the miscreant is covered at the end of the chapter.

Computer fraud is a rising crime, largely because as computers become more and more widely used in commerce and industry, so the number of people who know how to play around with them grows. Incidences of computer fraud start to move away from a technological variant of book-keeping fraud to more sophisticated scams.

A recent survey by the London office of accountancy firm Deloitte Haskins & Sells found signs of a shift in computer fraud, away from people 'merely manipulating an input document, to people with access to the system and the technology using that to divert large amounts of money on a one-off basis'. If you get away with millions once, you do not need to try it again elsewhere. And the thief is less likely to be a hacker from outside who breaks into the system and siphons off millions than from among the firm's own or external computer maintenance staff, or the boffins developing the system who know it inside out and backwards, or an analyst using the system. These all have the technical know how and the opportunity. If the firm treats its staff poorly or passes over an ambitious individual tactlessly, he or she may also acquire a motive. 'Unlike a classic manual fraud, you cannot detect a forged signature or see a changed amount: electronic Tippex is undetectable!' one expert points out. Combating this type of fraud makes as much use of common sense as of wizardry.

'When a bank or company installs new systems, there is more likelihood of error than fraud', a professional computer fraud troubleshooter explains. 'As organisations get to grips with that higher probability of error, the more they develop systems. Over time you get very rapid change, and a period of consolidation. But human ability moves in a straight line so as the pace of change increases, you are less in control. *This creates a critical risk window*. It could be because you are putting in new systems and getting used to how you use and control them. Therefore, the risk of a technician getting away with a one-off fraud is that much larger. Or you miss things you would, over time, have controlled. Fraud can be masked as an error more easily during this time too. For example, if you have a suspense account which should be cleared once a day, but you are so pressed that it is only done once a week: giving the criminal five times the chance to get the money away.

'Other threats to your system during this period are your dependance on technical staff not doing something bizarre, deliberately or accidentally. And there is always a danger that when you get behind with a computer system, you will cut corners on control because there is such a backlog. Business interruption is also very costly.'

In fact, it is one of the things that businesses fear most: hence all the back-up systems more and more companies are investing in away from their main place of business and the rise of 'concurrent technology': machines that keep going even when bits of them are being pulled out and fixed – 'very, very resilient, fault-tolerant systems', says one expert in this field.

It is not just money that is immediately at stake where computer systems are vulnerable: confidential information can be intercepted and might be of value to a competitor, willing to pay an employee for a bit of industrial espionage. Company strategies, business plans for acquisitions, confidential accounts, even records of investigations into suspect employees might be read. The pay-roll is another area potentially at risk.

Investigators of computer fraud and assessors of the risks of it happening, find that it is not always high on a company's list of anxieties. It is perceived as a lesser risk – 'A perception which is correct perhaps in terms of frequency, but people have not done a full risk assessment of the possible magnitude of fraud,' one investigator explains. 'It is partly because those who don't know how to work the computer do not always realise what the risks and opportunities are, and are not keeping up with the management security and control issues associated with that change.'

He, like others in all fields of fraud, finds that the majority of culprits 'tend to stumble across the opportunity [to commit a fraud] rather than plan it. It is mostly committed by people in a relatively trusted position who have the opportunity as part of their day-to-day working. They almost trip over the opportunity and suddenly realise they can get away with something – and then they think of ways of exploiting it. But the seed is sown by the opportunity.' Investigation into suspected computer fraud often reveals that security controls like passwords are very simple, while management has an exaggerated faith in them. It is very easy, even convenient, for people who work together to learn each other's passwords, and that part of the security system breaks down. Or there may be collusion between someone inputting data, and a programmer. 'There have been cases of people putting orders into the system and getting goods delivered to addresses they control' – while queries from the accounts department, the supplier or other clients can be attributed to incorrect accounts or records.

'A business can use a computer to cope with big volume, but that volume can also mask things. It is a factor which can be on the side of anybody who wants to defraud an organisation,' investigators also point out.

So much for some of what can go wrong. Once a firm suspects there is a problem and calls in the experts to check out what is going on, tracking missing money becomes a journey through the maze of the computer system. It has to start from the question: has the money, or valuable goods, actually been diverted, or just lost in the system? The investigator first must find out if the accounting entries are simply incorrect. Once he knows money really is missing, his next step is to find out how the system processes transactions which are fed into the control area where the loss was detected. Areas which are at risk may be revealed here.

'To a large extent you are using normal audit techniques to find these,' one consultant says. He then looks into each of these areas to see how a fraud could happen and who could do it. Could it only be done by collusion? Between what departments? 'You look for people in two departments who are good friends or living together – someone in a position to alter records, and someone in a controlling position. Or you could be looking for technical manipulation. If there is no evidence of abnormal use of normal transactions, the fraud must have come in via a technical route. Hackers, or someone in the DP department?' (The DP department is jargon for the maintenance experts and boffins.)

At this point the investigator may lose the audit trail: 'You could see reasonably straightforward access to someone able to dial into the system, or a programmer may be able to get into any part of the system – but your ability to narrow it down is limited by the evidence the company collects on a normal basis.'

Where high volumes of goods and entries are involved, it can be even more difficult to trace where money has gone to: and the problem could still be error not manipulation. 'The computer could be erroneously generating transactions and causing money transfers to take place. You look at the programs in great detail to find out if there is any possibility – testing it with increasing precision. It is very very difficult to come up with a check-list of how you trace the money: that is in the skill and knowledge of the investigator who is pitting his wits against the technical complexity of the system and against the individual who is manipulating the system.'

One case uncovered was that of the DP manager who had run up gambling debts and was trying to make the money he took out of the system look like the activities of an outside organisation. 'He had the authority, the technical know-how, the intellectual knowledge of how the system was constructed, and was able to manipulate it and get away with it for a bit.'

Ways of combating fraud include reducing the risk, on security, and attitude. 'We recommend to people that they do an assessment of the extent to which they rely on the computer system, and what impact on the business a loss or fault in the system would have. This determines the level of security which has to surround it. We then expect individuals' abilities to be locked out of various parts of the system.'

But in any system there will always be one key person who knows how the whole system operates, and several skilled technical staff who could probably bypass the checks that will foil most of the rest of the users. Management tends to forget that what bamboozles them may not be a mystery to others. Hence the importance of vetting, especially at a time when there is a shortage of skilled staff in the computer field and companies tend to settle for whoever they can get with the necessary basic skills – as happened in the City of London after Big Bang. On 27 October 1986, the UK securities industry moved over to telephone dealing against on-screen prices, and massive dependence on computer systems right across their businesses.

When skilled staff are in short supply and firms will snap up anyone they can get without checking his/her curriculum vitae and references, 'this is a fairly substantial risk area for one-off, large manipulations', consultants warn. If there is a computer crook playing the system, there is also the additional danger that the culprit may cause deliberate mayhem to cover his (or her) tracks, using his know-how to throw the whole system into confusion for long enough to get money transferred anywhere in the world from its first stop. Computer chaos can take two to three days to sort out, which is enough time for the culprit to take 'sick leave' and vanish before anyone connects him with the emerging disaster.

People in sensitive positions should be screened or in some way – tactfully – positively vetted. 'Companies have not yet realised the risks which they are running and the degree to which positive screening of individuals can have a very positive effect. And they should come down hard on the abusers,' consultants in this field recommend.

Security expert and writer Hugo Cornwall recommends thorough and detailed checking of all CVs of key technical people being hired to work on your computer system – but cautions against methods that may violate human rights and could upset or alienate staff.

Companies may corroborate CVs themselves or hire an outside agency: the expert investigators' advice is whatever route you choose, do make those checks. Cagey replies from ex-employers who are nervous for legal reasons of saying too much, could be warning bells. If the ex-employer is a business competitor whose own ethics are a bit flaky, it may not mind a rival firm getting lumbered with a bad 'un.

A resentful leaver may mess around with the system not for personal gain (or not solely for that), but to get his own back later on. If he is a clever saboteur, he may leave what the boffins call a logic bomb in the system – something pre-set to crash the system or cause chaos at a given date, or to be triggered by a particular event or even a routine computer entry. Another spoiling tactic is the computer virus, an event or a routine command that is set to mushroom exponentially and take up so much of the computer's capacity, as it tries to obey the spreading chain of commands, that it becomes clogged up or crashes.

Not all fraud is carried out to harm the firm. Some cases of false entries and manipulation of computer records have been by poor managers seeking to disguise their failings in the belief that they will be able to meet the exaggerated production, or sales, or whatever, levels later. Misleading performance printouts leading to eventual disaster for the division will almost always follow. All these possibilities explain why the emphasis on control has to change from being detective controls, monitoring what historically has gone on, to controls which prevent people from doing things. 'Limit their activities,' is the expert advice.

The question of how you mete out justice to an exposed culprit is a thorny one. The first step may be to try and get your money back, which may mean doing a deal with the fraudster: no prosecution in return for information on how it was done, and/or the return of the cash, dismissal but with references – or some variation on these themes. One of the difficulties about prosecuting anyway is proving electronic fraud satisfactorily in court: fraud can be hard to prove at the best of times but 'clean' electronic fraud (no Tippex, none of the tell-tale chemicals that leave their traces on forged documents), is harder still.

Companies may also fear the publicity attached to a fraud case. Others will prefer to use the grapevine to block the culprit from getting similar work. But some may just settle for instant dismissal and leave it at that: which makes it doubly important to check references when hiring experienced staff.

If it is any comfort, Deloitte Haskins & Sells' survey into computer risks found that there is still more danger to most banks and businesses of technical or systems failure than of fraud. But who needs either?

8

The Investigators

Investigating commercial crime is not just the purview of the national police forces or the FBI. Many other bodies carry out valuable work in this field, ranging from professional accountants to intelligence officers.

The Banco Ambrosiano tale (see Chapter 9), with all the ingredients of a major thriller, illustrates dramatically the kind of detective and investigative work that the accountancy profession may be called upon to do for their beleaguered clients. But there are plenty of other less dramatic and extensive, but just as demanding, cases that could use the skills of an experienced accountant to unravel. Some of the major accountancy firms provide specialist 'forensic' investigative services to root out fraud after the event, and consultants who will teach a company how to reduce the risks of becoming a victim of fraud of all sorts, including experts in computer protection.

Private agencies and consultancies also offer a host of other services, from discreetly vetting new staff to pursuing counterfeiters of their clients' products, and advising companies facing hostile takeover bids on what to do to protect their information and their secrets. Some companies will also ask their consultants to try and dig up a little dirt on the opposition.

Fraud prevention is clearly the best option – but with the explosion of sophisticated and international fraud cases, the official bodies whose task is to investigate, uncover, and recommend prosecution, are being strengthened too.

In Britain the traditional *fraud squads* of each of the forty-three regional police forces of England and Wales are being encouraged to co-opt more accountants and other appropriate experts onto individual cases – and in London, the *Fraud Investigation Group*, or FIG, system was set up at the start of 1985, to provide a pool of financial and legal

173

expertise to work with fraud squad officers on more complicated, selected cases. The oldest regional fraud squad is London's *Metropolitan and City Company Fraud Department*, set up in 1946.

The FIG system also made room for greater co-operation between the police forces and inspectors appointed by the British *Department of Trade and Industry* (DTI) under the Companies Acts, to look into dubious goings-on. Previously, DTI evidence was taken in a way that did not comply with the rules about how evidence must be presented in court, so if a DTI investigation was referred on to the police, all the evidence had to be re-examined and taken again, which slowed things down considerably. But now the DTI, which supervises the regulatory system for trading, insurance and securities firms, and also appoints inspectors to look into suspected insider dealing and suspected breaches of the new Insolvency Act – which covers the conduct of liquidators and of company directors – can give them powers to take evidence on oath that the courts will accept. This also makes gathering evidence a lot easier. Anyone refusing to answer the inspectors' queries finds himself in contempt of court and facing a possible fine or jail sentence, so most people are more inclined to help than hinder.

Into all these changes, Britain has also added the *Serious Fraud Office* (SFO), a new hybrid investigative body set up in 1987 after Lord Roskill's report into the prosecution and trial of fraud in the UK, to take on and speed up the investigation of the most complex and serious of fraud cases. It was fully operational by mid-1988 with statutory powers far wider than the scope of the FIG system. But its case-load should remain relatively small, probably not exceeding fifty to a hundred (average sixty) at any one time, and only concerning frauds of £1 million or over.

Under the Directorship of John Wood, formerly a deputy director of public prosecutions, the SFO aimed to build up a staff of eighty to one hundred lawyers and accountants by autumn 1988, to work closely with an attachment of police officers from the City of London Fraud squad. Other expertise would be co-opted (like Counsel's advice) as and when needed. Wood's budget for the first year of SFO work was £6 million of which half was earmarked for prosecution costs. As the SFO's director, Wood bears the same relationship to the Attorney-General and to Parliament as the Director of Public Prosecutions (whose office is now the Headquarters of the extended Crown Prosecution Service, or CPS): he can take the decision to press ahead and prosecute on the basis of the evidence uncovered. He can take over for the SFO any fraud case already under investigation elsewhere that he considers to be sufficiently grave or complex.

Cases may be brought to his attention by the fraud squads, the *Inland Revenue*,* the DTI, the CPS, the *Customs & Excise* men,* and possibly even the Self Regulatory Organisations (SROs) overseen by the Securities and Investments Board under the terms of the Financial Services Act that regulates Britain's securities trading and financial centre, the City of London.

The object of all this is to get on with the investigation and prosecution of the most damaging frauds as fast as possible from the moment it becomes clear that a major scam seems to have been in operation. That way trails have less time to grow cold and evidence is fresher when served up in court. New rules about how evidence may be presented, including the use of charts and diagrams, also resulting from Roskill's recommendations, are all part of the SFO's, the fraud squads', and the CPS's armoury, and the SFO soon started to look into the uses of computer graphics to present evidence.

At the time of setting up the SFO, City (securities) fraud was of major concern and the general expectation was that some of the frauds that would come under the 'most serious and complex' category for SFO treatment would arise in the City of London – where the Securities and Investments Board (SIB) has its own powers to carry out investigations of member bodies' (the SROs) conduct and can put unsatisfactory individual operators out of business by revoking their authorisation to offer investment and advisory services. High profile cases taken up by the SFO included the long-running Lloyd's PCW scandal, the Guinness affair, and the controversial collapse in the summer of 1988 of the Barlow Clowes gilts investment firm involving £138 million of small investors' savings (see final chapter).

The Stock Exchange (a recognised exchange and an SRO under the aegis of the SIB) has its surveillance and market supervision departments too. The latter tries to ensure orderly conduct of the markets, and the surveillance team, led by the tall, silver-haired Bob Wilkinson, keeps a sharp look-out for unusual share price movements at sensitive

---

*These bodies also have their own investigation departments. Inland Revenue offices have some powers wider than those of the police, but will liaise with them in major tax frauds. The Customs and Excise men also have wide-ranging powers and carry out many prosecutions into Excise frauds.

times in a company's year that might indicate a spot of insider dealing ahead of good or bad news. To help him, at the start of 1988 he took on board the services of a former leading Metropolitan Fraud Squad officer, Michael John. Wilkinson's task is to ensure that Exchange member firms and their staff keep the rules: that no one defrauds clients, that employees do not defraud their own firms, and that individuals do not try to line their own nests by trading on the back of, or passing on, information gained in confidence through their jobs. Geoffrey Collier, the British merchant banker who could not resist dealing on the back of information about his firm's clients' bid intentions, fell into that category.

The surveillance department has the power to make spot checks and detailed routine inspections of all Exchange member firms. Wilkinson aims to make at least two routine visits a year, but some firms may merit far more frequent attention. 'We will normally say we're coming, but we do have the right to knock on the door when the office opens and we have done it,' he once explained. 'We have a broad range of powers from a dawn raid to a chat on the phone to no-holds-barred access to their books and records.' It is a condition of Exchange membership that firms allow Wilkinson's men in when they call. Late in 1986, *Lloyd's of London* gave its chief executive similar powers.

All Stock Exchange firms must also have compliance officers who police the firm's staff and systems to ensure that the rules are kept, so that when Wilkinson's team calls by, all is well. Compliance officers must report to the Exchange cases of insider dealing uncovered by the firm. Cases of market manipulation go to the Exchange's market supervision team, overseen by Geoff Waters, who also maintains close contact with the surveillance department.

More secretive than the Exchange about the role of its members' compliance officers are the banks, whose in-house investigators and surveillance teams are kept increasingly busy. *The Bank of England* oversees the banking community. It has the Banking Act behind it to enforce liquidity and lending rules, and decides who and what can legally be called a bank. It is Britain's lender of last resort, and a power to be reckoned with when it comes to discreet policing of many financial fields. During the Guinness share support scandal of 1985-6 it intervened to tell merchant bank Morgan Grenfell, adviser to Guinness in its fateful bid for Distillers, that two of its top men must take the blame for not overseeing their pushier staff correctly – and go. When

US broking and banking house Merrill Lynch tried to hire one of them two years later, the Bank vetoed the appointment. Merrill needs a UK banking licence, so there was no argument. The man became a consultant instead of joining the executive staff. His 'crime' had been allowing the go-getters amongst his corporate finance staff at Morgan too much leeway – which one man advising Guinness appeared to have exploited beyond the bounds of legality in the share price support scheme Morgan's client operated. The Old Lady of Threadneedle Street expects men in high office to be firmer.

In the USA the chief banking authority and lender of last resort is the *Federal Reserve Bank* – the Fed. Securities trading matters are overseen by the *Securities and Exchange Commission* (SEC) whose by now formidable powers of investigation date back to its formation in 1934 to police the wave of legislation brought in from 1933 onwards in reaction to the horrors of the 1929 Wall Street crash. That was also when the first, US, anti-insider dealing law was brought in. The SEC is also a federal agency and does not come wholly under the US President's influence, retaining its political independence. Like the man at the top of the Fed, the SEC's chairman's term of office spans and survives changes of government, though he is a Presidential appointee on first assuming office.

Besides the chairman there are four other SEC commissioners, two appointed by the Democrats and two by the Republican party for balance. All five are subject to the advice and scrutiny of the US Senate, and the SEC is required to make financial disclosures and various reports to the Senate Committees. The chairman appoints the staff and there are four main divisions, overseeing investment management, corporate finance, market regulation and enforcement of the law and SEC rules. Though extensive, its powers to prosecute are civil, not criminal. If the SEC finds that the securities laws have been violated, it will file a civil law suit against the suspect. There was a time when the lack of powers to take out a criminal prosecution made it seem toothless. But latterly it has taken to working very closely with the US Attorney's office to share evidence and act together against wrongdoers. Thus Ivan Boesky, the insider trader exposed by others to the SEC, agreed to pay punitive fines and surrender his illegal profits to the SEC without actually admitting in law that he was at fault in a deal struck between his lawyers and the two authorities that gave him immunity from criminal prosecution on all but one charge – provided he had confessed all. He was finally sentenced to eighteen months in jail (the maximum term under the single charge would have been five). Any attempt to hide some of his profits or otherwise lying to the SEC would have made the deal with the Attorney's office null and void.

The SEC's policy is that it never brings a case until it is pretty sure of success – with the result nowadays that many actions are settled out of court with the culprit handing over his fines and profits without admitting guilt. The SEC reckons it saves the US taxpayer a small fortune in civil court fees this way. But in criminal cases brought by the US Attorney, it can act as *amicus curiae* to the court to give advice and evidence and supply interpretations of the federal securities laws. In this role – its office of General Counsel – it can also mediate in disputes between investors and their agents or brokers, and defend the SEC's own staff against angry subjects of investigations.

The SEC has been greatly strengthened by being allowed to levy punitive fines of up to three times the illegal profits made on insider dealing – and to fine the suppliers of price-sensitive information whether or not they benefited from passing it on. And its investigations are wide-ranging – from examining phone and credit card records to checking out personal links when looking for sources of a suspect's inside information.

Information about unusual or suspicious share trades around the time of sensitive information being made public is passed onto the SEC by the *New York Stock Exchange* (NYSE) whose Stock Watch computer monitoring system records all trades and 'flags' any unusual trading volume or trading patterns in any stock. The NYSE investigates first, like the UK Stock Exchange surveillance department, starting with the member firms who executed the trades to see who dealt and why. All NYSE firms have to keep such trading information and names and addresses of clients, preferably in computer-readable form, which the NYSE can demand at any time. The NYSE's powers extend to being able to take depositions, and has the power to bar from the securities industry anyone who fails to co-operate until he or she agrees to help. To a degree, it also relies on voluntary informants to get proof of illegal trading.

Most NYSE disciplinary matters go to a panel headed by an NYSE official and two others who are the defendant's peers in the industry. It rules whether the individual, who has an attorney and the right of reply to all charges, is guilty or innocent, and the penalties it can hand out vary from censure to fines of up to $25,000 per charge on individuals, and $100,000 on firms.

If evidence of insider dealing (like a link between the buyer or seller of stock 'flagged' by Stock Watch with someone in the know within a member firm or an investment bank) is found, the SEC is alerted. The NYSE had already reported suspicious patterns in trading from Bank Leu's Nassau branch to the SEC long before the customer concerned, Dennis Levine (who then led the investigators to Boesky), was finally trapped. Investigations were initially hampered by the bank's offshore status and Bahamian secrecy laws. But the Swiss bank, Bank Leu, also operates in the USA and was not keen to lose its banking licence there for failing to co-operate with the US securities authorities.

The SEC sharpened its teeth, wits and methods a good deal in the 1980s after the boom in mergers and acquisitions spawned a feeling amongst young Wall Streeters that the rules were being rewritten, if not thrown out of the window, in the rush for profit – for the firm, and then, as ethical boundaries were eroded, for the individual. The defence people rehearsed to themselves for insider trading on inside information was 'everybody's doing it, and nobody's getting caught'. The arrests of Ivan Boesky, Dennis Levine and others in the second half of the decade quashed that feeling and shook the sparkle out of many of the too-complacent younger stars on the Street.

The illegal games on Wall Street pale beside some of the scams seen in Canada on the *Vancouver Stock Exchange* (the VSE), before it cleaned up its act. Banco Ambrosiano may have been the best thriller of the financial genre, but a pretty good potboiler could be woven out of the VSE's New Cinch affair. False gold assay reports, million-dollar gains and losses and murder were just some of the ingredients. The assay reports were faked (the samples were doctored with added gold) to make it appear that a small Canadian company, New Cinch Uranium Mines, had struck it rich with the other yellow metal in the Orogrande in New Mexico. This was in late 1979. As the doctored assay results were released to the Vancouver Stock Exchange during the summer and autumn of 1980, where New Cinch shares had just gained a listing, its share price soared: from C$2.50 to C$29.5 in just four months. The early investors made a lot of money.

One keen buyer of New Cinch – 17% of the company – was Willroy Mines. It spent C$27.5 million on shares and warrants. Then the truth came out: that the gold assay results were fiction, that gold had been added to get good results, and the shares collapsed. By December 1981, New Cinch shares were trading at only 37 cents each.

Willroy sold out its stake as the shares tumbled, getting C$4 million, for a C$23.5 million loss on that investment (and later became part of Lac Minerals of Toronto). But in February 1981 it sued to get its money back: going not only for the officers of the company, its promoters and associates, the owner and staff of the assay company – but also suing the VSE for listing the company when, as it had since emerged, some VSE officials had been aware of conflicting and far less favourable assay reports which they had not released to the public at the time.

The story got nastier down in Phoenix, Arizona, where a young man called Michael Opp, who had worked at the company where the assays had been faked and who might have been a useful witness for Willroy, came to a sudden, untimely and violent end. Someone kicked his door down in the middle of the night and shot him in the head. The man later charged with the killing, said to have resulted from a row over a $24 television set and a marijuana deal, was called Hoyt Trujillo.

Trujillo had been 'shopped' by his girlfriend in a plea-bargaining session with the Maricopa County Police. But then she ran away and retracted her statement by letter. Trujillo was eventually acquitted. Before his trial, Opp's bereaved parents had apparently found a rambling eighteen-page document that explained why he feared for his life hidden under the carpet in his room.

It now seems unlikely that Opp ever wrote it. But it was put together by someone who knew a great deal about what had gone on between officials of New Cinch and the assay people – and who wanted the matter exposed. The letter claimed the assay company had been persuaded to falsify the assay in return for some of the profits from share dealings as the New Cinch price soared, as it surely would (a cinch, in fact). There was a great deal more besides about the bizarre personal lives of the principal players in the scam, in which Opp was said to have participated to some degree: drink, drugs and violent homosexual encounters, allied to promises of a slice of some of the profits on New Cinch share deals.

Whatever the provenance of the letter, Opp had often told his mother that he knew too much about the assay company, and that he had even been threatened with death if he said what he knew.

Who killed Michael Opp has never been satisfactorily resolved. But his death, and the letter, were widely publicised in Vancouver, and the New Cinch scandal led to a major shake-up of the VSE – some of whose officials were guilty at best of negligence and at worst of collusion in allowing New Cinch shares to be listed before seeing independent assay reports.

The shake-up was overdue: the VSE had become a byword for 'ramps' where worthless stock in small, often newly formed and floated companies soared in inexplicable demand, only to collapse once the share paper had been offloaded for handsome profits to some over-eager, but innocent, investor expecting in turn to make his fortune from it. Several oil and gas exploration companies quoted on the VSE acquired overseas listings in London in the early 1980s – only for their value to sink like a stone once UK investors were locked in. In most cases this was because the oil and gas industry in Canada slumped into the doldrums just then. But some of these outfits looked like ramps from the start. Greedy investors got caught by both sets of circumstances – forgetting the first rule of finance: that the return you expect to get on an investment is a measure of the degree of risk you are taking with your money in making it.

Willroy decided to sue in the New Cinch case, with spectacular results. But many organisations and businesses are reluctant to go straight to the police when they first suspect fraud for lack of definite information and fear that a police investigation may attract unwanted attention or publicity early on, scaring customers away. Banks are especially twitchy about word getting out that they have been defrauded, and companies may not want their trade creditors to know.

And so it is that, as in many of the best whodunnits, organisations turn to the service of *the private investigator* – or consultant, as many prefer to be called these days. Forget the image of the lone gumshoe, with belted mac and a witty line in repartee masking a befuddled intellect that is, nevertheless, still capable of flashes of extraordinary insight – and a dash of lust for any female villain or victim. Today's confidential fraud investigator is most likely to be an ex-fraud squad officer or even former secret service man running a highly successful advisory business. He leads a select team well versed in the arcane workings of accountancy, computers, the electronic movement of money around the banking system, as well as how to vet staff, debug boardrooms, spot the industrial spy in the ranks, track fake telexes, pinpoint who makes counterfeit perfumes in Hackney or Brazil, and zero in on the bit of arson behind the fraudulent insurance claim, for example. The private consultant's task is to find out what is, or has been, going on; how to stop it; and to advise the client on how to prevent it happening again. He will also give advice on the chances – and wisdom – of a successful prosecution of the perpetrator.

One of the biggest US private agencies is Jules Kroll's Kroll Associates, based in New York but with offices in other major centres. Its work for the financial services sector ranges from tracing missing assets to advice on mega-takeovers and uncovering art fraud.

Private investigators are perhaps best placed to see how the pattern of fraud has changed in recent years because not only are they big businesses' frequent first port of call when trouble is suspected, but they are also freer to investigate internationally than are most national police forces. The police are hampered by differences in legal systems and a host of problems relating to who prosecutes, and where. (This is despite the important services of international police co-ordinating body Interpol, whose work is described later on.)

British and US private investigators report that fraud is not only becoming more international – in that one fraud may range over several countries – but that it is becoming more organised. The big crime groups are moving in. 'Over the last few years product counterfeiting, for example – intellectual property crime – has been on the increase. It grew rapidly over five to six years and is now steadying off. It has passed its peak, but now you are getting big organised conspiracies instead. It's consolidating,' explained Vince Carratu, head of one of the larger and longer-established investigative consultancies, Carratu International, in October 1986. Based in southern Britain, 80% of its work lies overseas. Like many of his calling, Carratu – a bluff, stocky, moustachioed and outwardly jolly man – is a former policeman, ex-Scotland Yard, who went private in the early 1960s. Nowadays, 'bank fraud is very much on the increase', he reports. 'We are finding that more and more of the organised criminal elements or groups now realise they can make far more money out of fraud than other activities, and the chances of being caught are that much slimmer, and the penalty is lighter. You never hear of a fraudsman going to prison for life or twenty years, but they get away with far larger amounts than the bank robber. The [British] authorities are very slow off the mark. The writing was on the wall years ago.'

The rise in bank fraud is facilitated by the reluctance of many British banks to blow the whistle loud and alert each other to a potential problem. This has international repercussions. One major fraud against a large Hong Kong bank was perpetrated by a fraudster who had already swindled a major UK clearing bank of millions of pounds. Instead of alerting the Hong Kong bank when it proposed to take him on thereafter – unaware of his particular skill – the UK bank, in the words of one observer, was 'delighted to get rid of him'. 'I just wonder whether they are not burying their heads in the sand. How do you create a deterrent if you are not seen to do justice?' asked one seasoned fraud investigator.

One man who does encourage banks to alert each other, if in the course of one investigation he finds evidence of fraud against another bank, is John Davis of Farleigh Consultants in Croydon. Like Carratu, he is a former police officer, as are all Farleigh's investigators. 'Banks tend to regard it as fair game if they have a loan facility likely to go wrong, and another bank takes it over and asks no questions,' Davis confirms. 'I've tried to create a better form of liaison between banks, and if in investigation I find another bank involved, I go to my client and say, can I tell them?' When he gets a go-ahead – and that is not always the case – he finds the other bank 'is always grateful', not to mention surprised, for such courtesy.

There have been moves to create better liaison between banks from within the banking community too. As Carratu reports: 'Banks got together to form the International Banking Security Association a few years ago. It is not a secret organisation but it is not publicly spoken of, and amazingly quite a number of British banks don't belong because they feel they should do their own thing – which is disastrous because the exchange of information is so vital. But it's very important that responsible people at banks realise that unless they are prepared to co-operate, they will be victims, time and time again. On the Continent, banks consider themselves a group and work together – especially in the Benelux countries.'

Since Carratu spoke those words, new British banking laws have been introduced that spell out UK banks' duties to pass some information on to third parties – and the penalties for failing to do so (see Chapter 11).

The kind of work private firms are called in to do is wide-ranging. Farleigh Consultants' list is fairly typical, offering, for example, to look into the infringement of trademarks, industrial espionage, breach of employee contract, fraud or theft by staff and management (even directors), and will even vet prospective staff for corporate clients. For insurance groups it will check that theft or personal injury claims are valid. Banks might ask it to check suspected fraudulent loan applications. Other services can include advice on personal security for key personnel, how to protect gold bullion, or finding bugging devices. The much larger Carratu International's brochure offers a similar range of services. And, as it says, investigators are always discreet. Fraudsters are naturally secretive; many of their pursuers are equally shadowy.

So how do they do their job? 'Generally speaking, the client knows they have a problem which they can't handle themselves and do not know what to do about,' an investigator explains. 'We have to identify how much of it is internal or external, so we take statements, identify documents, look for forgeries – very much as a fraud officer would.' It is methodical, routine, thorough, often desk-bound work. At this stage people are often more willing to talk to a private, independent investigator than they might be to tell a police officer what they know, or think they know.

At the end of the work, a report goes back to the client, supported by documents, schedules, diagrams, flow charts – plus advice on whether or not a criminal offence has been committed and if it should be reported to the police. If the client takes this route, the private investigator can liaise with the investigating officer and may well appear to give evidence in court. Most companies prefer to go about things in this order because that way the investigation remains within their control and the information it yields belongs to them first and foremost. 'If the police are called in right away, the company loses control of the investigation. This way, the client knows what is going on, and at the end of the day he can decide whether or not he wants to involve the authorities,' explained one seasoned fraud consultant. 'Then when the matter is reported to the police there is sufficient evidence and the prosecution will be supported by access to the relevant company documents.'

When it comes to investigating counterfeiting, the client's main aim is to see the counterfeiter go out of business – at least in the line of those copied products. Carratu, an expert in this field and scourge of the counterfeiter, does not entirely buy the argument that counterfeiters are always stealing market share from the makers of the real thing, however – especially where high priced items are being copied for the low-budget hoi polloi. 'Look at Cartier watches. Counterfeiters produce thousands to sell in pubs, cafés and railway stations. None of the people who would normally buy a Cartier watch for £1,200 or £2,000 is likely to buy one in a pub or a station forecourt. So Cartier haven't lost the money. But they have in the sense that it costs a fortune to get the fakes off the market.'

Fake goods can damage the real manufacturer's reputation and may even be dangerous – as has been the case with goods ranging from copies of branded electrical plugs to useless car brakes, fake contraceptive pills, poor quality aero-engine components and lethal faked brands of alcohol. Carratu's collection of examples of the faked products his organisation has snaffled and stopped is legendary in the business: a cabinet full of famous brand names and rich men's toys. In the first eight months of 1986 alone, Carratu International collared:

36,000 bottles of various counterfeited perfumes;
almost 500,000 cartons of labels designed for counterfeit goods;
24,000 empty bottles copying famous brand shapes;
2,600 copies of branded shirts;
7,000 handbags;
over six miles of counterfeit cloth copying designers' work.

'How do you value that?' Carratu asked from behind a long, low, neat desk in his Surrey headquarters. 'One Brazilian counterfeiter making a famous perfume had a wider range than its own. He even improved on one pack and sold mini versions of their products to the airlines.'

That operation was run by a man in Sâo Paolo, who had built himself a mock castle and a large modern factory out of the proceeds. By all accounts the prefume he made was very good. But he stole the brand name to make his profits, and the true owners saw to it that he went out of business after they got wise to him.

The penalty for the counterfeiting was 'only minimal. Unfortunately people look on counterfeiting as helping the man on the street to buy things cheaper,' Carratu said. 'Kids go to the market for a "Lacoste" shirt. But it's ludicrous: Lacoste is a good quality shirt and its trademark is famous. Why should someone be allowed to import cheap nasty shirts from the Philippines and put a crocodile on them and sell them for a few pounds more?' The buyer may think he is getting

Lacoste or Lacoste look-alike cheaply, but he is often paying too much for sheer tat.

When it comes to electrical equipment, drugs and motor spares, 'consumers are gambling with their families' and their own lives by buying very cheaply off a stall'. Even reputable stores have been conned by suppliers and ended up selling counterfeit products on occasion, though these tend to be the better quality ones or they would be spotted sooner.

The work of anti-counterfeit investigators is not helped in Britain by there being 'no criminal offence in the UK of counterfeiting. You can do them under the Trade Descriptions Act for conspiracy to cheat and defraud but many cases get thrown out due to a decision which says you cannot conspire to cheat and defraud in the UK when the people being defrauded are overseas. So we need legislation more like the USA's. Or we have to go through the civil courts for trade mark infringement.'

Investigators like Carratu also have links to a *Counterfeiting Intelligence Bureau* (CIB) set up by the International Chambers of Commerce with others, and a sister body of the International Maritime Bureau (whose work is described in the chapter on the *Salem* affair). Run by Jack Heslop, another former policeman, the CIB pursues investigations for clients and provides an information and intelligence base from which to watch the pattern of counterfeiting around the world. Unlike the private investigators, it will help clients to negotiate with major counterfeiters where the legal position is confusing, perhaps because the country the counterfeiter operates from has no anti-counterfeiting or trade mark infringement laws. It has done a lot in this line with the Taiwanese government, for example, to encourage new laws and persuade some counterfeiters to go legitimate and make products properly under adequately protected licensing agreements with the owner of the brand name.

Carratu disapproves of turning selected counterfeiters into *bona fide* manufacturers, seeing this approach almost as an incentive to others to start copying goods. But for Third World nations graduating to more developed status and with increasing technical skills, this route may be one way of earning legitimate hard currency and joining the industrialised world on a more secure footing – and gaining extra markets for the manufacturers of the original goods.

The private investigators take a lot of the strain off the police, and relations are, by-and-large, good. As fraud grows, national police forces have had to find extra manpower to cope – and it is not always easy to persuade governments to find the extra money to hire and train them. Nor do many of the traditional entrants to the force come with the training needed to combat financial crimes – knowledge of accountancy, or the securities markets, for example – already under their belts. The Metropolitan Fraud Squad in London, under Commander Malcolm Campbell, took the need to gain these skills seriously in the mid-1980s, however, opting to work alongside a panel of accountants ready and willing to be co-opted onto individual fraud cases, for example, and looking into the use of specialist computer programs to store and analyse information.

The leader in this field is the *Ministry of Defence Police*'s serious crimes squad, which developed its own highly sophisticated computer system for use in investigating procurement frauds (systematic, long-term cases of overcharging for defence contracts by British and other manufacturers). In early 1988, the Met was hoping to be able to buy the program for its own use; and the American FBI seconded an officer to work with the MoD team and learn about the system. International co-operation like this is growing, but for many years the fraud squad officer has had access to the work of overseas police forces on the same criminals through *Interpol*.

Interpol's General Secretariat is an international organisation with 141 member countries. Each country's police force provides a National Central Bureau: London's is Scotland Yard. Only France does not belong, although the organisation is headquartered in Paris. The Secretariat provides a radio network which allows officers investigating a case – criminal or fraud – to be put into contact with any officer in another country investigating the same people, or aspects of the same crime, without having to go through the normal diplomatic channels. So an officer in Britain working on a case with a German angle, say, contacts his national central bureau at New Scotland Yard. The Yard goes through the Paris HQ's system to contact the West German national central bureau in Wiesbaden. This relays the UK request to the appropriate German police officer, and the two investigations have made contact.

Interpol is essentially a co-ordinating operation. It does not take an active part in investigations, itself, but it does have a number of divisions specialising in linking up certain types of criminal investigations. These include a drugs subdivision and a fraud unit – each with their own liaison officers who maintain contact with appropriate regions of the world and help to co-ordinate international investigations. Interpol keeps an index of all those whom it knows are being investigated somewhere in the world, so all the investigations can easily be cross-referred.

'It's not always a full picture, but bits and pieces of information primarily coming to us through telex traffic. We index names of companies and individuals under investigation by member states – if we are informed of it,' an Interpol spokesman explained. 'If there is a major bank fraud, and we see the fraudster is working simultaneously in several countries, we will get all the police together to develop a strategy. We very much play an advisory role. For example, there is the FOPAC group (it is a French mnemonic that translates as 'funds derived from criminal activities') working on the issue of tracing and identifying the assets of organised crime.'

FOPAC developed model legislation with a series of recommendations that would also give police access to financial information about the criminals and allow different police forces to exchange such information. The model, the result of a working meeting in the Caribbean, was sent to all member states. Interpol also sent it to the Customs Co-operation Council, a ninety-eight-state body based in Belgium, and to the United Nations in Vienna as an addendum to the UN's international convention on narcotics.

Interpol often makes recommendations to the UN and other bodies, but does not participate in the politics of drafting the international treaties that may follow. But it has compiled another useful compendium: a Financial Assets encyclopaedia which lists all member states who have notified it of their laws and procedures for seizing criminal assets – another useful tool for the fraud investigator. And it liaises also with the new Chicago-based International Banking Security Association which looks into the ways of combating the fast-moving electronic transmission of fraudulently gained funds. Interpol is a remarkable effort of international co-operation. Not even two world wars have destroyed it, though they did suspend it. Set up in 1911, the co-ordinating operation was out of action for the First World War and not restarted until 1922. After the Second World War, it re-opened more promptly in 1945.

A more recently established example of international co-operation, concentrating particularly on fraud cases and drug-trafficking, and one which is empowered to undertake investigations itself, is the *Commonwealth Secretariat's Commercial Crime Unit.*

Its brief is to prevent crime as much as to discover it. Its officers – whose skills range from oriental martial arts to English law degrees, as well as intelligence work and financial expertise – travel the world as and when necessary, and work closely with designated officers in the law enforcement agencies of the Commonwealth countries (such as Nigeria, India and the offshore centres like Grand Cayman), and some others including the USA. Through Interpol, the unit also has access to all relevant police records and intelligence; but most of its officers' extensive knowledge of the complex and murky world of commercial crime – be it securities frauds, banking fraud, commodities fraud, counterfeiting or computer fiddles – is based on their own information and wide network of contacts.

Since 1986 it has been empowered to act as the central co-ordinating authority for mutual criminal assistance on commercial and organised crime investigations throughout the Commonwealth; and increasingly liaises with other nations, particularly the USA and Japan, in combating organised crime – from the Mafia to the Japanese Yakuza, and Chinese Triads in Taiwan. It now splits into four divisions: two investigatory units looking into various cases, headed by a full-time officer with seconded staff (policemen, intelligence officers from Commonwealth countries); one intelligence unit tracing about twenty suspected fraud operations; and a training and technical services arm run jointly with the Crown Agents.

The unit targets and watches suspected fraudsters, alerts their potential fraud victims, answers requests for help or information, runs checks on financiers for governments borrowing money, and so on. In 1982, its first full year of operation, it unmasked attempted frauds totalling £11 billion on a very slender budget. In 1986, its brief was officially extended to cover drug trafficking and abuse – since drug money is so widely used to finance additional, commercial crime (and vice versa). The unit was set up in November 1981, after four years of mounting concern amongst Commonwealth law ministers that commercial crime was getting out of hand. It was back in 1977 that the Ministers, meeting in Winnipeg in Canada, first openly voiced their governments' concern that the rising tide of commercial crime, seen since the Second World War, had grave implications for the economies of some of the poorer or more financially embarrassed member states.

The risks of poor nations becoming poorer – and therefore more unstable – because of the activities of sophisticated financial crooks and conmen on a major scale, were not lost on the ruling governments of the day. So the Commonwealth Secretary-General was asked to look into how the 'special bonds' between Commonwealth countries could be put to work to combat fraud and other commercial crimes.

The most immediate result was a lengthy consultant's report on international co-operations to combat economic and commercial crime, whose recommendations were endorsed by the law ministers' 1980 meeting in Barbados – and the Commercial Crime Unit was conceived. It was originally meant to operate as a catalyst to co-operation between Commonwealth law enforcement agencies, but right from the start it was deluged with requests for direct help with specific cases or for information about individuals involved in particular deals, actual or proposed. This flood of requests, combined with the fact that many developing nations did not have a police force with the manpower to deal with commercial crime, meant that the law ministers decided in 1983 (meeting in Sri Lanka this time) to give the unit more money and more people, and formally extended its services into loss prevention. Various member countries also agreed to second staff to the unit for a year, to help out and to bring valuable experience and expertise in combating commercial crime back home. Then in 1986, ministers meeting in Harare to agree a scheme for mutual assistance in criminal matters similar to the European convention on the same, giving the unit the wider co-ordinating powers for the scheme described above, on page 189.

To some extent the unit now provides an alternative service to Interpol (which always supported the unit with its own services). It is also recognised and helped by the Customs Co-operation Council, the EEC, the Association of South-East Asian Nations, the International Chambers of Commerce and the International Banking Security Association. So its net is wide and it carries clout. 'The unit is increasingly operating as a supra-national investigating body on instruction at the highest level,' reported its head officer in summer 1988, 'though its operational budget remains small.'

In the more than 1,000 requests for help that came to the unit in the first few years of its life, were some very large and serious fraud attempts. The unit is highly sensitive about saying which countries have been in danger of being defrauded, or have actually lost money.

But, with a few names and some rather large figures left out, it is possible to give a few examples of the type of work it has done. A Chief Minister of one state asked his Commissioner of Police to find out more about an American and Swiss corporation that his government was about to get involved with in a 'substantial' (many millions of pounds) way. In its own words, 'The unit was able to provide information showing that the principal of the Swiss company was associated with a Mafia family and had been connected with a series of international frauds though they had never been convicted. In this particular enquiry the Swiss and American governments willingly gave a great deal of co-operation.'

Another request for help came from the Attorney-General of a British dependency. He wanted to know about the background of some people who had approached his government 'with a view to obtaining bank licences for a number of offshore operations.' The unit checked, and told him that 'persons associated with these individuals were highly undesirable and the licences were declined'. The dependency concerned did not want to be used as a money laundering or fraud depositary.

On one occasion, the unit received information about a major shipment of counterfeit video and audio tapes, and it co-ordinated an operation to track the shipment to its destination. The consignment was watched from Singapore, through Spain, to Nigeria, where it was seized by the Nigerian police, who also arrested the conspirators.

The unit has also given legal advice – on, for example, whether travellers' cheques could be considered valuable securities for the purposes of a criminal prosecution in Brunei. The answer was 'yes', and a successful prosecution followed. And it will help to trace money that has already gone missing: in one case a nationalised industry of one country had been defrauded and the national police force requested help in tracing the cash. The unit found it in another Commonwealth jurisdiction and arranged a court action to freeze the money and then get it transferred back to the outfit it really belonged to.

Behind these bare facts lie plenty of thrills and spills, and lots of hard work by the investigators. This is the slightly James Bond-ish end of the official fraud investigators' business: not licensed to kill but certainly licensed to operate somewhat covertly in order to keep member nations' goods and finances where they belong.

As well as working with other countries' more traditional police forces, the unit likes to touch base with other agencies – in the UK, for instance, it would maintain links with the Bank of England as well as the fraud squads, the International Maritime Bureau and the Counterfeiting Intelligence Bureau – and it keeps in touch with various self-regulatory bodies like London's International Stock Exchange. It is also on friendly terms with a handful of investigative and financial journalists.

In 1985, the unit was asked to use its intelligence network and database to provide vetting procedures for small states operating as offshore banking or investment centres and to check applicants for licences to do business from such places. This was an effort to combat organised crime's tendency to use these places to set up shell banks for money-laundering purposes. Partly because the unit has often found links with organised crime and drug money in the fraud attempts it has dealt with, it was a fairly natural step when the law ministers asked it to extend its growing brief to looking into cases of drug trafficking and to trace where that money washes up.

The unit is also supposed to train people from Commonwealth countries in the skills of combating commercial crime. With only four top officials and half-a-dozen seconded staff, the unit at first tactfully read this to mean running regular symposia on aspects of commercial crime and law enforcement – which it still does every year in Cambridge in association with that university, and the Centre for Commercial Law Studies of London University, Queen Mary College and the Secretariat of the International Chambers of Commerce. Law ministers, attorney-generals and other legal eagles, trade officials, top policemen, bankers, accountants and investigators from all kinds of business operations descend from around the world on the calm of a Cambridge college for a four-to five-day series of sessions on the hot topics of the moment. Valuable information is exchanged, contacts made during the sessions and in the bars afterwards, where it is not uncommon to see a brace of attorney-generals cheerfully trading names and fraud stories into the small hours. There have also been regional symposia held in association with the Crown Agents, in Singapore and elsewhere in South-East Asia, and the unit sets up courses in various countries on specific topics (money-laundering, customs fraud, and so on) when requested.

One area where the unit has found drug trafficking and fraud to overlap lies in the ingenious methods used to pay for drugs: for example, not in hard currency, but in valuable information. One case investigated started with a call from a non-Commonwealth country where a regulatory agency wanted help to trace some telephone calls from a Commonwealth country. Investigations in co-operation with the national police force revealed that professional advisers with price-sensitive information about certain companies, whose shares were traded on the securities market, were being used to pay for cocaine-dealing by being pressured into passing on this information to individuals in the Commonwealth country. They passed the information on in turn to their drug associates back home, who used it to time dealings in the shares concerned – and made money on the back of it. Drug traffickers were being paid with 'inside' information and no money was being seen to change hands. The proceeds did not even need laundering since they were simply the profits on some remarkably timely and successful share dealing. But the regulatory body spotted the success-rate, and grew curious. There have been other examples of corporate officials being bribed or blackmailed by organised criminals to supply price-sensitive, inside information.

Stocks and shares are favourite vehicles for laundering money, but Stock Exchange member firms in Britain who suspect their clients' money comes from drug dealing now have to report their suspicions to the police. In a letter from the Stock Exchange Council Secretary, Martin Fidler, in October 1986, all Stock Exchange member firms were reminded that, under Section 24 of the newly passed Drug Trafficking Offences Act, failure to pass on such suspicions is now a criminal offence punishable by fines or up to fourteen years' imprisonment.

Fidler advised member firms to spill the beans straight away, for delays would be hard to explain. He reminded them that the Act absolves them from being accused of any breach of confidence whether their suspicions proved right or wrong. The letter must have startled some of the more complacent members of the financial fraternity, whose attitude had tended to be, 'I don't care where my clients' money comes from as long as I am not asked to do anything illegal with it.'

The tide is gradually turning away from just trusting people to be honest and efficient to ensuring that they are, by introducing stricter, better systems (in-house and regulatory) and by letting people know that someone will be round to investigate and penalise the culprits when the rules are suspected of being infringed and abused.

9

Looking for God's Banker

Investigating fraud can have all the ingredients of a good whodunnit. Indeed, fraud cases can also become whodunnits in the sense that the occasional corpse bobs up. Remember 'God's banker' – Roberto Calvi – whose lifeless figure was found hanging from scaffolding beneath Blackfriars Bridge in London, with a brick or two in his pocket for good measure?

The bank he chaired and ran, the Banco Ambrosiano in Milan, was out of pocket to the tune of US $1.56 billion. Even more scandalous, most of the money had been loaned to the Vatican's bank, the Institute per le Opere di Religione (IOR for short); or, to be more accurate, to Panamanian and Liechtenstein 'shell' companies that the IOR apparently owned, in one way or another. The money seeped on through these shell operations and much of it had vanished.

At first the British investigators and authorities who had to react to the corpse dangling under Blackfriars Bridge thought Calvi had committed suicide. His bank was under investigation in Milan and the man had problems. But the manner of his demise – those bricks, and that bridge – and the emergence of his links with the scandal-ridden P2 pseudo-masonic lodge in Italy, run by a deeply sinister man called Licio Gelli, led many to speculate that he had been done away with.

Gelli was a Tuscan businessman who, amongst other things, allegedly dealt in arms and pharmaceuticals on the one hand, and people's reputations on the other. He masterminded the P2 lodge and its network, to which important members of the Italian political, judicial, military and financial worlds belonged. He was also believed to have sold the French Exocet missiles to Argentina used against the British Task Force during the Falklands War.

Roberto Calvi came to be completely under his thumb. God's Banker also became the devil's, allowing Gelli and his colleagues to spirit millions of other people's dollars out of Italy illegally. Calvi was used to provide and man the conduit for funds to bankroll Gelli's other, overseas interests. Once involved he would have been wide open to blackmail and other pressures to keep the sluicegates open.

Calvi once nurtured ambitions to enter the more glamorous worlds of publishing and the media. Under his leadership the Banco Ambrosiano was to participate in the reconstruction of Italy's biggest publishing house, Rizzoli, which bought the *Corriere della Sera* and used the paper as collateral – in hock to the Banco Ambrosiano. But Calvi did not foresee that the flow of events would also lead to his posthumous fame as the suspect subject of several dramatic books. It was not quite the role in publishing that he had envisaged.

He had learnt some of his slick financial skills from Michele Sindona, a financier who in 1980 was convicted in America of fraud and perjury and given a twenty-five-year sentence, after a new Swiss-American Treaty on Mutual Assistance in Criminal Matters had paved the way for US investigators to take a look at Sindona's Swiss bank records in Zurich and Geneva. These showed the passage of $15 million misappropriated from two Italian banks that Sindona controlled, via Switzerland, to the USA where he used the money to buy stock in two American businesses, the First National Bank and the Talcott National Corporation.

The $15 million had not officially been loaned to Sindona so he had filed false statements with the powerful and strict Securities and Exchange Commission in the USA to say that the monies were his own. Events conspired against him, however, and after his 1980 conviction – thanks to the evidence of the Swiss bank accounts – for conspiring to defraud US investors and filing false statements, he was extradited to Italy in 1984 to face charges there of financial fraud, and was convicted. He also died there, in prison, from cyanide poisoning. The fatal dose was in a cup of coffee. Suicide courtesy of understanding business contacts, or murder to keep his mouth shut? Either way he slipped through the authorities' fingers in the end. Others were to follow suit.

What Calvi had learned from Sindona was how to get round a tiresome Italian banking law that forbade retail (high street) banks to own non-banking interests (and vice versa). They did it by setting up a network of offshore shell companies in foreign tax havens that took a more relaxed view of financial affairs than many European countries.

Money was channelled from the Italian bank into the shell

companies through numbered or coded accounts in different banks. The shell companies would be owned by the banker and his friends, their identity masked by the use of these coded accounts, and the money would be used for financial schemes and deals that would have been illegal in Italy and some other European jurisdictions. The deals might be done by the offshore shell company that the money first flowed into or, to cover the trail better, might be channelled through another, similar outfit first.

This wheeze paved the way for further serious fraud. For example, if the money was put into stocks and shares or other assets that could be moved around from one shell company to another . . . and another . . . at increasingly inflated prices each time, then the owners stood to gain high profits from each transaction. Suppose shell company A buys shares in 'Italco' at 50p each, sells them to B company for 75p, and B sells them on to C at 100p. That makes considerable paper profits for the owners of A, B and C – who are, of course, all the same people – while absorbing, and supporting, their flow of secret money.

To ensure that the market price of the stocks and shares involved was never in danger of slipping too low back home in Italy, the Italian bank controlled by the financier(s) involved would start to buy the stock, apparently quite independently, on the Milan stock market. Since this is a relatively 'thin' market – that is to say, where securities change hands in fairly small parcels of shares – the price could easily be forced up or kept high by even quite modest buying forays from time to time. Moreover, as other unsuspecting investors saw the stock move up, they were tempted to share in its rising fortunes and would buy in at these artificially inflated prices. This allowed the crooked financiers to offload stock in careful stages, and convert their spiralling paper profits 'earned' on the original transfers, into hard and outwardly legitimate cash.

It was a clever scam that depended on thin markets, a good understanding of the Milan exchange, and careful manipulation of share prices. For a while it was very successful.

What made the Banco Ambrosiano's activities along these lines so shocking was not just the way Calvi and his associates defrauded Calvi's own bank and ripped off Milan's investors, but the fact that many of the deals had been set up through shell companies linked to the Vatican bank – the IOR.

The inference of the ordinary observer was that someone at the IOR must have known what was going on. The finger of suspicion pointed most at its chairman since 1971, the muscular Cardinal Paul Marcinkus – who denied all knowledge of Calvi's financial shenanigans, saying that Calvi had abused the IOR's financial naïveté for his own purposes. The Vatican is a separate state from the rest of Italy, and for a long time Marcinkus was able to shelter behind its walls and avoid answering embarrassing questions about what happened.

Italian businesses frequently operate like members of one big family, holding each other's shares. In many ways, joining Gelli's P2 lodge was a way into that family – a membership card, as one observer later put it. But even tightly knit family groups can founder at times. What ruined Calvi's speculation and his friends' schemes in the end was a series of changes in Italian law. In 1976, Italy made the illegal export of currency a criminal offence rather than a civil 'administrative' one as before. Calvi's scam had grown so big that the offshore shell companies had even borrowed extra money abroad for their speculative activities. The loans were repaid from time to time with the cash spirited out of Italy through the trustees.

The new law meant that Calvi could no longer risk paying off foreign debts with Lire spirited out of Italy but would have to repay it with more new money borrowed overseas, as the old debts fell due. Most of the borrowings were in US dollars. But the dollar was rising against the Lire just then: so the value of these debts kept rising in Lire. Worst of all, the 1976 law was retroactive: it applied to funds moved before the law was introduced as well as after that date. That gave Calvi a real headache. For by 1978, the Italian authorities were investigating his Banco Ambrosiano *for the third time*. The first two investigations, in 1971 and 1974, had led to a collapse in the bank's shares that Calvi had seized as an opportunity quietly to buy its stock through his shell companies.

Now the investigators were back, and this time they found evidence of Calvi's web of companies and crossholdings. What the inspectors could not prove, they certainly suspected – and Calvi, now a worried man, decided to do a little restructuring of his empire to cover his tracks more convincingly. It involved, in a complicated chain, increasing the Banco Ambrosiano's own share capital from 20 billion Lire to 30 billion. That meant the shell companies had to borrow even more money to allow Calvi to retain control of the bank as well as keeping the share price up on the Milan exchange.

Then, in June 1980, a real banking client, construction group Mario Genghini, went bust. Of its 450 billion Lire of debts, a third had been borrowed from Banco Ambrosiano. This disaster came just days before Italian investigators decided a major Calvi deal had indeed been an illegal export of currency – and Calvi was told to surrender his passport. The net was closing in on him.

He managed to keep out of its coils for a bit longer, however, despite another new law, insisting that Italian banks could only own foreign, non-banking holding companies if the Banca d'Italia checked them out first. Even then, they had to be based in countries where there was also proper banking supervision. The chain of shell companies Calvi used did not match these criteria.

That same year, 1981, the Milan stock market's ruling body insisted that Banco Ambrosiano shares had to move from being traded on the less-regulated, over-the-counter market (where shares were only traded once a week) to the open main market. This made it much harder for Calvi to exercise any control over movements in his bank's share price. Finally he could not keep all the balls in the air any longer. The whole charade collapsed and, in May 1981, Calvi was jailed for illegal currency exports.

Astonishingly, the bank kept going even with its chief executive behind bars, albeit briefly. For Calvi was soon out on bail, pending appeal, though he had to hand over his passport again. The appeal hearing was set for June 1982. Investigations into his bank's overseas interests were widening, however, and – even though Marcinkus and the IOR now helped out the increasingly desperate Calvi by providing 'letters of comfort' confirming that the Vatican's bank was the owner of nominee companies in Panama and Liechtenstein that had borrowed money from Banco Ambrosiano – Calvi's associates told him he now had to solve his problems for himself.

It was getting too risky for everyone else involved to help him out further. He tried: seeking respectability by bringing in a new deputy chairman – none other than the chief executive of the famous Olivetti group, Carlo de Benedetti – who also bought 2% of the bank's shares, for 50 billion Lire.

But de Benedetti resigned after just three months, saying picturesquely that he had come up against a 'wall of rubber' every time he tried to find out just how the bank was run. He even had phone calls threatening his family in terms the Italians usually associate with the

Mafia. The implications were that bigger forces than Calvi were really behind the bank's goings-on.

In May 1982, a few months after the bank's shares had become fully quoted on the Milan stock exchange, the Banca d'Italia pointed out to Calvi that Banco Ambrosiano had loaned US $1.3 billion to 'unspecified parties' through just three other banking operations. It was a lot of money to have been loaned out to so few, obscure outfits. Calvi again asked the IOR to say it was responsible for these debts, but this time he got no joy there. The game was up; and on 11 June 1982, a Friday, Calvi did a runner.

It was to be a trip that ended badly a week later under Blackfriars Bridge in London. But Calvi went first to Austria, on a false passport, calling himself Gian Roberto Calvini, on a last-ditch mission to salvage what he could.

Waiting in London a few days ahead of him was a man called Francesco Pazienza. Calvi had taken him on to help sort out the Ambrosiano affair. Some think he did just that (for someone else) by dispatching Calvi himself. Pazienza, believed to have Mafia connections, was also wanted for fraud and misappropriating funds in the Ambrosiano affair. In March 1985 the US customs authority held him, pending extradition.

When news of Calvi's absence from Milan broke on Monday 14 June, Banco Ambrosiano shares crashed once again. That week the IOR and the bank wrangled over who owed whom the $1.3 billion used to buy IOR's Panamanian assets. On 16 June, in Calvi's continued absence, the Ambrosiano board was dissolved. Calvi's body was found two days after that. He was dead, but for the rest of the world's banks, the Ambrosiano scandal was only just beginning.

Though the Banca d'Italia was the lender of last resort, and had to prop up and reconstruct Banco Ambrosiano in Italy to protect its genuine clients, it decided that it was not obliged to support its overseas subsidiaries – a decision which caused consternation in the international banking world.

The first of the subsidiaries to go under was Banco Ambrosiano Holdings (Luxembourg) – or BAH for short – and its subsidiary Banco Ambrosiano Andino (BAA). BAH owed 109 other banks $600 million all told. Eighty-eight of these got together to form a group to recover what they could, and others joined them as time went on.

BAH was the outwardly legal face of Calvi's efforts to sidestep the

Italian restrictions on retail banks. Under exchange control rules, Italian banks had permission to set up overseas subsidiaries which could trade without exchange control permission from home on every deal. Luxembourg is a favourite place for such overseas subsidiaries. Calvi set up BAH there and then raised money, in dollars, quite legitimately, on the Euromarkets to fund its operations.

BAH in turn had subsidiaries – one in Nassau in the Bahamas (BAOL), one in Peru (BAA), and one in Nicaragua (AGBC). Money would be raised by BAOL in Nassau and then passed on by BAH in Luxembourg to one of the other subsidiaries before it moved beyond the bank's own doors. It also owned a controlling stake of over 50% of Switzerland's twelfth largest bank, Banco del Gotardo.

When the Milan parent bank collapsed, the Banca d'Italia persuaded seven institutions to take on board the whole of the retail business of the Italian operation, leaving just a shell that had a few connections with the Luxembourg end – which was physically outside the Banca d'Italia's jurisdiction and which, it decided, did not come under its legal obligations as the Italian lender of last resort.

When the international banks whose money had gone into the Luxembourg holding company realised that the Banca d'Italia would not bail out the foreign subsidiary, they pulled the plug and put BAH into *gestion controlé*, a form of controlled administration. Its subsidiaries were handled slightly differently according to the local practice: BAOL went into liquidation in Nassau, BAA had court-appointed directors and so on.

The collapse had come in the summer of 1982. The complex Luxembourg legal process dragged on through the next twelve months, during which a British firm of accountants, Touche Ross, was asked to help the administrators who had been appointed by the courts to sort out BAH.

In July 1983, the increasingly restive creditors appointed three of Touche Ross' men as President and directors of the Luxembourg company to salvage what they could. Apart from its Bahamian interests, being unravelled by a local liquidator, Touche Ross took on the task of trying to track down the bank's money across the world. The work of unravelling the mess – or at least, the bulk of the mess – went on until mid-1985; and some of the legal actions to recover some of the money traced are still underway. They could drag on for years yet.

The investigators found scarcely any proper bank records to go on, and the quality of what records there were was horrific. Banking transfers and deposits had not been properly documented. A few bits of paper remained, but nothing of substance and it was hard to see what the background was to many of the transactions. The team had to take small pieces of evidence and build them up like sections of a vast jigsaw puzzle before they could start to construct a picture of the whole. It meant starting with an individual story or piece of evidence and working from it to try and document what had happened. From this work they could 'repair' the asset. This had to be done file by file. A rough calculation in the early stages of this painstaking work suggested that perhaps $200 million worth could be traced, with a lot of luck thrown in.

One of the earliest things the team was able to do, was to sell the stake in Banco del Gotardo to Japan's Sumitomo Bank for $144 million in 1984. But chasing up BAH's 'repaired' assets led them all even further afield around the world, ranging across fifteen to twenty countries – and involving complicated legal proceedings in other jurisdictions' civil courts. The team soon grew to forty accountants, and ten lawyers, working flat out. One of the smaller loans (these were around the $250,000 mark) was secured against a tannery in Argentina that had gone bust; another was tied to a deep-freeze plant in Venezuela. Argentinian law meant that the tannery's local creditors had to be repaid in full before anyone else, which locked up the asset – and the Venezuelan loan could not be foreclosed on or local rules meant that the action would be lost, making the loan almost as deeply frozen as the plant's other contents. And so it went on.

As some sort of order began to emerge out of the chaos of poor documentation and curious loans, many of the rumours that something very fishy had been going on turned out to have some substance.

Some of the loans were straightforward commercial arrangements. others had a whiff of power-broking, favours, and some smelt down-right dishonest. There was little outward logic in many loans, to South American politicians, to businesses, to Italians' overseas accounts. But the team needed only to establish the movement and provenance of the money, not the intentions behind the loan decisions.

Some of the money was found in the shares of unquoted companies, one loan went to the bottom of the sea in the form of an uninsured Caribbean fishing fleet, and a good deal landed up in property in Panama, Peru and Canada – but each transaction was 'peculiar'. The largest single sum to have gone out of the Luxembourg bank group was $95 million. From there, it was parcelled up into separate lots and broken up further thereafter. A substantial amount of it, however, found its way into the hands of Licio Gelli, and his friends and associates, many of them members of P2.

Gelli and his closest associate received at least $100 million each from the scam. Sums paid out ranged from $3 million to $50 million a time. They would appear in the bank's books as loans to Bellatrix, a Panamanian company with no paid-up share capital. From there it would move via bank transfers into an account in Switzerland and be divided up into a host of further transfers fanning out across the world. Charts drawn up tracing the flow of funds resembled a family tree.

What was the influence or knowledge that Gelli and his associates were able to exert over Calvi to make him agree to such outpourings of money? As one observer said, 'Once someone has done something wrong he can't get out of it. They say, "you can't say no to us because you did this last time".

'Once he was involved, it just increased, and in the 1978-79 period and 1980 it just got out of hand.'

For the investigative team, recreating and picking their way through it all was hard work. It was acting for the international banks whose money had gone into the Luxembourg subsidiary. Its members had none of the official muscle of a national police fraud squad investigating a crime. Nevertheless, many national authorities were helpful; and even where others were less keen to play ball, the team worked its way through the civil remedies open to them in each country to lift the veil of banking secrecy wherever possible.

At this point some of the banks who were now the creditors employing the team, found to their horror that they were also on the long list of banks who had allowed the missing funds to be moved so freely round the world.

Once identified the money gradually grew easier to follow even though its routes had been complex. Once found, the cash could be frozen. Tougher, however, was preparing legal evidence of good enough quality to satisfy the local court that the money belonged to the Luxembourg bank's creditors, and should be handed over.

Some of that work continues. But by early 1988, the team had successfully recovered 71% of the Luxembourg arm's international creditors' money. The only remaining assets were the legal actions still to be completed – and some of these could take years. Many of the actions name Gelli and his associate Umberto Ortolani, and substantial sums still sit in Swiss banks awaiting the outcome of legal proceedings.

But some of the money may never be recovered, hidden deep in the banking system which, because of its secrecy, favours those who spirited it away. Of the cash recovered, some came from the realisable assets that were found; some came from loans, legitimate and questionable, that were traced and recovered; and the rest came from a dramatic financial settlement with the IOR – the Vatican Bank.

Though the IOR's true role in all this will probably never be made fully clear, the Vatican did agree to a goodwill payment of $241 million to help repay the eighty-eight non-Italian banks who lost their original $450 million when the Luxembourg side of Banco Ambrosiano collapsed. What was originally agreed as a $250 million settlement, became $241 million after it was divided into three instalments. The first, $151 million, went to the 109 banks who had lent money to BAH and/or BAA. About $8 million went to BAOL's creditors, and $82 million was handed over as part of a discounted deal on payments due to the bank, and commuted to cash.

Thanks to these arrangements, the sale of Banco del Gotardo, and the accountants' perseverance, BAH's and BAA's creditors got back 71% of their money, while BAOL's creditors were repaid 89% of the $200 million deficit (for once backed with some real assets) in Nassau. And there, by April 1988, the sums rested – pending any other recoveries from continuing legal action around the world.

It was one of the greatest financial detective stories of the age and, as in the best whodunnits, Calvi's was not the only corpse in the affair. His unlucky secretary 'fell' from the bank's windows in the first week of the denouement: whether by her design or someone else's is uncertain.

And the rest of the fallout from this affair was even more sinister. Calvi's links with the Tuscan businessman Licio Gelli were first uncovered in 1981 when a raid on a villa the latter owned in Arezzo had yielded evidence of Calvi's fraud as well as Gelli's own activities, which included extortion, and Gelli had fled to South America. But in 1982, he was arrested in Geneva, trying to withdraw Swiss francs 120 million ($55 million at the time) from a numbered Swiss bank account set up by Calvi himself. But Gelli, a slippery fellow, did not stay in custody long: escaping from the Swiss high security Champ-Dollon prison just before he could be extradited to Italy – after bribing a warder – and vanished. In a saga that linked Calvi money to arms dealing and Gelli to blackmail of top Italian figures, it was assumed that Gelli had exercised his peculiar talents to the full to ensure he was not caught again.

But Gelli too had enemies, and when he needed major surgery in 1987 he reappeared in Switzerland and gave himself up – preferring to face the surgeon's knife in a Swiss jail than risk the more corruptible atmosphere of a commercial operating theatre.

With extradition proceedings pending, he finally returned to Italy to try to pull off one more deal. Under Italian law you can only be charged with the offence your extradition was sought in connection with. Wanted in connection with even more serious charges, opting to face the lesser Ambrosiano ones was a wise move. He may choose to lift the veil to his own advantage and to the consternation of fellow-conspirators. But, while he lives, many of the other people privy to the inner secrets of the Ambrosiano affair prefer to preserve their silence.

10

The Money Trail

One of the most telling scenes in the film 'All the President's Men' comes when Bob Woodward, played by Robert Redford, meets his deep throat contact in a Washington garage. 'Follow the money,' says the contact and it was through tracing cheques in the burglars' accounts which were originally meant as campaign contributions to the CREEP, the committee to re-elect President Nixon, that Woodward and Bernstein begin to unravel the complex Watergate story. In that case it was not so much fraud as political deception and double-dealing. But the money trail is all important in fraud. For fraudsters have to do something with the loot they make. They have to stash it away and the places they select for such supposedly safe deposits often provide the investigators with their clues. Like Woodward and Bernstein, fraud investigators follow the money and often discover the fraudsters.

This was most vividly illustrated when the Securities & Exchange Commission finally began to nail Dennis Levine, Wall Street's most notorious insider trader. In May 1980 when Levine travelled to Nassau in the Bahamas and opened an account under the name Mr Diamond at a branch of Bank Leu, a Swiss bank, he thought he had double protection. Switzerland has historically been the place to stash away money. In Switzerland banking secrecy is an article of faith with Swiss banks prevented from communicating information about tax or exchange-control violations to foreign governments. Evading taxes is not a crime and there are no restrictions on currency movements. The numbered Swiss account with the name of the customer known only to a few top officials in a Swiss bank is almost as much a tradition as Swiss cheese.

Strict banking secrecy laws had made Nassau, capital of the Bahamas, a major financial centre in the 1970s. Banking ranked next to tourism as a revenue-earner and many of the people attracted to Nassau banks knew that their secrets were safe because the country's banking laws made it a criminal offence for a bank employee to reveal the identity of a customer without an order from a Bahamian court or proper government official. Not surprisingly, Levine felt safe and in five years of insider trading made an estimated profit of $11.6 million on which he probably earned another million dollars in interest.

What undid him was the money trail and the persistence of the SECO. As seen in Chapter 6, in May 1985 Merrill Lynch in New York received a letter without a name and address but clearly posted in Caracas, Venezuela, alleging that two individuals in Merrill Lynch's Caracas office were indulging in insider trading. The letter was full of spelling mistakes and the writer(s) clearly had a shaky grasp of English, but named the two individuals. Merrill Lynch's investigators could work on this information and discovered that one of them had written two cheques totalling nearly $8,000 to Brian Campbell, who had left Merrill to work for another Wall Street firm. It was this trail that led Merrill and then the SEC to Bank Leu and eventually, after a great deal of persistent investigation, to 'Diamond' and Dennis Levine. Even then Bank Leu officials could only disclose Levine's name to the SEC after they had obtained the permission of the Bahamian government with their lawyers making representations to the Bahamian Attorney-General. While this was crucial, the initial impetus for the investigation had been provided by the money trail and the cheques traced to Campbell's account.

It is interesting to note that after the publicity surrounding the Levine scandal, the Bahamian government felt obliged to act. The cornerstone of their commercial operations was banking secrecy. In 1975 Sir Leonard Knowles, then Chief Justice of the nation's highest court, had said, 'The secrecy provision is one of the pillars of this part [banking] of our economic structure, destruction of which would lead to the collapse of the whole structure which it supports.' But having consented to Bank Leu breaching this basic structure, the Bahamian government felt it ought to do something. The whole Levine scandal had shown up offshore banking in a very bad light and the Central Bank of the island forced Bank Leu to remove the Bank Leu official whose testimony was crucial to convicting Levine. He had to go as general manager of the bank and central banking authorities also insisted that the entire local banking board of the bank be changed.

How much this will undo the damage the scandal has done to the

Bahamas is difficult to say, for since the early 1960s it has been the great money laundromat of the world. Criminals have always required a place where they can stash their money away. Gold was an historic way of converting and storing loot and there was also the age of the little tin boxes, but in the 1930s we had the first use of Swiss bank accounts by the American Mafia. Meyer Lansky, who counted Al Capone among his friends, had linked up at the 1932 Democratic Convention with Huey Long, the corrupt governor of Louisiana and a virtual dictator of the state. The idea, it seems, was that Long, in return for $20,000 a month, would let Lansky open slot machines which were meant for charitable purposes. Predictably, widows and orphans received just $600 and the rest was said to have ended up in Swiss bank accounts. That seemed to have started the tradition and later there were colourful stories of Mafiosi characters caught trying to spirit the money away to Switzerland. This happened to Bugsy Seigel, whose mistress, a southern beauty called Virginia Hill, flew to Zurich with the loot, and when Seigel explained to his fellow-criminals that she had gone there to get choice Swiss materials for the Flamingo, Las Vegas' first gambling place, Seigel received a few choice bullets. Miss Hill returned the money. Credit Suisse was one bank much favoured by the Mafia. Eventually the ingenious Lansky set up his own Mafia bank, the Geneva based Exchange & Investment Bank, which made sure that Mafia money went back washed 'in the Alpine snows'.

But it was in the 1970s, as Whitney North Seymour Jnr, US attorney in New York, told a Senate committee that bank accounts protected by thick veils of secrecy had replaced 'little tin boxes' for the criminals. 'Secrecy and subterfuge,' he said, 'are the white-collar criminal's best friends. The surest invitation to illegal conduct that man can devise is a hidden conduit for the transmission of funds safe from the eyes of law enforcement officials. That is exactly what secret foreign bank accounts do. Although such accounts may be used with perfect innocence by some depositors, they are too tempting a lure for the tax evader, the securities swindler, the corrupter of public employees, the fraud and the cheat.'

Legend has it that it began with a man who liked to call himself Jack van Allen. In the mid-1950s he had been convicted of distributing unregistered stock and debarred from access to US stock markets. But in the 1960s he used Swiss banks in a similar swindle, passing off worthless stock to the US public at $16 a share. What made the fraud novel was that it used a Swiss bank backed by a Liechtenstein trust. This is a marvellous financial instrument discovered by the land-locked state in the 1920s when it emerged from the ruins of the Austro-Hungarian empire. Its contribution to international finance is the anstalt, a single-shareholder company which enjoys tax-free profit distributions, reduced capital tax, absence of supervision and examination by the tax administration, absolute tax and banking secrecy, liberal formalities and low costs for setting up the entity and ensuring the anonymity of the provider of capital and the beneficiaries. Since its creation it has been the favourite vehicle of the rich to shelter their money.

In this case the Securities & Exchange Commission was able to get to the truth because one of the participants spilled the beans, almost the first time that a US agency had got behind Swiss secrecy. But such victories against Swiss banking secrecy remain isolated – though in 1982, as Levine was making his pile, the United States and Switzerland did agree to allow the SEC and the US Justice Department access to information about Swiss bank accounts in certain cases of insider trading in the US securities markets that might also have violated Swiss law. But this was hedged with all sorts of qualifications and the records could be withheld if a commission established by the Swiss Bankers' Association determined that the case did not really mean a violation of Swiss insider trading laws. They, needless to say, are much more liberal than the US or British versions.

The Mafia and insider dealers are not the only ones who feel the need for Swiss banking protection. Thurston Clarke and John J. Tigue in *Dirty Money* describe how heroin-dealers found the 'full services' of Swiss banks very useful. They found they could then 'store excess profits that cannot be safely spent and that are not needed to finance new shipments . . . transfer money to foreign suppliers . . . earn interest and pay, make investments . . . launder the money'. Switzerland had banks that were sophisticated, very secretive and worked in a very stable political environment. There were occasions when Switzerland was not used, for example during the bribery scandals that featured American corporations in the 1970s. At one stage during the Vietnam war much dirty money from drugs and dealing in arms was generated and found its way to Hong Kong. There it helped the colony become quite a centre for flight money, as the Chase Manhattan Bank put it in a 1966 report. But eventually even this found its way back to Switzerland.

However, in the 1960s and 1970s the Caribbean began offering centres that provided some alternatives to Switzerland. The rise of the Bahamas as a money laundering centre is recent, in terms of historic centres like Switzerland and the result of the fall of Batista's Cuba in 1959. This, while giving the right-wingers in the US something to shout about, also dealt a severe blow to the mob and its money. In the 1930s, as we have seen, the Mafia had discovered that it needed money-laundering centres which could wash its dirty money and return it without any tell-tale marks. Meyer Lansky decided to find another centre, and this is when the Bahamas became prominent. On the same time-zone as New York, but with much warmer weather, it seemed ideal and as in Cuba, where he had financed Batista, Lansky financed the rise to power of the black Progressive Liberal party which unseated the white Bay Street boys. The Bahamas attracted such distinguished visitors as Bernie Cornfeld, whose IOS had most of its infrastructure there, and also Robert Vesco, the man who succeeded in looting several million pounds from the IOS. Vesco supported Lynden Pindling, the Bahamian premier, until US pressure forced Pindling to deport Vesco.

International banks have long used the Bahamas as booking centres, to avoid the laws that limit their ability to attract deposits and offer loans. In 1983 there were 189 branches of US banks in the Bahamas, nearly all of them corporate shells. The Bahamian domestic banking system was controlled by four large Canadian banks, with the Royal Bank of Canada's branch on the island of Bimini attracting $12 million in cash deposits in 1983, all of this believed to be money made from drug-dealing. It was the expansion of drug trafficking through the Caribbean, particularly in the Bahamas in the 1970s, that led to the growth of offshore banking. A US Senate investigation in 1983 had said that the money that flowed between the US and offshore havens as a result of criminal activities like drugs was so great that it threatened the US banking system, probably accounting for the $75 billion in the US balance of payments that was described as 'errors and omissions'. A year earlier it had been estimated that 50% of the cocaine and much of the marijuana getting into the States was through the Bahamas.

Lynden Pindling is no stranger to controversy. A Bahamian Royal Commission found that he had more income than could be justified from legitimate sources open to a prime minister, and allegations regarding his business dealings were discussed before the Commonwealth heads of government meeting was held in Nassau in November

1986. Even Buckingham Palace wondered if the Queen should be a guest of Pindling. But in the end he did host the Commonwealth Prime Ministers' Conference. Pindling could argue that his regime is much better than the rule of the Bay Street Boys when, in the 1960s, as New York's then crime-busting US attorney Robert Morgenthau put it, 'It was extremely easy for anybody to form a bank in Nassau under conditions which made it impossible to get any information about the bank or its officers and directors.'

Things are a lot different in the Cayman Islands, and when it decided to clean up its image by making bad money unwelcome it was found that good money was attracted back to Grand Cayman. It still offers a tax haven, but now it is a respectable place for big business of the legitimate sort to stash away its profits. The biggest factor in this was when Cayman, a British dependency, exchanged letters of agreement with the US to lift the veil of bank secrecy in circumstances where US investigators had good reason to believe that the proceeds of crime were being moved there. Sound businesses had nothing to fear, their bank secrets remained inviolate, and their money moved into Grand Cayman. But crooks and racketeers knew their deeds could be uncovered and moved their money away to less scrupulous islands further south.

Another offshore centre that led the way in shaking out bad money in favour of good was Bermuda. Its second major source of revenue after tourism is international financial business, especially re-insurance. Bermuda took the attitude that 'the government will always co-operate in international investigations relating to prosecutions involving bribery, fraud, illicit drugs, etc., i.e. for offences which would clearly be criminal under Bermuda law'. This is the island's official policy and one that not all offshore centres practise. For Bermuda, it has brought prosperity. More than 6,000 companies were registered there by the mid-1980s, including most of the top 500 US companies, and the island scored a major triumph when the huge multinational Jardine Mattheson decided to move its head office there from Hong Kong.

While the money trail is important it need not be the only trail to try and trace possible fraudulent activities. The Sethia story, again, provides an example of a trail where goods, in this case ships, provided the main source of information. The action took place in the early weeks of 1984. As we have seen, Sethia's Esal was supposed to be shipping sugar in three ships to Nigeria. When the crash came two of the ships were sent to Rostov in East Germany and that is where solicitors from Linklaters, acting for Allied Arab Bank, tried to trace them and take possession. It is an intriguing story of chase and discovery and the attempt by one creditor, convinced he had been the subject of fraud, to obtain assets.

On the afternoon of 2 February 1984, Andrew Legg flew from London to Hamburg. Legg arrived at the Helmstadt border crossing between West and East, having driven from Hamburg, to find the East German authorities did not appreciate his urgency. He was kept waiting in the bitter cold for three hours before being allowed in. He got into his hotel in Rostov at about one in the morning. At 6.30 he was woken by the police to check his credentials. It set the pattern for his stay there.

Legg is a tall, rather professional looking man, with rimless spectacles and fair hair falling over his forehead who, despite his Yorkshire origins, had the reputation of being sensitive. For him, Rostov was a flat, bleak, dirty seaport and East Germany a very unnerving place. Even in London he was aware of how different and difficult things could be in the East. For a start, it was impossible for Western lawyers to contact directly East German lawyers and he had to use a professor in East Berlin to be his go-between. Normally lawyers all over the world strike up a spark, but the Rostov lawyer Legg was introduced to by the East Berlin professor could not speak English very well and so there had to be another intermediary.

The concrete monstrosity of the Rostov Hotel made Legg even more nervous. People seemed to be constantly coming in and out of the hotel and Legg had the strong suspicion that he was being watched. Suddenly on Saturday morning, with his mission nowhere near complete, he was told he must leave. The hotel was closing down.

It was not until Legg was safely back in Hamburg that he felt some of the tightness and sense of foreboding, that had gripped him in Rostov, slowly disappear. Throughout his stay there he had never felt entirely safe. This whole Esal fraud seemed so fantastic, he could not work out what the ramifications were. A week ago it was a matter of debt collection, interesting but part of the service Linklaters provided their clients. On that Sunday, weighing up the options in the Hamburg hotel, Legg wondered if it might be a matter of state. He decided that if he was to go back to East Germany he needed some support and so got another lawyer from London, Dominic Helps, to join him.

211

They flew from Hamburg to Tegel in West Berlin. This time the efficient intermediary who had interpreted for the East German lawyer seemed to have made all the arrangements. At Checkpoint Charlie, where they crossed into East Berlin, there were visas waiting for them. They were put up for the night at the Metropole near the Brandenburg Gate and on Monday they drove in an East German car to Rostov.

There Legg's unease was heightened when he discovered that the Rostov Hotel, which was meant to be closing down, was still doing business. This time they were lodged outside the town in a hotel packed with East German holiday-makers. For them this was an Eastern Blackpool. Legg and Helps could not wait to get away. Everything had to be done through somebody else. Under East German law there was no western-style separation of the state and the judiciary and Linklaters were, in effect, asking the state to arrest the ships. What was most galling to the lawyers was the fact that they could not attend court. It was Wednesday before the formalities could be completed. Then, since the ships were in the Straits of Rostov and had not actually docked, there was the problem of serving the writs. By the time this could be done it was Friday and Legg and Helps felt they could not endure another day at their hotel, which smelled of boiled cabbage, or possibly eat an East German meal again: steak like shoe leather served in a viscous liquid masquerading as gravy with processed vegetables. They heard that a Danish ship was heading west and they decided to take it. Almost the first thing they did when they got on the ferry was to head for the restaurant. Never did simple Danish food taste so wonderfully gorgeous.

As it happened, the misery that Legg and Helps suffered at Rostov was in vain. Both ships had already been mortgaged by Esal to the Middle East Bank and after Allied discovered this the arrests were lifted. This effectively marked the end of Linklaters' role as detectives, English solicitors imitating the more American style of lawyers acting as investigators. But it blew the Esal case wide open and made the task of investigating one of the biggest frauds ever seen in London that much easier. It also highlighted the various ways money and goods can be traced and the trail they leave behind, be it in Swiss bank accounts or on the high seas.

11

Regulation and the Future

In Great Britain the winter of 1985 saw a major offensive mounted against fraud and fraudsters. New laws touching on every aspect of the financial and commercial world from accountancy to securities dealing were drafted for enactment over the following three years. They brought dramatic changes in the legal obligations of professional advisers – who are now required to blow the whistle on crooks and conmen on pain of being prosecuted themselves for withholding vital information. In return, they are freed from the spectre of being sued for breach of confidence. This deprived the fraudster of the protection and niceties of privacy and confidentiality extended to bona fide business-men – traditions that for far too long most of the banking fraternity had cited for resisting requests for information from investigators, and refusing to tackle the thorny question of whether to handle money whose possessor or provenance was dubious.

Britain was not acting in isolation in introducing new rules. The seeds of many of these changes had been sown two decades earlier in the USA, and by the early 1980s concern about the rising tide of fraud and its financial, economic and social cost was reaching its zenith around the civilised world: as witnessed by the establishment of the Common-wealth Secretariat's Commercial Crime Squad, and a host of treaties to swap information about securities fraud, agreed by the US Securities and Exchange Commission and a clutch of other national regulatory bodies in the late 1970s and mid-1980s. This period saw an explosion of meetings between senior officials of sovereign states to exchange views and explore the creation of a network of broadly similar laws in which to trap the international fraudster – who is no respecter of boundaries, and gratefully exploits the shelter to be found in the gaps between differing legal systems.

In Britain it led to the introduction of five different sets of

213

legislation, between the winter of 1985 and the close of 1987, that tightened the net at that end. They were:

1. The Drug Trafficking Offences Act 1986, which for the first time allowed the seizure of a suspect's assets before his trial and, in some instances, even before his arrest.
2. The Financial Services Act, which revolutionised and regulated the sale of securities and financial products in the UK.
3. The Insolvency Act, which changed the procedure for company liquidations and brought in tough new penalties for wayward or merely incompetent company directors, in an attempt both to drive out the crooks and to pressure the rest into taking a more rigorous interest in the conduct of their companies' affairs.
4. The Banking Act of 1987, which, amongst other things, imposed the new obligations of disclosure on the banks in fraud and criminal matters.
5. The Criminal Justice Act 1987, which introduced a tough new investigative and prosecuting body, the Serious Fraud Office, just before the 1987 election, and which was followed with further legislation put before Parliament by the re-elected Conservative Government during 1988. This second act made insider trading an extraditable offence and toughened the maximum penalties from two years to seven years in jail.

These two Acts were the result of the deliberations of a committee set up in 1983 and headed by the Law Lord, Lord Roskill, to look into the fraught question of how the antiquated British legal system coped with the trial and prosecution of complex and confusing frauds. The Roskill Report was published in the winter of 1985, and recommended far-reaching changes in the way traditional British jury trials were conducted, and in the presentation of evidence. It even suggested the abolition of jury trial for certain frauds, an option yet to be taken up by a British government at the time of writing. But its main recommendation – that a new Serious Fraud Office be set up with wide-ranging powers to investigate and prosecute – was accepted. Enshrined in the Criminal Justice Act 1987, the SFO was up and running by mid-1988 and immediately took several major fraud cases under its scrutiny.

The workings of these Acts are described later on, but first it is worth looking back at why they were deemed necessary at all, and where they fit into the international march against fraud and economic crime. The seeds of all this activity – particularly of the first of the UK's 1985 campaign against financial crime, the Drug Trafficking Offences Act – were sown in the USA in the 1960s. That was when US investigators, trying to trap drug smugglers, decided to take a greater interest in where the drug profits went and how they were 'laundered' to look like innocent proceedings of legitimate business dealings. They reasoned that finding the money might help them find the drug barons.

The investigating officers found a fascinating trail. It led from suitcases stuffed with banknotes leaving the USA by air or sea to offshore banking havens, and from these, to the international securities markets. *En route* there were sometimes minor detours, not just to continue the laundering process but to perpetrate new commercial crimes in other jurisdictions, earning a bit more along the way: frauds, confidence tricks, and product counterfeiting amongst them. The link between organised crimes like drug smuggling and the use of their proceeds to fund other, commercial crimes, continues to be a major worry for many countries.

The successful drug trafficker has only one main concern, other than not getting caught: how to spend his drug profits in the country of his residence without attracting awkward questions about how he came by such riches. The same is true of the crime families who run prostitution, protection and other rackets. The bosses of organised crime tend to want to live in places that offer all the diversions and comforts of modern civilised life on which to lavish their money. But this also generally means living in a place that levies taxes, and the authorities tend to ask tough questions of those who seem to be living beyond their official means about whence their money comes, and which impose heavy penalties upon those who are caught evading tax on ill- or well-gotten gains.

It was for tax evasion that the US authorities finally nabbed the infamous Al Capone. Illegally earned though his fortune was, the authorities held that he was not entitled to compound his crimes by dodging tax on his profits (why give a gangster the double benefit of a tax-free income?). So it was for tax evasion that Capone finally went to jail, not for racketeering. As a result, the modern gangster needs a sufficient official source of income that justifies his lifestyle and on which he can pay some income taxes – and stay out of prison.

The Americans made their tax inspectors' and other investigators' lives a little easier by imposing a legal obligation upon US banks to declare to the authorities any sums of more than $10,000 that were moved from one account to another, or left the country. This ought to make it possible to keep track of large movements of money through the banking system, to check that there is a legitimate business reason for the money to be moving on, or for profits to be returning into an account. Banks that fail to óbey these rules and do not declare movements of clients' funds in size can expect serious penalties and lashings of public opprobrium in the press. But not all banks stick to the rules, and there are other ways of moving cash and assets around. In 1986, the US Treasury estimated that over $100 billion a year was being earned in the States alone from illegal drug trafficking. That is a lot of money to move without alerting the authorities to its where-abouts – and so money laundering is big business.

Drug barons, the men or women behind a string of prostitutes, or running a protection racket and advance-fee fraudsters are all running a business. They want to make a profit and to enjoy the proceeds, and like any legitimate businessman they want both to stay in business, ploughing back a certain amount into the operation, and to maximise their own present and future stream of income from it. Not for these people the tucking away of notes under the mattress or hiding them all in the safe to spend discreetly as and when needed. This is where the business of laundering 'dirty' money and the urge to use one's existing capital to make more money converge. For the professional crook, both can be achieved through the laundering process. For example, after taking cocaine profits abroad in suitcases and shuffling them through various offshore bank accounts in nominee names (to disguise whose cash it started out as), the best way to turn these deposits into legitimate earnings for tax purposes is to invest some of the money in an outwardly legitimate 'front' business that appears to generate a lot of cash. If the front business really makes money, so much the better. But if it loses there are always ways of transferring sums from one of the network of bank accounts so that the cash looks like profitable income from a business deal to make up the shortfall. If the front company is a fruit and vegetable importer, for example, these transfers might look like regular payments from clients purportedly buying perishable (and therefore, untraceable) goods. That way the money is laundered even if it does not generate anything extra in the process.

A whole string of such outfits makes the proprietor a big businessman, earning 'clean' money from legitimate operations. On that he will pay whatever taxes the law requires, after going through the usual business gyrations to minimise the apparent tax liability. No business is – nor in this case can it afford to look – keen to pay more tax than it must. But the criminal enterprise does not stop there. Once a reliable laundering process has been established, complete with a convincing final 'rinse' through a profitable front company, it makes financial sense to use some of the dirty money to earn some more illegal cash *en route*. Thus the network builds up. Drug money flows abroad to some poorly regulated offshore centre, offering maximum banking secrecy and minimum interference, in which it is easy to split the money into half a dozen bank or trustee accounts. These will ostensibly be opened by a variety of companies, registered in other offshore centres or even locally, without too many questions being asked. Some of this money will then be used to fund further drug deals: ploughed back into the basic business, already a secretive one, it will not need to be laundered. Part of this portion may go into other illegal rackets like pornography. Dirty money will do nicely for dirty business. Of the rest, once offshore, some will take a little detour and be used to earn more money, also illegally, from anyone who can be conned into parting with his own funds. These will eventually either flow into the front business or into a spin-off of the con-trick, which itself appears legitimate.

It is easy to see why countries are concerned about the damage done to their society and budgets by major inflows of illegal drugs into their jurisdictions. There is the health cost of addicts needing medical help and attention. There is the social cost of addicts unable to work and perhaps stealing or turning to other petty crime to pay for their habit. There is the cost of occasional users making an expensive mistake at work or perhaps behind the wheel of a car while under the influence. There is the outflow from the economy into the black market of cash from employed drug-buyers that might otherwise be spent on dom-estically produced consumer goods (or state-approved drugs like alcohol or cigarettes, a useful source of tax revenue to some countries' exchequers) and stay in the system.

Yet fraud has often been called a victimless crime, for its costs are less immediately obvious. This attitude overlooks the frequent link between the laundering of funds earned from street and organised crime and other frauds committed *en route* to generate extra cash – or

217

to get hold of financial securities that can be used to generate apparently legitimate profits in the laundering process.

The fraudster enters the commercial area trying to spirit something away and leave nothing in its place. He unbalances and nullifies the normal economic equations. The defrauded company or individual sees money or goods flow out of its hands into the black market. A large business' growth may be retarded, jobs may be trimmed or, at best, not created. A small business may even go bust, with knock-on effects on its suppliers too. The costs of fraud soon mount up.

A dramatic illustration of the damage that flows into the vacuum it leaves behind can be found in the advance-fee fraud, which enjoyed a bout of popularity amongst the fraudsters and their associates in the 1970s. It can either be set up in a small way to deprive individuals of a few thousands, or in a big way to defraud nation states to the tune of many millions in cash and collateral, securing securities that can be sold to generate apparently legitimate profits.

Basically, the advance-fee fraud takes the form of a fraudulent promise to provide someone with a service – usually a bank loan – in return for a set fee, payable in advance, that is non-returnable even if the deal falls through. The individual, company or country that goes along with this proposal will usually be unable to get a bank loan in the normal way, either because his/its credit is already poor, or it is overborrowed, or because the person seeking the loan has some dubious reason of his own for wanting to evade the normal channels. In the case of a country it may be a developing nation, seduced by the profligate lending policies of western banks in the early 1970s and now too deep in rolled-over debt and interest charges to be able to raise more cash on reasonable terms from its existing bankers. Along comes a smartly dressed, financially fluent, offshore 'banker' or lawyer representing some organisation or unnamed client prepared to lend the country millions of dollars at a rather – even very – favourable rate for a period of twenty years. The rate, the intermediary will explain, is a bit lower than the usual loan interest rates because the client wishes to remain anonymous and in return for secrecy will accept a lower financial return on his money.

Favourite ploys were to suggest that the client was a country for whom it would be politically embarrassing to lend openly to the borrowing nation. Another was that the client was a member of a wealthy Arab family, or potentate, with personal or political reasons for wishing to mask his identity. The borrower, strapped for cash to build much-needed schools, factories, hospitals or agricultural projects, is grateful for the chance of a cheap long-term loan. In twenty years the projects that the money could be invested in should prosper enough for the economy to benefit and the country be able to repay the loan. Even if things do not work out quite that well, the chances are that it will fall to a future leader or finance minister to reschedule the debt. Meanwhile, the current regime hopes to meet the low interest cost with ease. Part of the new loan could even be earmarked as a cheap replacement of some existing rolled-over debt. There is, however, the matter of collateral – the assets to back the loan should anything go amiss. The lenders' agent requires that government securities to the value of the agreed loan be deposited at a mutually satisfactory – say, Swiss – bank. This will be a real and perfectly respectable bank.

The important point about government securities is that they will be 'bearer' securities, or bonds: that is, whoever, holds them is automatically the owner and can sell them on the world's bond markets. This is usually done at a discount to face value calculated according to when the loans mature. Bearer bonds are therefore virtually cash-in-hand and, once sold, carry no trace of the seller. But the immediate object of the scam is the advance fee: usually 1% or sometimes 2% of the value of the total loan, payable to the smooth-talking intermediary. If the loan is $45 billion (and one attempted fraud of this nature was this size), that is a cool $4.5 million to be paid over in advance *and which the agreement states cannot be returned* even if the loan agreement falls through.

Dazzled by the thought of $45 billion to spend on developing their country – and perhaps getting re-elected for their pains – the President and his advisers may agree to the deal and hand over, through their national bank, the advance fee. They also agree to issue and deposit the securities at the Swiss bank of the lender's suggestion as collateral. Then the problems begin. There is a hitch, a minor delay, in getting the loan funds transferred to the borrower's bank. Or the borrower's paperwork is found to be not quite in order. Or the lender has simply found another taker for his money while the President took so long making up his mind. One way or another, the deal is off; and the non-returnable fee has been paid in vain. Goodbye $4.5 million that the country can ill afford to lose.

Worse, the delay may have cropped up after the bearer securities were deposited as collateral in Switzerland – and (with a bit of fast and forged paperwork) they have already been taken up by the intermediary posing as or 'acting on behalf of' the supposed lender. He has probably already encashed some of them through the international bond markets, where they will continue to be bought and sold as the genuine article – as indeed they are – until they mature in twenty years time *when they have to be repurchased at full face value by the country*. So it has lost $4.5 million up front and has the spectre of an extra $45 billion to find in twenty years time with nothing to show for either.

The moment it knows the bonds are missing, of course, the country's officials realise they were being duped all along. The bonds would not be spirited away if it was a simple matter of a loan deal falling through at the eleventh hour. But if the conman is happy just to pocket the advance fee, it is almost impossible for the country to know for certain that it had been dealing with fraudsters all along . . . unless by reputation.

Why? Firstly, because the fraudster always appears to have a legitimate reason for the deal falling through and an advance-fee agreement looks legally binding – even if the documentation is actually shot full of legal holes. Secondly, the defrauded nation may have been targeted precisely because of its current leaders' limited knowledge of the workings of the international financial markets and the unliklihood of anyone smelling a rat. Thirdly, whether they realise they have been ripped off or not, there is no way that the country's leaders want the other creditors to hear that it is now at least $4.5 million worse off than before. All sorts of loan roll-over agreements might be jeopardised, and who needs the political embarrassment anyway?

This argument applies even more powerfully when the securities are also missing. What country is going to announce to the volatile financial world that it has just issued up to $45 billion worth of bearer bonds that are not backed by anything other than a large dent in its already precarious finances? Its ability to make any further issues would immediately be dramatically reduced, possibly to zero.

Meanwhile, the country, already in financial difficulties and now $4.5 million worse off immediately, with the prospect of having to pay out the nominal $45 billion value of the genuine bearer bonds when they mature in twenty years time (or whatever their designated life is), may have to put on ice all those schools, hospitals, dams and other projects that the loans would have financed. Projects already underway may have to be limited or even abandoned. That means fewer jobs at home, setbacks to agricultural projects – and fewer orders of building materials, engineering and architectural services from other nations including the developed ones. European, Japanese and US companies may face lost and cancelled contracts. The knock-on effect goes beyond the victim's borders and spills over into world trade balances. Fraud impoverishes us all.

Within the defrauded country's borders, this sort of fraud is not only economically but also politically destabilising. In the short term, it holds a country back as jobs, food supplies and health programmes suffer. In the medium term, these handicaps can topple governments whether at the ballot box or in a coup.

The $45 billion case drawn upon here was foiled at the eleventh hour when a senior member of the government concerned asked the Commonwealth Secretariat's Commercial Crime Unit to run a quick check on the people offering the cheap loan. The unit found a web of links to known criminals and the deal was stopped. Although the bearer bonds had already been deposited with the bank that was (unwittingly) being used as a conduit for the fraudsters, they were retrieved and even the advance fee was recovered.

This was a particularly big loan deal – big enough to raise queries, admittedly rather late on. But many advance-fee frauds were for much smaller sums. One attempt concerned a loan deal arranged secretly by a minister who wanted to stage a coup with the money he believed he would raise. Another was for a corrupt minister who wished to line his own pocket with the cash while using his country's bonds as collateral – for which it would have to pay up, twenty years hence. Both examples show why the borrower was willing to do a secret deal with 'lenders' that wanted to keep their own identity under wraps.

Companies and individuals have been caught out this way too, though obviously for smaller sums. Sometimes instead of an advance fee as such, they agree to deposit cash in an overseas bank account to be used by the 'go-between' to cover the supposed costs of setting up the loan sought. The money gradually gets eaten up in 'expenses', but still no loan materialises. A string of reasons is given: the borrower has failed to find an acceptable bank for the loan money to be deposited in, his proposed collateral is not good enough, the lender is not satisfied that he is a good enough risk, and so on. By the time he realises that the loan is off and the deposit lost, the proposed borrower may be loath to blow the whistle. For one thing he feels embarrassed about his loss. A

221

company may not want its union officials to know jobs could be at risk. A businessman fears his reputation will be damaged if his peers hear of it. Or the prospective borrower may have been using money he himself does not want the authorities to know about to deposit in the overseas bank account as the go-between asked: extra cash he or his outfit had not declared to the taxman, perhaps. He has to chalk up the loss to experience and try not to get stung again.

But for at least one American advance-fee fraudster operating in London around 1984 just such a scam backfired somewhat when the defrauded client, an American, got nasty in return. Private detectives were hired to build up a dossier on his activities, and much of the information eventually found its way into the hands of the UK authorities, already keeping a watchful eye on the man's activities. Two fraud cases resulted; but − pre-Roskill and the changes his committee inspired in the presentation of evidence − such is the complexity of fraud and proving advance-fee fraud in particular, that in the first and smaller instance the man was acquitted only to end up in custody at Wormwood Scrubs jail awaiting trial on the second, larger fraud charge. He was sentenced on 31 March 1988 to three and a half years in jail on two counts − one involving obtaining property, and one of executing securities, by deception. A $20 million libel action he had taken out against the business magazine *Financial Weekly* for writing about some of his earlier activities, was finally dismissed with costs on 8 December 1986.

Advance-fee frauds have lost their charm for many conmen, though every now and again there is a resurgence of these attempts. For one thing, thanks to the Commonwealth Secretariat's Commercial Crime Unit and other agencies, advance-fee fraud has had a good deal of publicity where it counts − at heads of government and senior banker level. Also, fewer big loans were being arranged in the late 1980s than in the mid 1970s and potential borrowers are becoming more sophisticated and are more likely to smell a rat than they might once have been. Advance-fee fraud has grown a bit too risky; it has been given too high a profile by the fraud prevention experts for the perpetrators' comfort, and discreet offers of big loans for long periods at well below market rates now shout too loudly that there is something funny afoot for many money launderers to try that route to getting hold of legitimate bonds.

Whatever route the criminal's money takes some of it will eventually end up looking like the profits of a genuine business or the handsome gains made from canny share dealings, and will be repatriated, declared, and taxed. The securities, commodoties and Eurobond markets are natural choices for this final rinse because income and capital from the markets need far less explanation than business records, for example, involve. A stable of nominee companies can be used to mask the seller's identity and spread the proceeds around. All he has to do is declare his chosen 'income' from securities trading in due course.

US concern about all these matters – the ravages of the drugs business, its links with other, commercial crimes and the abuse of the major securities markets by money launderers – spread outwards and had become an international talking point by the end of the 1970s. In the early 1980s, heads of the British Commonwealth nations and others agreed in principle to try and re-shape parts of their legislation on drug trafficking and banking secrecy in a concerted effort to make it easier to pursue the criminals across national boundaries.

One of the major problems facing law enforcers was that a crime might be planned in Europe, perpetrated in the US, masterminded from Scandinavia, and the proceeds be spirited to Switzerland (one attempt took just this geographical form). How do you co-operate across frontiers to catch the criminals and recover or sequester their profits if half a dozen different police forces, working under half a dozen different and possibly clashing sets of laws, are involved? The nations decided that the answer lies in greater international co-operation based on greater reciprocity and new sets of laws drafted to complement each other's rules. Between 1982 and 1986 the American SEC signed memoranda of understanding on such matters with the Swiss, the British and the Japanese, while the US government made a similar agreement with the Cayman Islands. Back in 1977 the US had already signed a treaty on Mutual Assistance in Criminal Affairs with Switzerland (mentioned in earlier chapters) in which the Swiss agreed to extend the rules under which their famous banking secrecy laws can be suspended to aid US investigators in certain circumstances. It meant that the US could have access to bank accounts, and the records of money flows, of suspected criminals to find the evidence and proceeds of their activities.

The aim of all this was to stop fraudsters from hiding behind conflicting rules in different countries. They already have an unfair advantage over legitimate businessmen by being able to set up competing, front businesses with limitless and tax-free cash flow from their illegal operations. They already damage the markets and reputations of legitimate manufacturers by counterfeiting their best and highest margined products, often producing shoddy or dangerous items. It was high time a tighter net was woven in which to trap and catch the international criminal. But lifting secrecy also requires secrecy or you alert the crook that you are hot on his heels. The Swiss/US treaty operates within the existing domestic Swiss system under which a magistrate can forbid a bank to alert a client whose account is being investigated.

The responsibility of banks, lawyers and accountants to report, or not, to the authorities any doubts they might have about the origins of a client's money became a hot topic. Banks are traditionally discreet about their clients' money: confidentiality is the cornerstone of the services they offer. But it is also abused by individuals to mask the evidence of commercial crime. A bank may have no idea that its client is a crook whose money has been laundered before it arrives in that account. And if the bank has its doubts it can turn down the business, but how many actually have done?

All that changed in the UK with the new criminal evidence and drug trafficking laws, which spelt out just what the obligations of banks and accountants were to be and introduced a range of criminal offences for withholding from the authorities signs of a client's criminal earnings. These include hefty fines, and jail sentences of up to seven years for individuals at fault.

The new laws also gave investigators greater powers to take evidence. For example, DTI-appointed inspectors can make witnesses give evidence on oath. Others can seek a court order to see relevant documents and records. Anyone failing to comply with these orders also faces possible criminal charges, fines and a jail sentence. Few professional advisers are prepared to go to prison for their clients. Past reluctance to blow the whistle on clients was partly because banks and other financial advisers feared legal suits for breach of confidence and because they forgot the maxim that bad money tends to drive out good. Britain's new laws exempt them from any breach of confidence *even if, on investigation, their reported suspicions turn out to have been unfounded*.

This revolution in British legislation hit the statute book in October 1986, when the *Drug Trafficking Offences Act* became law. It was a piece of legislation intended to reflect similar new rules in other Commonwealth nations, and was drawn up along the lines drafted by the Hodgson Committee for the Commonwealth Heads of Government. The Committee was an early attempt to create a broadly uniform, and thereby reciprocal, set of rules in each member nation to combat drug traffickers. But some of the principles it established, were later also enacted in the wider *Criminal Justice Act* 1987, aimed directly at the fraudster.

Amongst the Drug Trafficking Offences Act's major innovations was the section making it an offence to assist drug traffickers by looking after the proceeds of their trafficking while knowing, or suspecting, that they were involved in that trade. There is now a duty to disclose the suspicion to the police. If this is done, the disclosure 'shall not be treated as a breach of any restriction upon the disclosure of information imposed by contract'. If the person looking after the money really did not know its origins, or had planned to disclose his suspicions but had a convincing enough reason for not yet having done so, he has a sound defence to the charge of assisting a drug trafficker. The Act gave bankers, stockbrokers, commercial lawyers and accountants some clear guidance about what line they must take – or face fines and the possible imprisonment of their officers. UK case law had already indicated a duty to disclose suspicion of crimes, but the banks had largely ignored it. These two new acts have spelt it out for them. But the main point of the Drug Trafficking Offences Act is to allow the seizure of criminals' assets so they cannot come out of prison and still enjoy the fruits of their crimes.

This revolutionises the British system, putting the onus on the defendant to prove, for example, that his assets are not from drug trafficking. (The British government intended to extend this rule to all criminal proceeds, but the original draft of the Criminal Justice Bill that would have done this was caught up in the timetabling of the 1987 British general election. The part of the bill setting up the Serious Fraud Office recommended by Lord Roskill's Committee went through as the Criminal Justice Act 1987, but the rest had to wait until later.)

Because a suspect's assets can be seized on or even before his arrest, with the necessary court order signed by a judge, he is not – in effect – any longer presumed innocent until proved guilty. The assets will be put in the charge of a receiver who will keep them intact, or run any legitimate businesses, until the result of the trial – when they are either forfeit in whole or in part; or returned on an acquittal.

225

Hand-in-hand with that new power goes a rule that stops a drug trafficker from giving his ill-gotten gains away to a trusted wife, friend, lover, associate or adviser to protect them. Such gifts can also now be confiscated by the courts, as can the assets of any company that the drug trafficker hastily puts into liquidation.

This rule links across to tough new laws in the *Insolvency Act* of 1986, which swept up the old Company Directors Disqualification Act, the 1985 Insolvency and Companies Acts, and brought them together as one code. It also added a new concept to British law: the offence of *wrongful trading*. Under this new rule, directors who allow a company to continue trading even when it is on the verge of bankruptcy can be made personally liable for all the debts of the company and will be disqualified by the courts from being a company director for at least two years. Nearly a year later, the total number of directors disqualified under the new rules since their inception, had risen to 153.

The new rules, policed by the DTI, put the onus on the company directors to wind up a company voluntarily before it reaches the point of disastrous collapse. The directors, realising that the company is in grave danger of becoming insolvent, can appoint an approved Administrator to run its affairs and mastermind an orderly winding-up. By the close of 1987 around eighty had been appointed. Going into compulsory liquidation brings penalties and disqualifications. By October 1987, the DTI said just over fifty directors had been disqualified under the new Act and another thirty or so had been disqualified under the old companies legislation.

The new Act also brought tough new rules for the liquidators and insolvency practitioners, who now have to be licensed. Before, any accountant could offer this service and about 4,500 did. By the close of 1987, when the Act had been law for a year, only 1,500 had obtained licences to carry on doing so. But the difference 'is not 3,000 cowboys', the DTI was at pains to point out. Many small firms and sole practitioners just decided not to bother offering that time-consuming service any more. The result is a smaller pool of greater expertise.

The Act effectively outlaws the fraudulent trick of starting up a company and then going bust without paying the creditors for goods or supplying clients who have already paid – only to start up another company to do the whole thing all over again. Some people who did this were just incompetent business managers, regular phoenixes who left a trail of wound-up companies and unpaid VAT bills behind them;

but some were calculating fraudsters who fully intended to take a supplier's goods, use them in the business or sell them at retail prices, and not pay the supplier. A version of this was the long-firm fraud, where a new company would establish a good rapport with its supplier(s) by paying its bills, for small orders, on time at first. Gradually the orders would get bigger. Finally the outfit would be ready for the sting: by now a trusted customer it would place a very large order for goods and vanish with them, leaving the supplier unpaid and possibly in danger of going bust itself.

New banking acts were also part of the overall UK offensive against fraud and trickery that began in the autumn of 1985. In 1987 an additional Banking Act – dealing with the protection of depositors and regulating the use of banking names – extended to this field the same disclosure rules (and penalties) in cases of supected fraud and chicanery as laid down in the Drug Trafficking Act. But the bulk of the much tougher rules and regulations for the conduct of banking – including much more stringent liquidity requirements and rules about the number and size of major loans, introduced in the mid-1980s – were in response to the lessons learned from the crash of Johnson Matthey Bankers (covered in Chapter 4).

For the financial services industry, the most far-reaching piece of new UK legislation, dovetailing with all these other Acts and dating back to concern in the early 1980s about general investor protection, was the *Financial Services Act* of 1986, which changed the whole picture of UK securities trading and the financial markets. It began as a piece of investor protection legislation based upon the researches of another government-appointed committee, this time led by Professor Sir Ernest Gower. But eventually it combined other moves to drag Stock Exchange practices into the modern world, and ended up revolutionising the world's largest agglomeration of financial markets – from trading shares and Eurobonds, to selling life assurance – the City of London, whose position it should help to secure in the future. Under this act, the Secretary of State for Trade and Industry handed over to a new body, called the Securities and Investments Board (SIB), his powers to regulate the securities industry. As long as SIB does its job well, it keeps these powers. But if it fails in its task, the Secretary of State for Trade and Industry can step in and resume the reins himself. SIB oversees all the UK-based financial markets, designating them as Recognised Investment Exchanges (RIEs), and sanctioning the body that runs each designated exchange, called a Self Regulating Organisation, or SRO.

The rules came into force in stages, with April 1988 set as the date from which, to operate on any UK exchange in future, firms or sole practitioners must either belong to a body that is a member of the appropriate SRO, or get authorisation direct from SIB. SIB also recognises certain professional bodies, like the accountancy institutes and the Law Societies, called Recognised Professional Bodies or RPBs.

That month it became a criminal offence to carry out any investment business, be it tipping shares or selling insurance, without belonging either to an SRO, an RIE (recognised exchange) or an RPB, or being authorised direct by the SIB. In practice such was the weight of paperwork that temporary, interim authorisations had to be granted to thousands of small practitioners who applied to the appropriate SRO for membership on time. The SIB and the new regulatory bodies spent the summer of 1988 weeding out the good from the bad and a stream of firms lost their interim authorisation, and were forced to wind up.

One was gilts investment firm Barlow Clowes, whose thousands of small investors had put £138 million into the firm's two funds – made up of £53 million originally invested in the UK fund, and £100 million in Gibraltar, including about £16 million that had been transferred from the London fund. Liquidators were appointed to track down the money and repay creditors as much as possible. Peter Clowes, who ran the business, was arrested by the Fraud Squad acting on behalf of the Serious Fraud Office. This affair, and other closures, triggered arguments about the compensation arrangements for the private investor under SIB rules. These, limited to £48,000 per investor, only came into force in August 1988, leaving a *lacuna* through which the Barlow Clowes investors seemed to be slipping. However, the liquidators were soon able to promise a substantial interim payment from the firm's UK fund at least; and also tried to set the wheels in motion to try and set up a voluntary compensation fund for the losers, with assistance from one or two major City institutions. Meanwhile, angry Barlow Clowes investors looked into suing the original direct regulatory body, the DTI, which had granted the firm a licence to continue trading despite unfavourable press reports and growing concern in some quarters about the firm's business conduct and its ability to pay the very high returns it continued to advertise.

SIB's vast rulebook had to be approved by the Office of Fair Trading to see that there were no anti-competitive elements to it, and 1986 and 1987 saw massive lobbying by interested parties, especially amongst the banks and insurance companies selling financial products, who wanted to keep the rules to a minimum or objected to some of SIB's proposals. But eventually the contents of this tome, which each SRO's own rulebook had to comply with in spirit and practice, were sufficiently thrashed out for the SROs to start finalising their own arrangements and putting themselves forward for authorisation. The process continued in stages into 1988.

Breaking the rules of SRO, RPB and SIB itself can lose you your membership and, therefore, your livelihood – not to mention the scope for fines, or up to two years' imprisonment that can be also imposed on miscreants.

If the SRO fails to investigate and move against a rulebreaker, it will lose its authority back to the Secretary of State for Trade. In turn, SROs, RIEs and RPBs that fail to live up to SIB's requirements may ultimately lose their status – jeopardising all their members' live- lihoods. So it is in members' interest to see that whatever body they belong to toes the line. 'We have statute-backed, practitioner-based, self-regulation – all things to all men!' joked the London International Stock Exchange's surveillance supremo, Bob Wilkinson, describing the new system as it got moving in early 1988.

The reason for this curious structure is more to pay homage to the old idea that the City is a place where self-regulation rules supreme, while introducing greater protection for investors of all shapes and sizes, than the Stock Exchange shibboleth 'my word is my bond' actually granted in the heady days of the long 1980s' bull market. It was always subject to abuse, and once unscrupulous people broke ranks and brought it into disrepute, the old City club was in danger of crumbling – as was shown by the outbreak of a rash of insider dealing scandals in late 1986 flushed out partly under the new rules, but also in response to embarrassment over revelations from the Ivan Boesky international insider dealing scandal in the USA.

The Financial Services Act was part of deal cooked up between the serving Stock Exchange chairman Sir Nicholas Goodison and the then Secretary of State for Trade, Cecil Parkinson. It was in response to a long-drawn out legal action initiated by the Office of Fair Trading, under the previous Labour government, alleging that the Exchange's system of charging fixed commissions on share and gilts was a technically illegal, restrictive practice. In those days the function of jobber (wholesaler of securities) and broker (the retailer) were separate. The broker charged clients the set commission and the jobber made his money on the 'turn': the difference between the price he sold the stock ordered by the client to the broker, and what he had paid another broker for it. As Goodison and Parkinson got together, the action that was finally about to come to court – and the Exchange was anxious to avoid having rules imposed upon it by the judiciary, preferring to make its own and preserve the old gods of self-regulation. Goodison and Parkinson agreed that the case would be dropped in exchange for the Exchange abandoning fixed commissions for negotiated ones – while the Gower Report into investor protection would form the basis of a new securities law that would still leave room for self-regulation.

But the plan to end fixed commissions on 27 October 1986, known as Big Bang in the City, very soon led to other things even before that day was reached. The imminent advent of negotiated commissions led the Stock Exchange to liberalise its rules limiting the percentage of a member firm that foreign or other institutions – like banks – could own. Stockbrokers could see it might be harder to make a living from negotiated commissions alone, and that the firms would need new capital – especially to invest in all the computer equipment a modern Exchange uses. The money would have to come from bringing in new shareholders and owners of the firms. Selling the firm also allowed older partners to take their personal fortunes out of the business, clearing the way for younger men, though many stayed on as salaried directors within the new company afterwards. There was more cash too for the next level of staff, and huge salaries chased bright young men and women around the City for two glorious years (before and after Big Bang) until Black Monday dawned on 19 October 1987 when markets around the world saw share prices and trading volumes crash – and, with them, the firms' precious commission income.

If an outsider, say a bank, could buy both a broker and a jobber, then it seemed sensible to end London's old 'single capacity' system and let market-makers (jobbers) and agencies (brokers) be owned by the same parent. This was 'dual capacity': one firm offering both functions under the same roof – a roof which could also include all the other types of financial service. Banks, merchant banks, Japanese brokers and US securities houses all flocked to the big sell-off, and huge new financial combines emerged during 1987 ahead of Big Bang day on 27 October.

The Stock Exchange brought in new rules to keep certain divisions' work separate from others in the combine. Insider dealing law made it necessary to enforce imaginary 'Chinese' walls between departments so that confidential, price-sensitive information could not leak out ahead of time – for example, to stop corporate client departments who were planning share flotations, rights issues and bids, from whispering to market-makers and agency analysts what was going on until the time was right to announce it officially.

But, as the joke goes, Chinese walls always have 'chinks' in them and some information did leak out. The case of Geoffrey Collier, the ambitious merchant banker who could not resist trading on the back of his firm's knowledge of client's bid plans, highlighted the problem and led to tougher penalties for insider trading offences (see Chapter 6). Soon after Big Bang, and as the Financial Services Bill came closer to enactment, the Stock Exchange itself merged with the International Securities Regulatory Organisation, ISRO, another recognised investment exchange, to become the International Stock Exchange, with New York and Tokyo as her larger competititors. Another chapter had opened in the evolution of London as a major financial centre.

The more international London's financial centre becomes and the faster Tokyo and New York grow, the more important it becomes for London to keep out the fraudsters and the dirty money. But the more international it is the more it will also attract laundered money, because the best place to give such money the final 'rinse' is a fast-moving international market where nothing will look more natural than to cash in what appear to be profits from dealing in securities and take them home, pay some tax on them, and live off the rest.

Though the Drug Trafficking Offences Act marked the opening shot of the UK's 1980s assault on the economic criminal, Lord Roskill had been asked to chair his committee to look into improving the efficiency of jury trials for fraud cases three years earlier, in November 1983. He reported in late 1985 having concluded that the public rightly 'no longer believes that the legal system in England and Wales is capable of bringing the perpetrators of serious frauds expeditiously and effectively to book'. The system was 'archaic, cumbersome and unreliable . . . an open invitation to blatant delay and abuse'.

The eight-person committee made 112 recommendations to alleviate this sorry state of affairs, most of which the Home Office took up in

231

its new Criminal Justice proposals. But it shied away from the major recommendation, from which one member of the committee also dissented at the time of the report, which was that jury trial for complicated fraud cases be replaced by trial by a tribunal of a judge and two lay assessors. The debate about this had centred on whether modern fraud was so complex that ordinary people on juries could no longer follow the ins and outs and were therefore too inclined to acquit; or whether a panel of expert jurors drawn from the financial world would be too tuned-in to the custom and practice of the 'club' and be equally prone to acquit even though they understood some of the technical talk. The Home Office has decided in favour of improving the presentation of evidence and speeding up procedures and shelved the tribunal idea for the time being. But it did decide to set up the Serious Fraud Office, described in Chapter 8, a statutory body with its own Director that will take over the investigation and prosecution of the most serious and complex frauds.

British courts are now able to use visual aids for the better presentation of evidence, and even video links to hear evidence from foreign witnesses, and for the first time will be able to arrange for overseas authorities to take evidence on commission for use in British courts. This was not previously allowed, and if witnesses did not come to give evidence in person in the UK, their stories were not admissible. Prosecutors will be able to transfer serious cases straight to the Crown Court, avoiding Magistrates' Court committal proceedings, and to help the jurors, judges can now arrange preparatory hearings to sketch out the main ground before the full trial gets embroiled in the detail.

'The government has accepted ninety-five per cent of what we recommended,' Lord Roskill (now retired) said in reaction to the first news of the Home Office's plans. 'I'm extremely pleased. It's a very big advance forward – and many of these are reforms across the board, not limited to fraud. I think they will have a long-lasting effect.'

Fraud investigators, like the men at the Ministry of Defence police who have developed sophisticated computer programs to analyse fraud cases, report delightedly that Roskill's recommendations make the presentation of the evidence their programs yield and prepare infinitely clearer to juries. Some of the improvements Roskill recommended – like more use of accountants by the police force – were already being brought in little by little. In October 1985, the Metropolitan and City Company Fraud Squad, then led by Commander Malcolm Campbell, got together with an ebullient accountant Douglas Llambias, at the latter's suggestion and with the approval of government ministers, to experiment with an new Accountants Panel made up of accountants willing to work with police investigators on fraud cases. It was an enormous success, reducing the amount of time investigations took, and helping to improve how evidence was presented.

About the same time the Fraud Squad under Campbell's leadership began to change its approach to presenting fraud cases. Instead of gathering every shred of evidence, however complicated, to prove a huge fraud – say an accumulated £10 million worth – and risk confusing the jury with too much detail, the Squad's own prosecutor suggested they single out a clear cut (say £250,000) example of the type of fraud committed by the accused and home in on that. This proved a simpler way of getting a conviction, and since penalties for fraud handed down by the judges had tended to be much the same for a few million or few thousands of pounds worth, the sentence was little different than it would have been for the full whack. It remains to be seen if the new Serious Fraud Office will adopt the same tactic. The cases it follows are by definition complex, and the first trials to result from them should start in 1989.

Economic crime, as Commander Campbell often points out, is not regarded by society with the same outrage as murder, rape or even burglary. Yet it can affect jobs, trade, our individual and our national prosperity, and even our political systems far more than most people ever imagine. 'Fraud is like VD,' Campbell once said. 'If you've got it you don't talk about it.' But left to fester, it becomes a cancer: not so much VD, but more like the AIDS of the economic system.

Once it gets hold, fraud seems almost impossible to eradicate from the body economic. But there is a cure: good systems, good sense, adequate precautions and strong deterrents. But these only come in, and stay in, when society begins to recognise the damage that fraud, the hidden crime, can really do. Talking about it in the early 1980s yielded a brand new system to try and cure the cancer. The 1990s will reveal the results.

Bibliography

Cornwall, Hugo, *Data Theft* (Heinemann Professional Publishing 1987)

Frantz, Douglas, *Mr Diamond* (Bloomsbury 1987)

Klinghoffer, Arthur Jay, *Fraud of the Century* (Routledge 1988)

Kochan, Nick and Pym, Hugh, *The Guinness Affair* (Christopher Helm 1987)

Short, Martin, *Crime Inc* (Methuen 1984)

Walter, Ingo, *Secret Money* (Unwin Hyman 1985, Unwin Paperbacks 1986)

'Inquiry into the Management of Syndicates by Richard Becket Underwriting Agencies Limited', published by Lloyd's of London, July 1986

Lloyd's interim report on the Unimar affair, 1986

Assorted compilations by the Commonwealth Secretariat's Commercial Crime Unit

The Roskill Report; The Drug Trafficking Offences Act; Criminal Justice Act 1987; Insolvency Act 1986; Financial Services Act 1986; Banking Act 1987 (HMSO Publications).

Index